LITIGATING INTELLIGENCE

LITIGATING INTELLIGENCE

IQ Tests, Special Education, and Social Science in the Courtroom

ROGERS ELLIOTT
Dartmouth College

 Auburn House Publishing Company
Dover, Massachusetts

Library of Congress Cataloging in Publication Data

Elliott, Rogers
  Litigating intelligence.

  Includes index.
    1. Discrimination in education—Law and legislation—
United States.   2. Educational tests and measurements—
Law and legislation—United States.   3. Socially handi-
capped children—Education—Law and legislation—United
States.   4. Afro-American children—Education.
5. Intelligence tests—United States.   I. Title.
KF4155.E45   1987   344.73'0798'0269   86–32068
ISBN 0–86569–156–8   347.3047980269

Printed in the United States of America

FOREWORD

No more troubling examples of the inadequate union of law and the social sciences can be found than those presented in this book. That two reputable judges can reach opposite conclusions from essentially the same evidence presents the dilemma in stark outline. Where do the Constitutional issues prevail, and where are the social science results relevant?

As the author notes, the first hearings in the cases were separated by eight years, so that the Chicago *PASE* case occurred in a climate of less hysteria about affirmative action than the California *Larry P.* case. But the witnesses were the same adversaries, and the legal issues were the same contest between psychological prediction and school placement. Yet, the decision in *Larry P.* was for the plaintiff, a decision that barred the use of IQ tests in the assessment of black children for placement in special education classes, whereas the decision in *PASE* was to permit the Chicago school district to continue to use IQ tests, among other assessments, to assign minority children to classes for the mentally retarded. Professor Elliott provides a detailed comparison of these cases—the background, evidence, testimony, arguments, and surprising outcomes.

In the case of *Brown vs. the Board of Education*, the Supreme Court declared unconstitutional the segregation of black students into "separate but equal" schools on the basis that separate cannot be equal. But references to psychological studies of black children's self-esteem muddied the Constitutional issues. In *Brown* there was no reason to refer to social science evidence about the psychological effects of segregation on black children, because such effects are not relevant to Constitutional issues. Even if racial integration has harmed black education (and there is some evidence that it has), the Constitutional demand for equal treatment under the law must dominate other considerations.

v

Similarly, Constitutional issues were invoked in the segregation of black children into classes for the educably mentally retarded (EMR) or other groups similarly labeled. Is the issue a Constitutional one or a matter of social policy that may benefit, or handicap, young minority children? And if the issue is Constitutional, then is the disproportion of minority children in special education (especially EMR classes) an affront to the guarantee of equal treatment under the law? On the other hand, if special education classes worked to bring minority children up to the achievement levels of the majority group, would there then be less outcry about their disproportionate presence in special classes?

If special education actually worked, which it does not, and minority children assigned to EMR classes in the primary grades eventually reached the same level of reading and math achievements as children in regular classrooms, I doubt whether the plaintiffs in these cases would have brought suit. A major problem in the educational system is that special education, even with smaller classes and better trained teachers, still does not work to bring such children up to par. Rather, special education classes perpetuate educational disadvantage.

Is it realistic to believe that special education or other interventions can bring educationally disadvantaged and minority children up to average levels of achievement? Probably not. At least there is no evidence that educators know how to accomplish such feats; and, in general, the limitless optimism of those who hoped for great things from the schools alone has not been justified. Only the most extreme interventions, such as the adoption of black infants by white middle-class families, appears to bring such children into the normal range. Black children reared from infancy by white middle-class families achieve in primary school at much the same levels as other children adopted into mainstream middle-class families (Scarr & Weinberg, 1976). Thus, it is realistic to believe that young minority children can be served by the public schools if they share the culture of the schools; if they do not share the culture of the schools, they cannot be reasonably served, and they are relegated to special classes.

But what implications does this observation have for the courts, who have been asked to decide the proportions of minority children who may be assigned to special education classes? Perhaps, none. If Constitutional issues are to prevail, then the social science findings of the day may have no legitimate standing. If, on the other hand, courts attend to social science findings, the ability of minority children to benefit from exposure to the majority culture may persuade them to encourage such exposure through special educational classes, not for the retarded, but for the culturally different. Much could be learned from this exercise, and minority children could benefit.

This book raises all of these issues and more. In writing a thorough and dispassionate account of these lawsuits and by providing a wide-ranging discussion of the many issues that arose in them, from the meaning of culture to the meaning of intelligence, the author is to be applauded for his acute sensibilities and his social conscience.

SANDRA SCARR
Commonwealth Professor and
Chair, Psychology Department
University of Virginia

PREFACE

In 1980, after two decades in psychology and education, I took a sabbatical for a year's study of law at Stanford. I had become interested in (among other things) questions of educational equity through a half-time appointment in the Education Department at Dartmouth, and since my graduate training in clinical psychology I had been interested in ability testing. One of the reasons I went to Stanford, in fact, was to learn more about *Larry P.*, a case that banned IQ tests, at least for some purposes, in California.

It made no sense to me that a judge should do that; and what was even more startling was a comment made to me by one of the plaintiffs' lawyers, Edward Opton (he was also a psychologist), to the effect that there was no evidence that IQ tests predicted validly the school performance of black children.

It seemed to me that it might be worthwhile to find out something about the process that led judges and lawyers to such surprising opinions. Circumstances made my doing so easier than it might otherwise have been: The lead attorney for the plaintiffs, Armando Menocal, was teaching at Stanford in 1980–1981; and the defense attorney, Joanne Condas, let me use a small office to peruse all of her files once or twice a week during 1981–1982. (I had contrived to continue at the law school for a second year.)

The sheer mass of material was at first a little daunting—there were at least 13,000 pages of testimony, exhibits, pleadings, motions, briefs, and depositions, not to mention a large volume of correspondence, memoranda, and relevant case law. But I was utterly fascinated, as I slowly came to understand why the case worked out as it did; I continued to make my trips to the attorney general's office with unflagging enthusiasm.

The findings of fact and law that one reads in published opinion are far too abstract and selective for the real understanding of a complex case, and I wanted to get and report "the real story."

Much has been written about *Larry P.*, and much of that is
excellent. But I thought that despite my sympathy for the defense
position, I could, by immersing myself in all the materials of the
case and listening to people on both sides, add something to the
story—a kind of case study in social science and the law. I could
not have learned as much as I did without the very generous
cooperation of both lead attorneys, and I am happy to acknowledge
their kindness here.

Within a few months of the publication of the *Larry P.* opinion,
its impact was given emphasis by contrast: The *PASE* opinion, from
Chicago, found IQ tests not racially biased, and it was clear that
Judge Grady in Chicago heard very differently several of the same
witnesses who had appeared in *Larry P.* This circumstance made
issues about social science in court even more salient because fairly
direct comparisons were possible.

Since I was not going to school in Chicago, I had to rely on the
good offices of Christine Cheatam, a defense lawyer in *PASE*, and
Margaret Myers to copy the transcripts, pleadings, and exhibits.
William Winters, the lead plaintiffs' attorney, was generous with
his time in phone interviews, as was Sharon Weitzman, an executive officer of Designs for Change, an organization monitoring
consent-decreed changes in the Chicago public schools. My knowledge of *PASE* is relatively limited—I didn't have access to the
memoranda and correspondence that provide color and context to
trial records. Even so, I feel sure that a reading of the testimony
would have averted some of the harsher judgments of Judge
Grady's opinion, just as I think that I know why *PASE* came out so
differently from *Larry P.* (The impatient reader can skip directly to
Chapter 11 for the answers.)

Telling the story whole, though it is what I wanted most to do, is
not all I wanted to do. This book is not a treatise on school equity
law, or even on the law of testing, most of which concerns
employment testing. And it will not educate psychologists who are
part of the consensus concerning the measurement of abilities in
general and test bias in particular. But many lawyers and psychologists do not know much about that consensus, and many psychologists have little idea about what happens to social science data in
the adversary system, and for them, as for students in psychology
and education, the book will, I hope, be instructive. The chapters
on the effects of these lawsuits, on policy issues arising from them,
and on social science evidence and the adversarial system will

show why I am wary of judge-made resolutions of very complicated social issues.

Attacks upon ability testing will be with us for a long time. That would be true even if there were no ethnic or racial groups, since resource and credential allocation based on test results would be correlated with class position. The legacy of past white mistreatment of blacks exacerbates the issue by giving it a racial identity, including an incarnation known modernly as the underclass, whose scholastic achievement or ability scores are going to suppress the black average for a long time to come. Since tests are often quite useful, it seemed to me worth examining why killing the messenger is so popular a response to this bad news.

I thank the Dartmouth Faculty Research Committee for underwriting the costs of getting and copying the voluminous raw material of this research, and of readying the manuscript; the Stanford University Law School, whose deans and committees granted petitions for several unorthodox features of my program there; and the Stanford Law School and Psychology Department, who granted me the training fellowship in law and psychology that speeded progress on this work.

Finally, I am pleased to be able publicly to acknowledge my gratitude to the two psychologists with whom I began and ended this enterprise: First, to J. McVicker Hunt, whom I have never been adequately able to thank for his generosity, who let me read his treatise (*Intelligence and Experience,* 1961) while he was writing it in 1959–1960, thus sparking my interest in intelligence; and last, to David Rosenhan, my colleague, friend, and adviser at Stanford, who, every time he had a chance to help me, did so.

THE AUTHOR

CONTENTS

Chapter 1

BACKGROUND OF THE LAWSUITS

The two cases surveyed in this book were primarily concerned with the role of intelligence testing in assigning black children to special education classes for the very slow learning but in most respects normal children, known usually as the educably mentally retarded (EMR) or educably mentally handicapped (EMH). The first, longest, and most discussed of this pair was *Larry P.* v. *Riles* (343 F. Supp. 306, 1972; 495 F. Supp. 926, 1979), in which Federal District Judge Robert F. Peckham banned the use of individual IQ tests in placing black children into EMR classes in California. The specific complaints were that the six black children in San Francisco had had irreparable harm done to their educational careers by being inappropriately and pejoratively labeled and stigmatized and placed into "dead-end" (Judge Peckham's word) EMR classes primarily because of scores obtained on IQ tests said to be racially and culturally biased against blacks. Plaintiffs sought and finally got relief in the form of a test ban and a quota controlling the proportion of black placement into EMR classes at the level of black representation in the school population generally.

No one disputed the fact that black children were represented in classes at over twice their proportion in the general school population. But all of the chief terms of the pleadings, and some questions implied by those terms, were hotly disputed at the trial—that is, the meanings of *culture, test bias, intelligence, mental retardation, stigma;* the nature of EMR education; the role

1

of expectation in education; and the power of the schools to repair academic deficits. The case was, as much as anything else, a debate among psychologists and lawyers about the scientific status of tests of intellectual ability, and about the social and political implications of what such tests had to say about race and disadvantage.

Judge Peckham affirmed nearly all of the plaintiffs' contentions, finding that standardized IQ tests were biased against blacks and played a critical role in the decision to place children into EMR classes; that EMR classes constituted very bad education, being rather a burden than a benefit; that "intelligence" meant something innate; that a fair test of intelligence must yield equal scores for two racial groups unless those groups are different genetically, which they were not; that bias in an intelligence test was therefore manifested by group differences in its scores; that *socioeconomic* differences were not sufficient to account for black-white differences in "intelligence," though *sociocultural* differences were sufficient to account for differences in scores on IQ tests; and that the average black deficit in school-related abilities could probably be repaired by appropriate educational interventions.

The companion case (*PASE* v. *Hannon*, 506 F. Supp. 831, 1980), with the same complaints, and featuring several of the same plaintiffs' witnesses, was filed in Chicago in 1975 and tried in 1980. Here, Judge John Grady of the U.S. District Court found that the tests (save for a total of nine items) were not biased or discriminatory, that socioeconomic differences *were* sufficient to account for black-white differences in IQ, and that "cultural" differences were of little or no effect.

In many respects these cases, interesting as they are to educational psychologists and observers of the fate of social science evidence in the adversarial system, are more generally of interest as another battle in the continuing saga of racial conflict: Race is the pivot of much of American political and social history and the typical focus of the tension between equality and liberty or between equality of result and freedom of opportunity. Myrdal's great study, *An American Dilemma* (1944), poignantly illustrated the effects of centuries of the unusually harsh, deracinating oppression and denial that were part of American chattel slavery and, later, Jim Crow laws that remained in place until the great civil rights movements of the late 1950s began, when American blacks at last began to find their voices in protest and American whites, at least outside the South, by and large encouraged their claims.

The Egalitarian Optimism of the 1960s

The decade of the 1960s, marked at its beginning by the election of Kennedy, enhanced the burgeoning aspirations for social equality. The engines of the Great Society worked to make the hopes of egalitarian optimism a reality. The youth movement, spawned in huge numbers and reared in an affluence that seemed to make any desire attainable, provided enthusiasm and idealism. The war, offering as it did a rare opportunity for middle-class conscience and self-interest to march together, made anti-establishmentarianism respectable and added yeast and ferment to an already effervescent brew. In part, the goal was simply removal of barriers to opportunity, and the Civil Rights and Voting Rights Acts of 1964 and 1965 endorsed the dismantling of Jim Crow laws and de jure segregation everywhere. But it was recognized from the start that the conferring of equality of opportunity, if done too late in the life of an individual, is illusory: Giving the right of access, say to higher education, will not help people whose education has left them unfit to avail themselves of such "opportunity."

The governmental effort to upgrade black educational attainment was therefore considerable, at least in funding a variety of compensatory education projects, and it rested upon the American faith in the plasticity of behavior and the power of environmental intervention. No one will be surprised to know that schools were usually the site of these interventions—the faith in education as the vehicle to success and good citizenship was shown to be the almost sacred belief it is when it got the imprimatur of constitutional approval in *Brown* v. *Board of Education* (347 U.S. 483) in 1954.

The well-known efforts of Gray and Klaus (1970; Klaus and Gray, 1968), Karnes, Hodgins, and Teska (1968), Levenstein (1970), Garber and Heber (1977, 1981), Weikart, Epstein, Schweinhart, and Bond (1978), Bereiter and Engelmann (1966), and the Headstart and Follow-through programs were conceived in this period. The theoreticians of this movement were J. McV. Hunt, whose book *Intelligence and Experience* (1961) provided the rationale for hope by supporting the view that intelligence is enormously malleable and thus improvable; and Bernard Bloom, the chief promoter of "mastery learning," a doctrine that implied that as many as 90 percent of our students can learn "what we have to teach them" (Bloom, 1968, p. 1).

Signs of Trouble

There were, however, portents of trouble that most citizens, and
certainly those in the civil rights movement, were not ready to
hear; they ignored what they could and shouted down what they
could not ignore. The three major ones were substantial reports by
Moynihan (1965), by Coleman and others (1966), and the notorious
paper by Jensen (1969), "How Much Can We Boost IQ and
Scholastic Achievement?" Moynihan described the disintegration
of the black family in words that are, if anything, more pertinent
today than they were when written: ". . . the Negro family,
battered and harassed by discrimination, injustice, and uprooting,
is in the deepest trouble" (1965, p. 4). In dozens of tables and
figures, he detailed the elements of what he phrased "the tangle of
pathology": Extensive rates of father absence, illegitimacy, school
failure, low test scores, crime rates, drug use, and welfare. He
issued a call for a national effort for policies that were family
supportive, but he had no specific proposals.

Moynihan's view, and his recent book (1986), has of late become
not only acceptable but fashionable among all segments of society,
including black civil rights leaders. But twenty years ago his view
was vilified as a disgraceful attack upon the victims whose welfare
he purported to espouse. Though he had quoted E. Franklin
Frazier's (1950) similar analysis, and noted that nothing had improved since that time, the civil rights movement at that time did
not feel that it could cope with a problem that, though caused by
white oppression, was now self-perpetuating and unresponsive to
the simple removal of discrimination. Ryan's (1965) response was
typical: The report was overstated, it inappropriately blamed the
victim, and the real problems were discrimination and lack of
education.

The issues of this controversy have pervaded all later debates
about the role of compensatory education in ameliorating the
general condition of blacks. If basic, early socialization experiences
in families have powerful effects upon the development of those
skills and motives that equip the child to deal effectively with the
middle-class world and its artifacts, including schools and tests, or,
however malleable such effects, if current nonschool environments
far outweigh the influence of the school, then schools will have
only limited effect in repairing any deficits that children bring to
them. The implication is that the family and home environment

ought to be the focus of improvement and that effective remedies would be not curricular but economic and social.

On the other hand, if disadvantaged black children are not so much intellectually disabled by circumstances as potentially capable representatives of a different culture, needing only to be taught the white man's ways in the white man's schools, then more exposure to such schools should provide substantially more improvement. This, of course, was the rationale for early intervention. The extreme form is adoption, but, short of that, there have been programs (Garber and Heber, 1977, 1981; Ramey and Haskins, 1981) that have altered the daily environment of poor black children from infancy onward.

A strong variant of this view was one that criticized the early intervention model as trying "to establish programs to prevent deficits that simply were not there" (Baratz and Baratz, 1970, p. 47). Relying primarily on the observation that black children have language and, hence, deep structure competence (in the Chomskian lexicon), the Baratzes agreed with those who saw poor blacks to be different but not deficient. What they wanted, however, was not more exposure to the white man's schools but an education that capitalized on black cultural difference. What blacks needed were not basic skills so much as methods for decoding and translating the alien culture. Both these latter views, asserting fundamental and equal innate black competence, were very prominent in the first trial examined in this book, *Larry P.*

In the year after Moynihan's report, Coleman and his colleagues (1966) issued theirs, *On Equality of Educational Opportunity*. As with Moynihan's, the interpretation of it has varied with time and political fashions. The finding most taken up at the time of its appearance was the conclusion that blacks educated in mostly white schools performed better academically than other blacks—this finding is often misstated to say that blacks who *moved* into mostly white schools did better, and that form became part of the social science foundation for affirmative integration of schools. Less popular at the time was the finding that school characteristics per se made little difference in measured abilities or achievement, since this result is not encouraging to the exalted view of schools as powerful engines of change. And least popular of all—the sort of finding that Jensen (1969) but few others highlighted—were the data showing that the ability and achievement scores of black students lagged those of whites by about 1 standard deviation

(S.D.)[1] at every age tested, from grades 1 through 12. That is, the difference appeared to be present at the arrival of children at school, which did nothing subsequently to reduce it. Associated with this last finding was one even more obscure; namely, that in grades 3 and 6 (the only primary school grades from which data were gathered), the correlations[2] between verbal and nonverbal ability tests and tests of reading and mathematics achievement were very nearly the same among blacks as among whites. This meant that typical ability tests did not appear to lose their validity as predictors when used with black children. Thus the Coleman Report could have, and has, been used to justify integration, preschool intervention, and the use of tests with minority children.

The civil rights arguments for large-scale compensatory education and affirmative integration, based as they were on the assumption of the potency of environmental change and the assumption that intelligence is innate capacity equally present in all races, did not go unopposed. I refer to Jensen's famous (1969) paper, "How Much Can We Boost IQ and Scholastic Achievement?" which summarized a set of results then becoming quite clear: that to upgrade either the educational attainment or the IQ scores of poor black children was very difficult. Even more notoriously, Jensen reminded everyone that the intelligence of American blacks, as measured by IQ scores and other mental ability tests, was a standard deviation (about 15 points, or about the difference between the 30th and 70th percentile on a test) below that of whites, and he marshaled support for the view that about 80 percent of differences among us in our intelligence is associated with differences among us in our genotypes (that intelligence in our population is highly heritable). Finally, he offered as reasonable the hypothesis that the race difference itself is largely associated with race differences in gene frequencies.

While Jensen was suggesting a deficit more basic than even the most serious view of the effects of early experience would impute, he also suggested the possibility of different curricula for different sorts of learning abilities. Like Baratz and Baratz, Jensen thought that the environment in which poor black children were reared played little role in producing any deficit, he criticized the hegemony of the standard curriculum, and his argument went to issues of innate competence. As is frequently the case, the extremes on the right and the left had much in common, even though they differed on the probable answer to the fundamental question, whether there *was* any innate deficit.

Debates over Testing

Jensen's paper highlighted the IQ tests as measures of intelligence, along with related tests (for example, the Armed Forces Qualification Test, or AFQT, and school achievement tests) that yielded large black-white differences. In so doing he featured the Coleman Report data and the reference in the Moynihan report to AFQT differences. The problem thus appeared: If intelligence was something innate and equally present, on average, in all races, then the tests could not be measuring it—they must, that is, be invalid, unfair, and biased when used with blacks, Hispanics, and so forth. This "folk definition" (so called by Humphreys, 1984) sees intelligence as a fixed innate capacity for which the degree of realization depends upon the adequacy of environment; this view is pervasive still and was more so in the late 1960s. Environmentalists are prone to believe that normal persons are about the same in the amount of this capacity they possess, their differences on tests being purely a matter of differences in test-relevant environments; hereditarians would say that test differences are almost wholly hereditary; but both sides, it should be noted, would conceive of intelligence as innate capacity.

The view of scientific psychology is that innate intelligence is not measurable and not useful as a concept and that the only intelligence worth discussing is the average measure of current performance on a variety of cognitive, intellectual, problem-solving, and school-related tasks. Hebb (1949) made this distinction between innate ability and actual performance and labeled them as Intelligence A and Intelligence B, respectively, but it had not worked its way into the public consciousness by the time *Larry P.* was filed in 1971, and, as we shall see, the folk definition carried the day.

Whether the tests measured something innate or not, doing badly on them was usually not helpful either to one's self-concept or to one's life chances. Scoring low on the AFQT, for example, meant not being taken into the armed services at a time when they offered secure employment, and the failure rates cited by Jensen (1969) were 68 percent for blacks as compared with 19 percent for

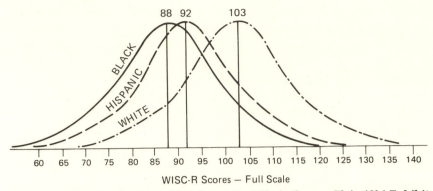

Figure 1. The Distribution of IQ Scores by Ethnic Group: Plaintiffs' Exhibit in *Larry P.*, Incorporated in the Opinion.

whites. Scoring low on school achievement tests, teacher-made or standardized, led to referrals for special education, and scoring low on the school psychologist's IQ test led, often, to placement in segregated EMR classrooms, where one might remain until age 18. Scoring low on employment tests meant, often, not being hired or not being promoted, and scoring low on high school tests and college selection tests might cut short one's education.

And blacks did score low, just as Jensen had said, on all such tests. Figure 1, taken from Judge Peckham's opinion in *Larry P.*, shows the distribution of IQ scores for whites, Chicanos, and blacks in California a decade ago. The distribution is typical. In fact, it was and still is a durable, well nigh universal finding in the field of ability testing that the black-white difference in America is as shown and that it exists at every age examined from preschool onward (Loehlin, Lindzey, and Spuhler, 1975; Jensen, 1980; Reynolds, 1983; Coleman et al., 1966; Reschley and Sabers, 1979; Oakland, 1978; Hall and Kaye, 1980), on every variety of tests of mental ability and their criteria (Jensen, 1980; Hunter, Schmidt, and Raushenberger, 1984; Klitgaard, 1985; Manning and Jackson, 1984; Wigdor and Garner, 1982).

Blacks fought the tests, alleging that they did not tap innate capacity; that they were culturally biased against blacks; that intelligence could scarcely be defined or, if it could, there was little consensus in the definitions; and that test scores systematically underestimated and underpredicted black performance on various criteria. The issues usually reduced to the question of criterion validity—that is, whether the tests predicted any relevant behavior, like grades or job performance, to some substantial degree; and, even if so, whether the tests were differentially valid, predicting for blacks differently than for whites. If the tests were not valid for blacks, their argument went, blacks ought to be admitted to the arena of performance (in regular classrooms, in colleges, in jobs) without having to cross any testing barrier and to be given the chance to prove themselves by a direct chance at the criterion itself. This argument was one for a sort of open-admissions policy, and it took the view that beyond some fairly low minimum cutoff (if tests were to be used at all), everyone was potentially equal as a performer.

By the turn of the decade, just before *Larry P.* was filed, it was not clear whether testing predicted job performance for blacks as well as for whites (Hunter, Schmidt, and Rauschenberger, 1984). The Supreme Court, in *Griggs* v. *Duke Power Company* (401 U.S. 424, 1971), had held for the Equal Employment Opportunity Commission's (EEOC) stringent view that tests must be newly validated for each job they are used to select for and must be shown to be specifically job relevant, thus rendering unlawful the unvalidated screening use of general ability tests. The decision made far more likely the simple use of quota hiring, because its use made the avoidance of race discrimination charges much easier.

It was clearer at the time that such tests as the SAT did predict about as well for blacks as for whites (see the review by Breland, 1979), though the issue was hotly debated because at that time colleges and universities were beginning to open up to black students in far greater numbers than before. The comparative prediction of primary school students, however, was less well established. Furthermore, it was even more controversial because of growing concerns having to do with handicapped children. There were five main elements of this concern. The first was the desire to take into public schools, and if possible to mainstream, physically and mentally handicapped children. The impetus to do this, seen in the famous cases *Mills* v. *Board of Education* (348 F. Supp. 866, 1971) and *PARC* v. *Pennsylvania* (343 F. Supp. 179, 1971), and represented in educational psychology by Dunn's (1968) critique of the EMR system, was running at full tide. The second was the disproportionate number of black children scoring low on ability tests.

The use of ability tests to allocate children to EMR classes or EMR-like "special tracks" was dealt a stunning blow by Judge

Skelly Wright, who, in *Hobson* v. *Hansen* (269 F. Supp. 401, 1967), abolished the test-driven track system in Washington, D.C. that had placed blacks into the EMR track in a proportion that exceeded their proportion of the total school population. Compared with the racial disproportions in California *(Larry P.)* and Chicago *(PASE)*, those in Washington were mild: 90 percent of the total elementary and junior high school population was black, and blacks accounted for 95 percent of the EMR track.

Judge Wright, granting that there may be bases of classifying students that do not offend the Constitution even though they produce racial disproportion, nonetheless insisted that ability classification must be done on the basis of *innate* ability, and since the test used (a mixture of group standardized aptitude and achievement tests) did not do so, especially in the case of disadvantaged blacks, they did not pass constitutional muster.

Judge Wright cited three other related concerns having to do with quality of education, expectation effects, and stigma. He found the special track to be an inflexible straitjacket, one that did not educate children well, and one which children seldom rose out of, and he made much of the effect of labeling and stigmatization on both the children and the expectations of teachers about children. Here was the introduction of the Pygmalion theme (Rosenthal and Jacobsen, 1968), to the effect that black and other disadvantaged children do badly in school in part because their teachers expect them to do so. The Rosenthal–Jacobsen book *Pygmalion in the Classroom* had great influence on the thinking of plaintiffs in civil rights schooling cases (see, for example, Wolf, 1981, for another example in the school desegregation litigation of *Bradley* v. *Milliken* [408 U.S. 717, 1974]), and Judge Wright's opinion was very influential with Judge Peckham.

To review, then, by the turn of the decade, 1969–1970, the issues of black intellectual competence, of the fairness of some of the tests purporting to measure it, and of the fairness of the educational system to black children were very controversial, and there was a great deal of political and legal support for the black positions on them. In 1969, at the American Psychological Association (APA) meeting in Washington, D.C., the Association of Black Psychologists was formed, and high on its agenda was a call for a moratorium on the IQ, achievement, and ability testing of blacks, because, among other alleged effects, these tests improperly classified black children. Robert Williams, a witness a decade later in

PASE, was the most eloquent and passionate spokesman for these positions (Williams, 1970):

> *The Association of Black Psychologists fully supports those parents who have chosen to defend their rights by refusing to allow their children and themselves to be subjected to achievement, intelligence, aptitude, and performance tests which have been and are being used to (a) label Black people as uneducable, (b) place Black children in "special" classes and schools, (c) perpetuate inferior education in Blacks, (d) assign Black children to educational tracks, (e) deny Black students higher educational opportunities, (f) destroy positive growth and development of Black people.*

The organization issuing the manifesto had much to do with bringing the *Larry P.* lawsuit, and California and San Francisco were, indeed, hospitable venues for it.

California and Larry P.

In the late 1960s in California, minority groups in general had become increasingly concerned about their disproportionate representation in classes for the educable mentally retarded (EMR).[3] In 1967, Chicanos in the Magnolia and Santa Ana districts were complaining, and those and other complaints were heard in the legislature, which passed resolutions expressing concern (H.R. 444 of 1969, H.R. 262 of 1970). In 1970, *Diana* v. *State Board of Education* (C-70-37 RFP, N.D. Cal., 1970) was filed in the United States Federal District Court of the Northern District of California, the case going to Judge Peckham, a judge with a sufficient reputation as a liberal that civil rights litigants were relieved to be assigned to him. The retesting of Chicano children who had been placed in EMR classes was the device used by the plaintiffs, and, when retested in their own language, eight of nine plaintiff children had scored above the IQ cutoff for EMR, some showing dramatic increases (see Bersoff, 1980, for an excellent review of this case).

Diana was resolved by various consent decrees (though there were still negotiations as late as 1979). The important features of the decrees—testing in the child's native language, using more than one assessment device, assessing adaptive behavior (AB) outside of school, and reevaluating students in EMR and giving transitional assistance to those (the "decertified") who were returned to regular classes—were quickly legislated (Chapters 1543 and 1569 of the 1970 Statutes, and Chapter 78 of the 1971 Statutes). More to the point, *Diana* resulted in a stipulated agreement that there would be a quota for Chicano representation in EMR classes. The 1970 legislation also required, for the first time, an IQ cutoff such that no child could be eligible for EMR unless he or she scored more than 2 standard deviations below the mean and that one of three individual IQ tests (WISC, Stanford–Binet, or Leiter) be employed. In 1971 the legislature declared that there should not be disproportionate representation of minority groups in EMR classes (California Education Code Section 56504) but did not mandate any action.

In fact, there was enormous disproportion for blacks. Of the 57,148 total EMR enrollment in 1968–1969, 25.5 percent were black children, though less than 10 percent of the school population was black. By 1971–1972, after the 2 standard deviation rule, EMR had only 38,208 EMR enrollees, but 26.7 percent were black. In 1976 to 1977, after the *Diana* order and the statewide IQ test moratorium, there were 19,289 EMR enrollees, but 25 percent were black (Peckham, 1979, p. 942). Another way to look at what happened is to consider rates of EMR enrollment. For blacks, the rate declined from 3.2 percent in 1968–1969 to about 1.25 percent in 1976–1977. But for whites and Chicanos it went down as well, so that in the year before the trial (1976–1977), according to Alice Bryant, a special education defense expert from Los Angeles, the black rate in that city was 1.25 percent, the white rate .28 percent, and the Chicano rate .37 percent. These figures represent (Bryant, RT[4] 8902) an undiminished disproportion of black students, even though the *numbers* involved were not large in any ethnic group. It will not have escaped attention that the Chicano EMR rate, two years after a quota was imposed, was within range of the white group, whereas the black rate, despite the statewide banning of the IQ test for use in determining black EMR eligibility, remained relatively high even while the absolute numbers were cut by 60 percent.

In the meantime, complaints of segregation in northern as well as southern cities had become more frequent during the late 1960s. In San Francisco, such complaints, which included the alleged "dumping" of black children into EMR classes, resulted in a lawsuit, *Johnson* v. *San Francisco Unified School District* (339 F. Supp. 315, 1971), filed in 1970 in the same district court that later heard *Larry P.* The court decided for the plaintiffs in July 1971, on the eve of the *Larry P.* litigation. (See Kirp, 1982, for an excellent review of the history of this legal and educational conflict in San Francisco.)

By 1970 black psychologists had formed the Bay Area Association of Black Psychologists, which included among their number Dean Asa Hilliard of San Francisco State University, the plaintiffs' expert on IQ bias; Dr. Harold Dent, a former coordinator of Pupil Services in Berkeley, and at the time of trial working at West Side Mental Health Services; Dr. William Pierce, also of West Side Mental Health Services; and Dr. Gerald West, Professor of Counseling at San Francisco State. They had initiated meetings with Morton Dean, head of special education in San Francisco, and with the State Department of Education (SDE). No government officer seemed ready to give up testing or to impose quotas. The state, in fact, set up a committee, chaired by Lee Cronbach, to assess its testing program, but the committee did not include any black psychologists. (The committee subsequently found the state's testing program to be reasonable.)

The Lawsuit

At some point, then, in the summer or early fall of 1970, a number of groups interested in the civil rights of minorities coalesced on the IQ testing and disproportionate EMR-placement issues. According to Drs. West and Dent (RT 994; 3838) there were present at the meeting representatives of the Bay Area Association of Black Psychologists, the Association of Black Social Workers, and the Urban League; lawyers from the NAACP Legal Defense Fund, Neighborhood Legal Assistance, and California Rural Legal Assistance; and parents, teachers, and concerned community people. West, Dent, and Pierce took on the assignment of selecting names, calling parents, and doing the IQ retesting. As West said (RT 1318), reporting on the statement of an attorney at the meeting, "if this is going to be a case, there has to be some plaintiffs." These plaintiffs came from a list of not fewer than seven and not more than twenty names of children thought to have been misclassified (it was never clear just how large the list was or even where it came from).

The action was begun in November 1971, when plaintiffs filed for a preliminary injunction asking for the elimination of culturally biased IQ tests, reevaluation of all black EMR children, supplementary assistance for those returned to regular classes, and a quota such that black children in San Francisco would no longer be assigned to EMR classes in proportion beyond their representation in the district school population. The judge did not ban the tests (they continued in use until 1975) but only restrained defendants (at the time, school officials in San Francisco only) from placing primary reliance on them, and he said he was "particularly wary of plaintiffs' proposed ratio system, for it leaves fulfillment of the needs of retarded black students at the mercy of white parents . . ." (Peckham, 1972, p. 1315). He did order, in his preliminary injunction order of June 1972, that black EMR children be reevaluated and that those who returned to regular classes be given special help.

In that 1972 opinion, Peckham said that there seemed no dispute that the tests were, in fact, culturally biased (p. 1313) or that qualification of placement in regular classes depended upon having the innate ability to learn at the pace at which such classes proceed (p. 1310). The idea is simple: Black children would score higher if they had better opportunities to learn, but they don't have such opportunities. Their low scores are wrongly interpreted to say something about their innate ability. A culturally fair test would show their innate ability to learn to be as high as that of whites. Thus a culturally fair test is one that would somehow tap innate ability and produce equal scores for the two groups.

Although Peckham's injunction was "preliminary," the fact is that in its modified form in December 1974, which broadened the class to all black children in California who may have been or might in the future be classified as mentally retarded on the basis of IQ tests, the judge found as a conclusion of law that plaintiffs were likely to succeed on the merits of their equal protection claim. He also found that defendants had failed to show that IQ tests properly account for the cultural background and experiences of black children and that black children suffer irreparable harm by being mislabeled as mentally retarded and wrongfully placed in EMR classes. If the attitudes of judges are as affected by previous public commitments on controversial issues as those of other mortals, the defense had a difficult uphill battle confronting it whenever the trial on the merits might commence.

Two other sets of events occurred prior to trial in October 1977 that changed the nature of the trial, one concerning the psychology of intelligence and the other, the statutory context of mental retardation. In 1974 Leon Kamin published *The Science and Politics of IQ*, a recounting of the racist views of many of the chief figures in the early intelligence testing movement in America and a critical analysis of the evidence for the heritability of intelligence. It was a very influential book.

In 1975 the APA Committee appointed in 1969 to examine the question of cultural bias in IQ testing issued its report (Cleary, Humphreys, Kendrick, and Wesman, 1975). The conclusion was that there was little or no evidence for bias in the prediction of academic performance, but perhaps the most important part of the article was the definition of intelligence as being current intellectual performance, with no implication either as to innateness or to permanence. The report and its definition were greeted with anger from the spokesman for the Association of Black Psychologists (Jackson, 1975) because, by its definition and its data, it said that blacks *were* less intelligent than whites.

The statutory context of the lawsuit was altered by the passage of PL 94–142, the Education for All Handicapped Children Act of 1975, and Section 504 of the Rehabilitation Act of 1973. The emphasis of each act was on mainstreaming handicapped children, so that, together, the acts appear to disfavor separate EMR classes. With regard to screening, they require multifaceted and multidisciplinary assessment, so they appear to favor a strong emphasis on nonschool adaptive behavior. Both acts also insist on the use of tests that are not culturally or racially discriminatory, are validated for the specific purpose for which they are used, and are not designed merely to provide a single general intelligence quotient. These last regulations also seem to favor an attack on the typical use of the IQ tests at issue: At least one test (the Stanford–Binet) produces only a single score; none was *specifically* validated for the placement of EMR students; and raising the questions of cultural discrimination gives sanction to it as an issue. (The idea of validation for a specific purpose appears to have been borrowed from the EEOC regulations that required validation to a specific job performance criterion, thus making test development expensive and the disparate impact resulting from tests therefore less common.)

The plaintiffs' motions to amend their complaint by adding these statutory causes of action were granted. Defendants' motions for dismissal in late 1976, and for summary judgment early in 1977, were denied. It then became clear that the trial on the merits

would, at last, take place. Morrison and Foerster, the second
largest firm in San Francisco, associated with Public Advocates as
pro bono co-counsel and assumed a very large responsibility for
major parts of plaintiffs' case; discovery proceeded apace. In
August the Office of Civil Rights joined plaintiffs as amicus.

The Trial

In September, at the second of two pretrial conferences, the state
of affairs is illustrated by the following remarks. They are deliberately extensive, so that the state of issues, especially in the mind
of the judge, can be illustrated as they stood a month before trial.

> *The Court:* Perhaps it would help me, because I don't have it right at
> my fingertips, does anybody have that definition of educable men-
> tally retarded handy?
>
> *Ms. Condas:* I don't have an education code with me, but it basically
> requires a child who is failing to profit from the regular classroom
> instruction. And when the teacher or some other person determines
> that the child is failing to profit from the regular classroom instruc-
> tion, he is then referred for a diagnostic process, which includes the
> whole litany of things that you heard so many times; the home visit,
> the adaptive behavior scale, where it is in use, the IQ test, medical
> data that have been gathered, and a get-together by an assessment
> team.
>
> So that it is not a simple definition.
>
> It is triggering mechanism, which is a child who is a non-reader,
> or a non-mathematician, or someone who is sitting in class for some
> reason or other seeming to learn nothing there.
>
> *The Court:* How do you distinguish, though, between somebody
> who just didn't have any sort of a childhood so he didn't have any
> aptitude and he would appear, but he would need some sort of
> remedial assistance, but not maybe be mentally retarded?
>
> *Ms. Condas:* . . . if you have a child who fits the description that you
> are talking about who has had that kind of a childhood with no games
> to play, no puzzles to put together, and he comes into the classroom
> and when assignments are given out, he is unable to read, he is
> unable to cipher and he is unable to seem to understand what is
> going on in the classroom, then from the point of view of what the
> school system has to offer, it really makes relatively little difference
> whether the cause of that is pre-natal malnutrition or impoverished
> home life. You have to look at what the school has available to offer
> him.

And the remedial help that can be provided can be of various sorts. If the diagnostic testing that is done discloses that what he has is some kind of a tendency to reverse letters so that it is a kind of learning disability, then he can be put into a class where they work on techniques not to reverse letters. If it seems to be a general low level of performance, then he does need the kind of class that is devised for the slow learner.

Now, if he is a child in which his background is entirely based on cultural deprivation, it isn't going to take him a great deal of time to make some progress.

Of course, that's the whole premise of things such as the Head-start program. Now, that's a remedial kind of program in a sense. It is remediating a childhood experience which never took place.

All right. That is in essence what the EMR program can be for the kind of child whose incapacity, as manifested at this moment, is from that kind of cause. Now, it may be that it is not from that kind of cause. It may be that he didn't have that bad a home life. It may simply be that he has limited mental endowment and he will not have the ability to outgrow that.

The Court: How do you distinguish between the two? They go to different remedial classes, don't they?

Ms. Condas: They really may not, Your Honor. If a child is a non-reader at the age when he should be beginning to learn to read, there are only a limited number—

The Court: Is he mentally retarded?

Ms. Condas: We are not talking about innate ability. That's not what these tests test.

The Court: Isn't that what this is all about?

Ms. Condas: No, it is not about innate ability.

The Court: Then why do you call these people mentally retarded?

Ms. Condas: Because some of them do have limited intellectual endowment.

The Court: I appreciate that. What about the ones that don't, that are disabled temporarily?

Ms. Condas: All right. But they are still disabled. . . . They still need the same kinds of remedial treatment that the person who is not going to get any better requires until their level of functioning is increased so that they can be reabsorbed into the mainstream.

Now, some children who are at a point in time diagnosed as mentally retarded, that's because that's the level at which they are functioning. And when we get to trial, if we do, you will see that on the cumulative records of all of these children there is repeated reevaluation of them, in some cases yearly, to see whether the placement in which they were put was the appropriate placement . . .

The Court: (We all agreed) at the Friday meeting that there are youngsters for one reason or another who need, the term was compensatory education. Now, you know, it would be somewhat of a—I don't know—I don't want to say tragedy, but irony if after several weeks of testimony and assembling of these 25 experts if we all sort of ended up by saying: yes, that's true, and the methods used in the state put the truly educably mentally retarded, if you use the definition—the mentally retarded, let's say, that still can learn to some degree, that have an innate limitation, and then also, you know, we don't know, maybe there are 40 percent others that appear the same way, but that do not have that limitation and capacity and when given the opportunity, if properly motivated, they can pull themselves up and get on up into the mainstream. If that's what all this is going to lead to, you see, that's what I was really addressing myself to on Friday, then what is really—I say this respectfully— what is this all about? . . . The plaintiff's concern is that there are persons who are stigmatized by being put into the EMR who are not innately lacking capacity. . . . In a sense you are saying there may be some people who need remedial attention who do get put in here by these measurements, but they may not be innately incapacitated or limited.

Ms. Condas: The tests don't purport to test innate intelligence, Your Honor. The tests purport to test what the child is capable of doing and performing and understanding at this moment . . .

The Court: Excuse me. No matter whether environmental or innate causes?

Ms. Condas: Yes. Yes, Your Honor. It's a sample of behavior . . . you use the test to try to find out what his functioning level is at the present moment. The test does have some considerable ability, along with other tests and other techniques, to identify whether it is more probable than not that that indicates a deficiency that is not going to be remediated, or whether it's a specific learning disability, or whether it's questionable. . . . You make the best educated guess you can about where he ought to be placed in the school system . . .

The Court: How do you distinguish between those two, EMR and this other one, this compensatory education category?

Ms. Condas: Frankly, I'm not entirely clear that they are mutually exclusive . . .

The Court: . . . To me this is extraordinarily important, because it makes it sort of an illusory lawsuit, you see, if the issues aren't joined. Then I don't know what these people are going to be addressing. I mean, I imagine all of the plaintiffs' experts are going to say many of these persons, for environmental reasons or otherwise, will need some compensatory education perhaps, but this test isn't fair in its classification of them as mentally retarded.

And you are going to come back, I gather, or your experts, I suppose, will come back and say: well, but these people are handicapped for the moment because of prenatal, post-natal malnutrition or poor environments, learning environments, et cetera. And there won't be any conflict perhaps, except on whether or not it's fair to classify somebody who isn't truly limited in his capacity as an educable mentally retarded person.

You see, I think that's what is offensive is the classification . . .

Let me ask you this to take a little different approach to this: with respect to these traditional—these three IQ tests—do the proponents of them, the defenders of them, do they take the position that, oh, except for perhaps a few degrees, that a person's IQ does not change?

Ms. Condas: I don't believe they take that position, no. No.

The Court: So there is just a measurement of the moment?

Ms. Condas: That's right. It is a small sample of behavior. The reason that it is used at all is that it is the most efficient and objective sample . . .

The Court: . . . Let me ask the plaintiffs, if I may, how will the plaintiffs' experts disagree?

Mr. Menocal: On what point? The last one, as to whether or not IQ changes?

Our experts will certainly—our expert will certainly say that it does change.

The Court: Yes. I assume that.

On this use of the tests—I don't want to try to oversimplify this, but again I get back to what I said Friday that, you know, I'm really concerned about this, that it ends up just sort of a label.

Mr. Menocal: Your Honor, I would say this: Your Honor's characterization, in terms of the—the first characterization you made in terms of where we may be a month from now, experts showing that there is a lot of children in these programs, some of whom are truly retarded and others are there for some sort of environmental—for some reasons unrelated to retardation, and I would say that that is a characterization with which we would agree.

And we would object to that happening certainly in part because of the stigmatization which occurs to the child, but I think Your Honor is possibly relying too much on that fact alone.

We also are going to show that once that happens to a child and a not truly retarded child is put in that environment, that child is permanently set back in his future, in his chances—

The Court: Consequences of the stigmatization—

Mr. Menocal: And the program, Your Honor. What happens in that class is not compensatory education. The curriculum that goes on in an EMR class is not what you would have in a compensatory education class. And the defendant's own witnesses will tell you how the reading level is five, eight years behind what may be going on somewhere else, and they don't expect the kid to start shortening that gap . . .

The Court: So it is simplistic to say that you would have just one big compensatory education class?

Mr. Menocal: That's correct.

That curriculum is designed for a child who is there because of limited intellectual capacity. Those other children who are there who have a normal intelligence but aren't performing well in a classroom, they need help, and we don't argue with that. We want to see them get that help, but they don't need the help that is provided in the EMR class. The only chance they have of getting help in the EMR class is if it is a small class. It is approximately—usually runs half the size of a regular class.

It is for that reason, I would surmise, that some of those kids get lucky and get out.

But we are going to show that for the majority of them, they don't get out. They don't, unfortunately, have the opportunity to get back on their proper educational track and have the same future educational and employment opportunities.

The trial lasted from October 11, 1977, until May 30, 1978, consuming sixty-five trial days and generating over 10,000 pages of transcript. Over 250 exhibits were proffered by the parties and the amicus, and over 200 were received in evidence. Some of these were enormous reports, studies, and compilations.

More than fifty witnesses were called, most of them experts. Those to be referred to in this volume are listed here, with a brief identification and description of their testimony. For the most part, they will thereafter be referred to simply by last name.

In addition to the black psychologists already mentioned (Hilliard, Dent, West, and Pierce), plaintiffs' experts included the following:

Dr. George W. Albee had served as president of the American Psychological Association (APA) from 1969 to 1970 and thereafter served on the Board of Directors of the APA. A recipient of the Distinguished Professional Contribution Award of the APA in 1975, he had been appointed by President Carter as a member of the President's Commission on Mental Health. Dr. Albee specialized in prevention and testified concerning retardation.

Dr. Reginald L. Jones was professor of education and chairman of the Afro-American Studies Department at the University of California at Berkeley. He was a member of the President's Task Force on the mentally handicapped. He testified primarily on stigma.

Dr. Leon J. Kamin was former chairman of the Psychology Department at Princeton University. He was author of *The Science and Politics of IQ* (1974) and spoke on the history of IQ testing.

Dr. Jane R. Mercer was chairman of the Department of Sociology at the University of California, Riverside. She was author of the book *Labeling the Mentally Retarded* (1973), and she testified on the inadequacies of the IQ tests to predict grades, especially of minority pupils, and on the need to assess nonschool adaptive behavior.

Gloria Johnson Powell, M.D., was the director of the Child Psychiatry Outpatient Department of the Neuropsychiatric Institute, UCLA Center for Health Studies, and professor in the Department of Psychiatry, Division of Child Psychiatry & Mental Retardation at UCLA Medical School. She testified on the etiology of retardation and on socioeconomic status and black culture.

Dr. Alice V. Watkins was a professor at California State, Los Angeles; her classes dealt with methods of teaching handicapped children, including the learning disabled, emotionally disturbed, and mentally retarded. She had taught EMR children in Los Angeles. Dr. Watkins testified concerning EMR placement and curriculum and mainstreaming.

The defense experts included the following:

Dr. Jerome E. Doppelt was director of the Psychological Measurement Division and vice president of the Psychological Corporation, the publisher of Wechsler IQ tests.

Dr. Herbert Goldstein was a professor and director of the Curriculum Research and Development Center at Yeshiva University and was regarded as a leading expert in curriculum design for the mentally retarded. He spoke on EMR curricula and their effects and on the nature of mental retardation.

Dr. Robert A. Gordon was an associate professor in sociology at

Johns Hopkins University. He testified as a critic of Mercer's work and on intelligence tests and their validity in general.

Dr. Herbert J. Grossman was a professor of Pediatric Neurology at UCLA. Dr. Grossman was editor of the *Manual on Terminology and Classification of Mental Retardation* (1977). He reviewed the data on the effects of poverty and prenatal and perinatal trauma on mental retardation.

Dr. Lloyd Humphreys was professor of psychology at the University of Illinois and editor of the *American Journal of Psychology*. He spoke on intelligence, intelligence testing and psychometrics, and race differences.

Dr. Nadine Lambert was a professor of education at the University of California at Berkeley and the developer of an adaptive behavior assessment device approved for use by the State Department of Education. She spoke about assessment, the role of IQ tests in it, and the validity of IQ scores.

Dr. Leo Munday was the vice president and general manager of the Test Department of Houghton Mifflin Company, the publisher of the Stanford–Binet test and other tests.

Dr. Jerome Sattler was a professor of psychology at San Diego State University and author of *Assessment of Children's Intelligence and Special Abilities* (2nd ed., 1982). He was a consultant to the defense and testified on the construct and predictive validity of the IQ tests.

Dr. Robert L. Thorndike was former chairman of the Department of Psychology at Columbia University and a developer of the Lorge–Thorndike Intelligence Test. He discussed intelligence and its measurement.

Dr. C. E. Meyers was a professor of educational psychology and special education at the University of Southern California. He testified concerning mental retardation, the EMR curriculum, and the status of the large number of erstwhile EMR children who had, because of legislation and litigation, been returned to regular classrooms.

Donald Ashurst was superintendent, Diagnostic School of Neurologically Handicapped Children, Southern California, an agency of the state. He testified concerning mental retardation and the past and present mental status of the named plaintiffs.

Frederick Hanson was consultant in the education of the mentally retarded for the Office of Special Education. He testified concerning the preparation of the list of IQ tests approved by the state for use in EMR placement and on his view of the causes of ethnic disproportion in the numbers of EMR classes.

Leslie Brinegar was director of the Office of Special Education and testified concerning the role of his office in monitoring and correcting school districts with respect to ethnic disproportion and concerning the department's view of the causes of disproportion.

Frances Caine was retired supervisor of classes for the mentally handicapped in San Francisco. She testified about the placement of the named plaintiffs, about placement generally, and about the EMR curriculum and classrooms.

Alice Bryant was a school psychologist and specialist, Psychological Services, in the Los Angeles school district. She testified concerning placement procedures in the huge L.A. district and about the causes of disproportion there.

James Colwell, a school psychologist in the San Francisco district, testified about the placement of the named plaintiffs and about the placement process generally.

Nancy Burenstein was a teacher of EMR and TMR classes. She described her classroom and daily curriculum and the behavior of some of the named plaintiffs.

Marilyn Stepney was a teacher of EMR and regular classes. She described her classroom and curriculum and the nature of the EMR children in her charge.

Finally, we ought to mention the principal defendant, Wilson Riles, the Superintendent of Public Instruction, a high elected official, and one of the most influential black educators in the nation. The fact that he had succeeded the very conservative Max Rafferty must have made doubly ironic his position as a defendant alleged to have racist intent to deprive black children of appropriate education by use of biased tests.

The lead attorneys in *Larry P.* were Armando Menocal III, leading a group of several lawyers and other assistants for the plaintiffs, and Joanne Condas, essentially alone for the defense.

Chicago and PASE

The initial trial of *PASE* came eight years after *Larry P.* was first heard in 1971, and much had happened in psychology and law, in addition to the already noted Cleary et al. (1975) report to the APA and the passage of PL 94–142 in 1975. As the decade wore on, the limits of mainstreaming, of compensatory education, of preschool intervention, even of affirmative integration itself became clearer, and optimism about the possibilities of change became very much muted where it still existed at all.

In the law the momentum of federal court involvement in large urban school districts was slowed by such cases as *Pasadena Board of Education* v. *Spangler* (427 U.S. 424, 1976, holding that initial integration plans need not be updated with every change in population) and *Milliken* v. *Bradley* (418 U.S. 717, 1974, holding that Judge Roth went beyond his authority in ordering a huge busing plan for Detroit that would involve the surrounding suburbs). *Washington* v. *Davis* (426 U.S 229, 1976) directly involved the racially disproportionate effect of an ability test, and the Supreme Court upheld the use of the test even though black candidates for police training in Washington, D.C., failed it more than twice as often as whites. This view, that a showing of disparate impact resulting from a relevant test without any showing of intent to discriminate was not sufficient to carry the day for plaintiffs, became clearer in various testing cases, with the Court showing less and less deference to the strict views of the EEOC (see Lerner's 1978 review for details), that racial disproportion was per se evidence of discrimination.

In psychology, reviewers like St. John (1975) and Stephan (1978) questioned the value of integration in helping black children. Other scholars—Gottlieb (1981); MacMillan, Jones, and Myers, (1976); Meyers, MacMillan, and Yoshida (1980)—reviewing the effect of mainstreaming on EMR children, found little if any effects upon their academic achievement and mixed effects upon their self-concepts. Even more generally, a consensus about ability testing and race was developing and spreading, partly because of the dismay among psychometricians with the result arrived at in *Larry P.* where the *premier* tests of ability, including the venerable Binet, were banned by judicial fiat. Two of these unhappy psychometricians were Gordon and Rudert (1979), who were responding directly to what they perceived to be inadequacies in the evidence and reasoning of *Larry P.*, and whose paper along with others that made the empirical point that ability tests are equally valid both for different races and for different classes (Guterman, 1979; Miele, 1979) were exhibits in *PASE* and much referred to there. (Both sides in *PASE*, in fact, had whatever benefit they could find from the *Larry P.* record, and the plaintiff team had had observers at the *Larry P.* trial.)

By the end of the 1970s, a clearer social science consensus had developed or been reestablished about many of the issues in dispute in these lawsuits. By consensus is not meant lack of controversy. Rather, what is referred to is agreement among psychologists most experienced and most expert according to the standards of their peers (for example, Breland, 1979; Cleary et al., 1975; Cronbach, 1984; Humphreys, 1979; Hunter, Schmidt, and Hunter, 1979; Linn, 1975, 1982; Sattler, 1982; Scarr, 1981; Thorndike and Hagen, 1977; Vernon, 1979). According to this consensus, there is a general mental ability usually called intelligence and consisting primarily of verbal facility; problem-solving ability; logical and quantitative reasoning; facility in learning, discriminating, and generalizing; and facility in forming concepts and applying them in novel situations. Measures of mental ability are fairly good predictors of academic success and most job performances and, in these uses, are as good for blacks as for whites. There was also a kind of consensus that the question whether population gene frequencies accounted for any part of the black-white differences in measured ability was not fruitful.

There was (and is) less consensus about the sources of intelligence in nature and nurture, though some degree of heritability in the range .2 to .8 is almost universally assumed. There was (and is) little consensus among experts about the plasticity of mental ability and about the power of known educational methods to alter it. Finally, few agreed (then or now), because few if any really know, about how best to educate children who are slow learners either generally or in particular areas—how best to deal, in short, with the mildly retarded or learning disabled (and in the case of the latter, how even to diagnose it).

Like many other northern cities, Chicago had been sued to integrate its schools, and it negotiated throughout the 1970s with plaintiffs and federal agencies, but the case never got to trial (it was finally settled in 1981). *PASE* very nearly did not get tried at all because of the imminence of a settlement that might have mooted the test issue (see Chapter 8).

The local context of the issues was very different in Chicago from what it had been in California. *PASE* had begun as a small organization (Parents in Action on Special Education) that was

largely Hispanic. Its organizer, one Dan Marquez, was an education student interning in an EMR classroom in a heavily Hispanic
district, and he thought most of the students in it really had
problems of culture and language rather than of low ability.

But the state had passed a strong bilingual education law in
1975, and the number and rate of Hispanic students in EMR
declined precipitately thereafter. One result was that the *PASE*
complaint was amended to eliminate all of its Hispanic plaintiffs.
Another was that there was no counterpart to *Diana,* setting a
precedent either for how to pursue this sort of lawsuit or for
minority relief by quota.

There was also no Chicago Association of Black Psychologists
pushing the lawsuit. Chicago has a large black middle class, and
the Chicago Board of Education (CBE) by 1980 was heavily staffed
with black professionals, many of whom used the questioned tests
in serving a predominantly black clientele. Black school officials
and psychologists testified for the defense in *PASE;* in California
the defense was carried almost exclusively by whites.

The large number of blacks in Chicago had another effect, that of
attenuating the apparent extent of disproportionate placement into
EMR classrooms. In the general school population, blacks were 60
percent; in the EMR population, they were 80 percent. But the
excess amounts to 125 percent of parity, as compared with the 200
percent of parity representation of blacks in the California EMR
system. A related difficulty for the plaintiffs had arisen with time.
Over the decade from 1970–1971 to 1979–1980, the white school
population had dropped from 199,699 to 95,528, and their rate of
EMR placement had gone up by a third, from 1.1 percent to 1.44
percent. Black losses were smaller, from 316,711 down to 290,021,
with EMR rates going from 2.8 percent to 3.7 percent (Plaintiffs
Suggested Findings; Designs for Change, 1982). The decreasing
absolute numbers of whites would make more and more difficult
any scheme that turned on an argument against segregation. Strict
proportionality might dictate nine black and three white children
in every EMR classroom, whereas in fact the average was about
ten blacks and two whites. The differences might be hard to notice.
Similar "numbers problems" might have affected San Francisco,
but *Larry P.* was modified before trial to make the entire state, and
not simply the city, the defendant. In the state the average class
should have had about nine whites to every black, and the excess of
black children was far more noticeable.

Finally, the special education system used by the CBE incorporated all the features made legally necessary by PL 94–142 and Section 504 of the Rehabilitation Act. The procedures, at least on the books, were the very model of a careful and legally mandated multimodal and multidisciplinary assessment and planning system for the handicapped, including the mentally handicapped.

PASE was a far shorter trial than *Larry P.*, lasting for only three weeks, with just under 2000 pages of testimony and argument, and with comparatively few witnesses. All of the experts of national note appeared for the plaintiffs. They included, in addition to Kamin, Albee, and Powell, who were repeaters from *Larry P.*, the following:

Dr. Robert Williams, professor of psychology and Afro-American studies from Washington University, was the deviser of the famous BITCH test (see Chapter 4) and appeared as an expert in testing and the black culture.

Dr. Richard Berk, professor of sociology at the University of California, Santa Barbara, testified to a study he directed, using the school records data of nearly 6000 referred children in Chicago, to assess the relative influence of IQ and other factors in the decisions to recommend and to place children into EMR classes.

Dr. Dale Layman, professor of special education, University of Illinois at Chicago Circle, testified on mental retardation and its assessment.

Dr. Robert Stoner, a private consulting school psychologist for the Joliet, Illinois, school system, retested the two plaintiffs in the case and testified as to his diagnosis of them.

Mr. John H. Brough, a registered occupational therapist, a private consultant in special education, and proprietor of a diagnostic and remedial learning center, testified as to the learning disability status of the two plaintiff children.

Mr. Albert Briggs, assistant superintendent for special education and pupil personnel for the Chicago school district, testified concerning referral and placement procedures and ethnic proportions in various special education categories.

The witnesses for the defense, all administrators for the CBE, included the following:

Ms. Barbara Williams, the due process coordinator for the CBE and a former regular and special education classroom teacher, described special education procedures and safeguards. She was a member of several black political organizations.

Mr. Elmer Smith, administrator of the Child Study Program for the Bureau of Child Study, testified on test bias and on socioeconomic factors in intellectual performance.

Mr. Terrence Hines, a director of one of the CBE's five Pupil Services Centers and a school psychologist for over twenty-five years, testified as to the role of school psychologists and their use of tests and gave his expert opinion, as a black psychologist, concerning bias of certain items.

Dr. Alice Zimmerman, director of the Mentally Handicapped Development Program for the CBE and former EMR teacher, testified concerning the EMR curriculum, the relations of poverty to EMR placement rates, and the referral and placement system.

The lead attorney for the plaintiffs was Wallace Winter, assisted by four others. The school board team was led by Patrick Halligan, assisted by two board attorneys. The city supported its team a good deal more than the state had supported Ms. Condas, and, with a smaller case and more lawyers, the defense in *PASE* was more evenly matched with the plaintiffs than was the case in *Larry P.*

Overview

Finally, it needs to be emphasized that among the differences in the backgrounds of these cases are the different histories that each judge had with his case. Judge Peckham, as we have seen, had made a preliminary decision in *Larry P.*, issuing his initial injunctions on the basis of an estimate that plaintiffs would prevail at a full trial on the merits of the case. The defense was thus handicapped at the start, and that would have been true even had Judge Peckham not been known to be the civil rights liberal that he was. Judge Grady had neither the previous commitment nor the reputation.

As will be seen, plaintiffs in Chicago won, by virtue of a settlement in the integration suit, what they did not win in *PASE*— that is, the banning of the IQ tests for use in evaluating children referred for special education placement. We will examine the effects and policy implications of these similar outcomes in Chapters 8 and 9, after considering the status of the plaintiff children (Chapter 2); the evidence in the two cases concerning the culture, socioeconomic status, and home environment (Chapter 3); the definitions and assessment of intelligence (Chapter 4) and mental retardation (Chapter 5); and the issue of test bias (Chapter 6). Finally, in Chapter 10, we will discuss the matter of finding truth in the domain of social science within the adversary system of Anglo-American law.

The two cases considered here would have been interesting to social scientists even had they both come out alike. Had the *Larry P.* opinion prevailed, for example, we would have the intriguing case of the failure of expert consensus in a venerable area of psychological research to prevail in the political arena. Had the consensus prevailed, as in *PASE*, we might have learned less about science and politics even while we were encouraged more by the persuasive power of the data. But the opposed opinions invite scrutiny, so as to discover what might be behind the difference, and to begin to see what strategies or tactics might improve the weight of good, and make clear the deficiencies of bad, social science evidence in the courtroom setting.

Endnotes

1. A standard deviation is a measure of the spread of the scores on any characteristic, like height or IQ, that is "normally" distributed: see, for example, the bell-shaped curves of Figure 1. In IQ, a standard deviation is 15 points; in grade-point average, it is about .5 (where A = 4, B = 3, and so forth). Another way to express the size of a standard deviation is to say that if the average score of the lower-scoring group is at the 30th percentile, the higher scoring group will score, on average, at the 70th.

2. A correlation is a measure of the degree of association between two variables and ranges from 0 to 1. The correlation between, say, fathers' height and sons' height is about +.50; between years of education and income, about +.60; between month of birth and height, about 0; and so on.

3. These classes typically kept their pupils segregated from other pupils for most of the day, except for recess, lunch, and P.E.

4. Record of trial.

Chapter 2

THE NAMED PLAINTIFFS

Both lawsuits were class action suits. The named plaintiffs represented the classes and were the living instantiations of the plaintiffs' claim that black children had been misplaced into EMR classes because of the racial bias of tests they took. The outcome of complex class action litigation does not by any means turn on who the representatives are. But when the issue is to some extent the degree of possession of some trait like intelligence or scholastic ability, the chosen representatives—the named plaintiffs—will themselves furnish more vivid evidence than would any class representative in, say, a securities fraud case.

Larry P.

The ambiguity of the issues was nowhere better illustrated than in the *Larry P.* testimony concerning the mental status of the named plaintiffs, the five black children who were identified from the list at the 1970 meeting. West drew for retesting D. L., soon to become famous as *Larry P.* He was nearly 12 when West came to his home to test him, and the record of that test, and more generally his passage through the school system, is not unrepresentative for the plaintiffs as a group.

D. L. had begun first grade in 1964 in a black school in Georgia when he was 5. He did badly, getting D's and E's, and whether it was youth or lack of ability, his first experience with school was of failure. He repeated first grade in San Francisco, where he was in a predominately black school (as were the other plaintiffs—these

30

were predesegregation days), and at the end of that year, in May of 1966, he was given the first of several WISCs, on which he attained a Full Scale (FS) score of 59.

For the next two and a half years he remained in the regular classes in second, third, and the first half of the fourth grade, and his achievement test scores were in the 1st to 6th percentile, with especial difficulty in reading. In February 1969, when he was aged 10–2 (10 years, 2 months), he was placed in an "ungraded" (the district's euphemism at that time for EMR) class, where he made some gain in reading achievement, with a Wide Range Achievement Test (WRAT) grade-level equivalent (GE) of 3, 1.5 grades better than what it had been in the regular class. (WRAT reading scores, however, represent vocabulary more than comprehension.)

That September he earned an FS score of 75 on a second WISC, establishing a pattern that persisted, with the exception of West's test, through 1977, when he was tested for the trial. That is, he scored lower on the Verbal Scale (71), and higher in the Performance Scale (85). By May 1970 the Admissions and Discharge Committee of the District Committee recommended that he return to regular class instruction part time, and by September 1970, when he was 11–9, his grade-level scores for reading achievement were 3.0 for reading and 4.6 for math (RT 8196 et seq.). Three years later, in Tacoma, Washington, to which the family had removed in 1972, he attained grade equivalents of 4.8 for reading, 5.0 for language, and 4.0 for math in achievement testing (RT 1057). He was then 14–10, and if one translates the grade equivalents into chronological ages, it is possible to calculate rough IQs (MA/CA) of 66, 67, and 61. In fact, a WISC given in September 1973 resulted in an FS score of 67. The examiner noted, however, that D. L. could do better when very much encouraged to do so and that he seemed uninvolved and uninterested most of the time, even to the point of making seemingly random responses (RT 1338). He offered a second score, estimating a higher potential of 76.

D. L. had not graduated from high school in Tacoma, though he had marched with his class at the ceremonies. The last set of grades put into evidence (RT 1076) were E's in history, typing, and math; D's in English fundamentals, reading workshop, and individual reading; C's in art fundamentals and wood technology, B in P.E., and A in Advanced P.E. D. L. had been a varsity football player (cornerback) and had some skill in crafts. He was unemployed and unskilled. He spent his days sleeping late, eating, playing cards, and watching TV. He did not drive and had no license.

In his final assessment before trial, supervised by Ashurst, the state's expert, D. L. scored FS 73 on the Wechsler Adult Intelligence Scale (WAIS), but, again, the examiner noted that he was far more forthcoming and clear after the testing than he was during it (RT 1016). On the Ravens Progressive Matrices, he scored at the 20th percentile of young adult norms (RT 8342), a result consistent with his relatively better scores on Performance tests.

Of the Wechsler tests that D. L. had been given by school psychologists (the second of whom was black), he scored (FS) 59, 75, 67 to 76 (the tester offered a range), and 73. In October 1970, preparatory to filing the lawsuit that goes by D. L.'s pseudonym, West went to his home, chatted with him and his mother for an hour or so, then tested him for an hour and a half or so, and left, writing his reports a few days later (RT 1300 et seq.). The test produced an FS score of 94, 20 points higher than scores on the same test earned one year earlier and three years later.

West's administration was a focus of controversy, as were those of Dent and Pierce. It was clearly in their interest to have plaintiffs with IQs as high as possible, the better to demonstrate alleged misplacement, and they did produce atypically high IQs, as Table 1 makes clear. For all five plaintiff children, the intervals from first to

Table 1.   Summary Scores, in Chronological Order, of IQ Tests Given

	Test Administration					
Child	1.	2.	3.[a]	4.	5.[b]	Ravens (1977) Percentile
DL	59	75	94	67–76	73	20
JL	68[c]	74	99		77	35
MS	70[c]	—	91	77	80	"average range"
JH	68[c]	62	79	69	78	55
SW	59	—	87	71	60	20
Average	64.8		90		73.6	

[a]Tests in this column given by members of Bay Area Association of Black Psychologists.
[b]Tests in this column given for trial in October 1977 at the Diagnostic School for Northern California, under supervision of Donald Ashurst, an expert witness for state defendants.
[c]Stanford–Binet IQ.
NOTE: The entries are keyed to the administration given for initial litigation in 1971, in column 3; those given by the defense for trial in 1977, in column 5; and the first test given by the school district in column 1. Other tests, where in the record, are set in order.

last test averaged just over nine years (range from 6–9 to 11–5), and the average FS score for the group over that period changed very little, from 64.8 to 73.6; but the "for litigation" scores averaged 90.

West's departures from standard administration and scoring provide the explanation for this discrepancy, at least in part. For example, when he asked Darryl how scissors and a copper pan are alike, he accepted the answer "that they are both iron" as fully creditable because it had the idea of metal; he accepted "acting bad" as the definition of "nonsense"; and when he asked what the color of rubies is and D. L. did not know, he prompted him, finally eliciting that the stones in a king's crown might be pink, a color he identified by pointing to something pink in the room. When West asked Darryl why criminals should be locked up, Darryl seemed not to understand the question, so he rephrased it, identifying criminals as people who sometimes break the law (RT 1296–1309).

West's view of standardized testing, clearly shared by his colleagues, was this: "If the purpose of psychological testing is to tap psychological function and if by asking a child a question different than the way it is posed in the manual affords me to tap that function, then that appears to be much more important to me than to be somewhat compulsive and concretistic in mentioning every word that is listed in the manual" (RT 1003).

Pierce tested J. L. and M. S. He, too, was loose with his administration, to the point where a reviewing committee of the California Association of School Psychologists and Psychometrists (CASPP) said he had created a new test. Pierce, in turn, criticized them for their "strict, almost pathological adherence to the manual" (RT 3114). He went past the discontinuation limits on subtests, rephrased questions, accepted nonstandard answers (for example, to the Similarities item "How are a yard and a pound alike?" he credited the answer "A yard has leaves, and a dog pound has dirt" (RT 3102), and even made up a new item—"How are a basketball and a football alike."

Plaintiff J. L., under such conditions, scored at FS 99, 25 points higher than he had gotten three weeks earlier with a school psychologist (though Pierce didn't know of that prior administration). J. L. had had no success in schools. He had been retained in kindergarten, again in first grade, and at age 8, went into the "ungraded" class, where he was reading at the preprimer level, did not know the alphabet, and was at first-grade level in arithmetic.

He was in the EMR class for two years, made some progress,

and was retested in March 1971 for possible placement in the EH (educationally handicapped) program.[1] At his parents' request, he returned to regular fifth grade classes in 1971, at age 10, and was reading at second grade level by the end of the year. He remained in regular sixth, seventh, and eighth grade classes, where his failures became progressively deeper. He was a behavior problem, often absent, and reading at third grade level in grade 8, where he was the furthest behind in a class that was itself behind in grade level (ranging in achievement GE's from 4.0 to 6.7). At the time of trial, at age 15, his grades were five F's and a D.

Plaintiff M. S., Pierce's other examinee, was very slow to learn, and in kindergarten had difficulty with naming colors and body parts, simple counting, and knowing different coins or his address and phone number. He repeated first grade, and then entered EMR in 1969, when he was age 7–8, where he remained for the better part of two years. He "tested out" of EMR in 1971 (FS IQ = 77) and entered grade 5 that fall, with special tutoring. He repeated fifth grade, tested at GE levels of 2.0 for reading and 1.6 for math, and returned to EMR programs in 1973 at the request of his parents, where he (and his parents) remained content. In the year prior to trial he was age 15, in grade 8, with a reading GE score of 3.4.

Dent tested J. H. and wrote the report on S. W. (who had been tested by one Sylvia O'Bradovich, whereabouts unknown at time of trial). J. H. was another student who, shortly after beginning school, had been assigned to an EH class, where he remained until he was 8. At that time, in September 1969, he could not print his name, read beyond the preprimer level, or count to 20 without confusion, and he was hyperactive. He was placed into EMR and remained there until September 1973, when he was 12, by which time he could read at second grade level and do simple fundamental computations. He went back into EH programs but made little progress. He was a poor attender and a behavior problem, and at the time of trial, when he was 16, he still read at second grade level and did math at fourth grade level.

S. W. also repeated kindergarten, repeated grade 1, and then was placed in EMR in 1969, where she remained until 1971, the year she became a plaintiff. At that time, at age 10, she was reading in the second primer. Her attendance in her first year of EMR was the best of her entire career—she missed only 28 days. She returned to fifth grade and continued to fail. At the time of the trial, at age 16, she was still in half-time attendance in junior high school, four to six years below grade level in reading comprehension and in arithmetical concepts and computation. No one knows how she attained her high scores on the test reported by Dent, since the actual tester was not around to testify.

This recital of multiple school failure is a short version of what the state presented in its brief on appeal, a remarkable document that went on for sixty-seven pages before it got around to legal argument, and which plaintiff respondents found to be an irrelevant and *ad hominem* attack. The class had been certified in 1974, and, as Judge Peckham noted in his opinion (1979, p. 987), "the interests of unnamed class members do not depend on the particular validity or even mootness of the claims of the individual class representatives." But the judge also noted that, having observed plaintiffs and having heard the testimony already reviewed, he did not regard them as retarded.

It may have made no difference if he had so regarded them, but their cases do tend to give color to the issues and to highlight the ambiguities inherent in them. The main allegations of the plaintiffs were that biased IQ tests had played a primary role in misplacing nonretarded children into "dead-end" EMR classes, thus doing them irreparable injury. If these children were selected as the most likely candidates to prove misplacement, it is hard to imagine that there was much egregiously bad misplacement going on. All had been identified as unusually serious failures in predominantly poor, black schools; and the choice for them was either the regular classes they were failing in or the EMR classes which carried a label that most observers, and certainly the black parents and professionals involved in this action, found stigmatizing and demeaning, a flagrant instance of blaming the victim. It was a Hobson's choice. One set of parents (of M. S.) requested his return to EMR; others were distressed at their children's continued failure in regular classes and asked for special help, but not a return to EMR placement. That, of course, would have been very hard to do while the trial was pending.

Plaintiffs argued (Mercer, RT 1753–1759), and the judge seems to have believed (1979, p. 932) that "it is not unusual for (black) high school students to be reading at the third grade level and performing at only the fourth grade level in mathematics." That is surely wrong. What Mercer found was that blacks in California perform at between the 15th and 20th percentile in reading, or just slightly less than a standard deviation below whites. That means that black twelfth graders read at between the eighth and ninth grade level, which is considerably higher than what plaintiff children were doing. On the other hand, the plaintiffs showed occasional performances that exceeded the fourth grade level usually considered asymptotic for persons mildly (educably) mentally retarded. J. H. scored at the 55th percentile on the Ravens Matrices,[2] S. W. was at grade level in word naming and had a fine memory for details of the lives of entertainment heroes and heroines (she would be in Jensen's, 1970, scheme, a secondary retardate—one with average level I ability and better prognosis for successful living than a primary retardate more uniformly retarded); D. L. actually performed a bit above GE 4 on many achievement tests, was a varsity athlete, and was skillful at certain crafts. M. S. was an excellent athlete; and J. L.'s Ravens score was at the 35th percentile.

Several testers cited in the school records, including those under Ashurst's supervision, commented on the lack of motivation in the children both in school and in test situations—they appeared to expect to fail and did so. Thus, D. L. was reported to answer questions after the test was over that he had just failed during it. And in virtually every record there was some suggestion that the child might be "more EH than EMR." The CASPP review stated, "in every one of these cases, a staff psychologist at some time questioned the appropriateness of the diagnosis of EMR and specifically noted the possibility of some other reason for poor performance" (RT 3861).

As will be seen, the labels "mildly mentally retarded" and "educably mentally retarded," though both refer to an IQ range of about 50 to 70, are different in their emphasis on nonschool related adaptive behavior (AB). There is plenty of evidence (see Mercer, 1973, who also presented it at trial, where it went pretty much undisputed) that before the effects of the mainstreaming movement took hold, most EMR children in the years before they entered and after they left school were not seen as so unusual that they warranted the label "retarded," which now requires, in addition to significantly subaverage intellectual functioning, impairment in everyday adaptive behavior (Grossman, 1977). But to say that a child in that IQ range is *only* retarded in school is to say that he is a failure for nearly half his waking hours during twelve years of his life. This dispute involved more than the definition of retardation because if nonintellectual adaptive behavior is a part of the definition of retardation, it may also be part of the definition of intelligence in general. We will deal with these matters extensively in Chapters 4 and 5.

The two sides talked a good deal about adaptive behavior, but they were each remiss in their attention to it in the named plaintiffs. The black psychologists scarcely troubled themselves to find out anything about the children's school records, health or developmental history, or behavior in home and neighborhood—they took their IQ score and made their judgment that the children were not retarded in just the very cursory way they complained that the school had used to decide that they were. The government did better than this but was still slipshod by any rigorous view of the official standards. The CASPP report found all records inadequate with respect both to AB and to health and development history (RT 8393). Ashurst had to admit that his own judgment of retardation was not based on any adequate knowledge of home and community lives of the children (RT 8472).

The judge did not appear to be pleased by the state's attempt to establish the retardation of the plaintiff children. At one point, after some testimony by Ashurst about J. H.'s lack of motivation in school, he cut off Condas to ask sarcastically, "Is he hopeless . . . should people be put in EMR classes for lack of motivation?" (RT 8450), and he took the role of cross-examiner after Ashurst had conceded that he knew little about the AB of the children: "I suppose it is possible, hypothetically, that the addition of that information, if it was all very positive with respect to the youngsters, might change the ultimate determination?" to which Ashurst answered, "Correct!" (RT 8422).

PASE

In *PASE*, the status of the two black plaintiffs played comparatively little role in the suit, and not because they were any more clearly ineligible for EMH (the Chicago acronym equivalent to EMR). The two girls were retested in 1974 by plaintiffs' expert, Robert Stoner, a black psychologist who, unlike his San Francisco counterparts, was a certified school psychologist (since 1965) and a registered clinical psychologist (since 1972), had been staff and then chief school psychologist in the Joliet system for thirteen years, and was well-qualified in the use of the tests at issue.

Again, unlike his San Francisco counterparts, he gave off the signs of competence in psychometrics: He knew and accepted the notions of general intelligence and the variable loading of different subtests on it, he knew the standard error of measurement of the WISC and explained it well to the judge, and so forth. Stoner thought that the tests were biased against black children (though it was unclear what he meant by that), but he insisted, even in the face of a strongly skeptical judge, that he administered the test as he taught others to do: exactly according to the manual (Grady could not believe that testers really enforced time limits in "the Draconian kind of way" prescribed [RT 997]). Stoner did, however, "test the limits" following his standard administrations, in an effort to learn more about the intellectual potential of his clients.

B. B., who was 16 when retested in 1974, was the daughter (one of ten children) of a welfare mother who did not read or write. Despite a record of reading, pronunciation, and vocabulary problems, B. B. had been promoted up through regular grades in predominantly minority schools until 1972, when, at age 14, she transferred to a predominantly white school in seventh grade. At this school she was tested, found eligible for, and placed into EMH. She remained in EMH through high school, graduating in 1977. At the time of trial, she was in a special program at Malcolm X Junior College. She could not fill out job applications.

Stoner found her to have an FS IQ of 75, with a very low Verbal score but a Performance IQ of 85. He found her achievement scores on the WRAT to be lower than the IQ would predict and concluded that placement in an LD or EH class would have been preferable for her, since he did not find her mentally retarded. (Her achievement levels were 2–4 for reading, 2–6 for spelling, and 2–9 for arithmetic.) He did note in his report, however (RT 1051), that her score of 75 put her in a "borderline" category and might make her eligible for an EMH class. Her age equivalent level on the Bender Gestalt Test was estimated at 6 to 6½ years.

A. J., born in 1962, and the girl in Marquez's class, was the other plaintiff. At the time of trial she was age 17 and in her junior year at Phillips High School and was reported to be doing average work in the regular program. Her mother was studying part time for a nursing degree and had six other children. Like B. B., A. J. had

had a record of reading difficulties from 1969 on, and sometime in the 1970–1971 school year she was tested, found eligible, and placed into EMH in the predominantly Hispanic Youngman school. She remained in EMH until 1976, when the board of education acceded to her mother's request that she be removed from EMH. She then repeated eighth grade as an LD student, following which she went on to high school.

Stoner had found scale scores averaging 5 for the verbal subtests of the WISC and 7.4 for the performance scales for an FS IQ of 72. Given the prevailing professional definition of mental retardation (calling for an IQ at least two standard deviations below the mean, or, in this case, 70, and significantly subaverage adaptive behavior), he concluded that A. J. was not retarded. Her Bender score was at the 6½- to 7-year level. Her achievement scores were below grade level but consistent with her IQ. Stoner, again pointing out the differences between her Verbal and Performance scores, said that she would be better categorized as LD or EH, just as he had done with B. B.

It seems likely that the two plaintiffs in *PASE*, having lower IQs than their counterparts in *Larry P.*, were more arguably mildly retarded. I did not see the school records, but their attorney told me that the IQs recorded in the school records were about a dozen points lower than those reported by Stoner. The CBE, however, did not seem interested in establishing their retardation. In California, plaintiffs were questioned extensively, with the purpose, to some degree at least, of displaying their deficiency. None of that happened in Chicago, nor was anything made much in argument about how "truly" retarded they were. The defense said they had been appropriately placed, of course, and it argued that the LD alternative was not a useful or even a very different one; but most of its argument did *not* concern the specific status of the two plaintiffs. The defense certainly did not attack the validity of the retesting—there was little reason to do so.

The introduction of LD as the more probably "true" classification of the plaintiffs, and the emphasis it was given by the defense, was unique to *PASE*. More will be said about that in the chapter on retardation. For the moment we may note that it provided a way of accounting for poor performance without imputing retardation, and it depended in part upon looking at variation among subtests, which therefore were accorded some utility and validity by the very side attacking the test of which they were parts.

Conclusion

We began this section by commenting on the ambiguity of the status of the named plaintiffs in *Larry P.* Notwithstanding the nonstandard test administrations given by the black psychologists in that lawsuit, the plaintiffs met the EMR standards of 1969, when they were placed, but even then they were near the effective borderline of 75 that prevailed, especially for minority children, in San Francisco. It is unquestionably true that a few years later they would not have been placed, except perhaps for S. W., and that, under Judge Peckham's quota, they *could* not be placed, as the discussion in Chapter 5 will make clear. In *PASE,* it seems even clearer that under the standards prevailing in Illinois in the early 1970s the two plaintiffs met the standards for placement since an IQ level of 80 then prevailed.

As will also be clear, the elimination of the "borderline retarded" category (IQs of 65–80) as one conferring eligibility for special education has left large numbers of very slow learning children in a no-man's land of education, between the rock of failure and the hard place of stigmatization. The plaintiff children, again perhaps excepting S. W., were in fact like the children who were taken from EMR programs by the thousands during the 1970s because of the lower cutoff and because of legislative pressures; but they were also like many children who never had been placed into EMR and, though four to five years below grade level, managed as the slowest students in slow classes. These also will be described in Chapter 5.

Endnotes

1. The EH program at that time gave special remedial instruction to children from regular classes who have some specific learning handicap, neurological disorder, or emotional disorder.
2. The state's expert Ashurst tried to minimize the weight of this fact by claiming that the Ravens was merely a test of "perceptual adequacy rather than intellectual capacity" (8141). He (and the plaintiffs) may have been surprised to learn that one authority (Jensen, 1980) regards it as "an excellent culture-reduced measure of fluid 'g,' probably the surest instrument we now possess for discovering intellectually gifted children from disadvantaged backgrounds . . ." (p. 648).

Chapter 3

GENES, SOCIOECONOMIC STATUS, FAMILY BACKGROUND, AND CULTURE

How could the large black-white test score differences described in Chapter 1 be accounted for? Much depended on the sort of answer developed for the judges. A genetic hypothesis had little chance; even if it were possible to support it, courts are to a large degree representative of public opinion, and American public opinion tends to be highly environmentalist in outlook. In any case, it is scarcely imaginable that a liberal judge like Judge Peckham could have approved such a hypothesis. But if the genetic hypothesis could be eliminated, the explanatory factors that remain are test bias, cultural differences. socioeconomic or psychosocial factors common to the two races, or combinations of these. All of these terms are very difficult to define, as witness the following dialogue from *Larry P.* (RT 245ff):

> *The Court* (to Condas): Is it your position that all of your people take the position that the IQs are not culturally biased?

> *Ms. Condas:* Well, Your Honor, I think one of the things that is going to have to surface here eventually is there is no definite agreement on what the term "culturally biased" means. I think that's part of the problem.

> *The Court:* Now, those terms are not synonymous, "racially" and "culturally." I want to be sure we agree on that.

> *Ms. Condas:* They are not.

41

The Court: So if the contention is made in defense that the IQ test is not racially biased, or racially discriminatory, but it is culturally so based on socioeconomic levels, then where are we in terms of the statutory claims?

Ms. Condas: I think, first, we have to ascertain whether "culturally" has the kind of connotation in that regulation. My guess, for example, it would mean that it would be more distinction between the black and the Chicano problem; that racially biased would be because of the kind of thing that we are hearing so much about today.

Culturally biased would be a matter of perhaps not speaking English, or speaking Chinese, or speaking Spanish, or something, or having a cultural background that is foreign.

The Court: How would you distinguish the poor whites of Appalachia from the children at Beverly Hills High School? Is there a cultural difference?

Ms. Condas: Again, Your Honor, it's not my role to define culture.

The Court: One may be predominantly "Wasp" and the other may be perhaps European heritage, Jewish perhaps in faith.

I mean, would you not say there is a cultural difference—

Ms. Condas: I don't think that's—

The Court: [continuing] between Appalachia—when you say culturally discriminatory, I mean, I'm concerned, though, about how slippery these terms are.

We do agree—and I wanted to be sure that I established that. I assumed that was so, but I wanted to be sure that we understood each other; that the terms are different, "racial" and "culture." They may overlap, but they are not the same thing necessarily.

What I am really getting at is whether or not a finding that the IQ tests were discriminatory with respect to lower socioeconomic groups, whether the plaintiffs, if they established that, would be entitled to win on that issue. This is just really an extension of the discussion that I initiated at the earlier of the two pretrial conferences.

I will be quite frank. I still don't understand whether your principals really understand what the issues are here; I mean, really, what has to be applied here in terms of law. And I say this because, as I indicated to you, this is all very fascinating, but, you know, six weeks of trial time, if we are all going to be about where we are now with the same disagreements and shadings, with the same concessions that I gather are found among the discovery material on the part of the defendants, unless it has been totally misrepresented here, that it's not racially biased, but there is a bias, socioeconomic bias of the test.

The concepts were no easier to pin down in *PASE;* consider the following (RT 1555–1557):

The Court: Maybe it is just the term "middle class" that confuses me, and maybe it has no—in other words, maybe it is no big deal. Everyone is saying "middle class."

Mr. Halligan: I don't think it is.

The Court: Who is middle class? Is the blue collar plumber who makes $30,000 a year—

Mr. Halligan: He is.

The Court: Is he middle class?

Mr. Halligan: I think he is.

The Court: Well, how about the school teacher who makes $13,000 a year? Is he or she middle class?

Mr. Halligan: I reckon. Let me tell you what we are driving at—

The Court: Are we talking about money? Are we talking about education?

Mr. Halligan: We are talking about the curriculum content.

The Court: We are not teaching people to live in Greece or Tasmania. I understand that. I don't think anybody says we should be.

Mr. Halligan: Well, I don't know about the plaintiffs' witnesses. I think it is important to mention these things. To me it is obvious, and to Dr. Alice Zimmerman, too. Maybe we are belaboring the obvious. I think we need to, to develop my next question, and I hope you will bear with me.

The Court: I am not even sure about white, either, and again I don't know if this goes to the nub of the case, but I think there are many, many black people in the society that speak the identical language and learn the identical things and hold the identical jobs.

Note that the question of a separate black culture pervades the other issues. At one limit, a translated IQ test might be considered unfair if used, say, on native Africans, even if it had criterion validity (predicted performance in American schools), because both school and test might be inappropriate institutions in an alien culture. That is, it might truly be the case that persons in such cultures displayed social and physical problem-solving skills in ways far more independent of test performance than would be the case in American society.

If, therefore, American blacks are seen as being part of a different culture, then what appears to be an intellectual deficit may be something more neutral, simply a difference. Such a view carries the implication, realized to a degree in the case of bilingual and bicultural programs, that there ought to be a special curriculum for a separate culture.

Knowing just where to place American blacks, however, is difficult. If being of a different culture means having a distinct language, a unique kinship system, particular sets of norms for interpersonal relations, characteristic religious and moral values, all combining in different "lifestyles" and life goals, then the hypothetical African tribe or nation surely has a different culture. Of American blacks, however, two things are true: They have a unique shared history and experience, and they are part of American culture, sharing for the most parts its language and its values. A unique, shared experience is what is common to several ethnic groups; some of these shared experiences seem more different from American culture than the black experience.

The more that blacks are seen as part of a separate culture, the easier it is to see IQ tests as an unfair imposition of an artifact of the mainstream culture on them. (The fact that the test might predict success in another mainstream institution, the school—that is, the test of equal criterion validity—will be dealt with in Chapter 6.) On the other hand, the more that blacks are seen as but one of several ethnic groups sharing the language, values, and aspirations of the mainstream culture, the more their intellectual deficit might be explained in terms common to all such explanations: by adducing socioeconomic or psychosocial factors known to act in similar ways regardless of ethnicity.

The two lawsuits were very different in the way the defenses dealt with concepts of genes, culture, and socioeconomic or psychosocial factors. We now turn to each of them.

Larry P.

Menocal's opening statement made it clear that the spirit, if not the person, of Arthur Jensen would be present at the trial. The state had not contended in 1972, at the preliminary injunction phase of the trial, that the reason for the excessive number of blacks in EMR classes was a racial genetic inferiority with respect to intelligence. The same luck of the draw that had provided a liberal judge, however, also provided a state's attorney, Joanne Condas, who was sympathetic to the Jensen hypothesis. During the years of discovery she consulted with Jensen and accumulated a file of his papers labeled "genetic factors" (which she obligingly put into the hands of plaintiffs' attorneys). Most damagingly, moreover, she permitted Leslie Brinegar, the director of the Office of Special Education, to sign under oath the answer to interrogatories (Nos. 13 and 14, filed August 3, 1976) asking why there was such a disproportion of black children in EMR; part of the answer included the phrase "perhaps even a poorer genetic pool for all races who are ghettoized in the inner city." An amended answer followed that referred to the number of EMR persons as being "highly dependent on such factors as circumstances of heredity and birth, adequacy of health care, economic conditions, and family circumstances." It was not much of an improvement.

A few weeks before trial the state said it would definitely not use as a defense evidence of a poor genetic pool among blacks. But the damage had been done. The named defendants (Wilson Riles and the members of the State Board of Education [SBE]) disavowed any suggestion of genetic inferiority in blacks. But the professionals and bureaucrats in the Office of Special Education (OSE) all maintained what they termed an "agnostic position." All five were asked whether they believed that black people had a poorer genetic pool than white people, and they all answered in the manner of Brinegar, "I don't feel I have enough data to support or deny that" (RT 4695). The answer is scientifically impeccable, but it is not the sort of testimony that will persuade a liberal judge of the purity of one's intentions.

In any case, the plaintiffs saw to it that the name of Jensen recurred throughout the trial, much to the discomfort of the defense (see RT 4121, where Condas complained of their doing this after the state had foresworn the use of the "poor genetic pool" defense, and the latter portion of Riles's examination, where Menocal details the fact that Condas consulted Jensen). The state was left with two defenses. It could try to prove that the differences in intelligence were real and that the IQ tests validly predicted scholastic achievement; it could then try to prove that an adequate explanation of the differences lay in the average differ-

ence between the races in socioeconomic status (SES) and family
background variables common to the races. The plaintiffs knew
this, of course, and there followed a very odd confrontation
between a proponent (Condas) of an SES explanation, whose heart
was not really in it, and a plaintiffs' counsel (Menocal), who, though
an environmentalist, had to try to categorize as many as possible of
SES and psychosocial effects on IQ as racial or "cultural" and
otherwise minimize SES effects on IQ.

The Literature

At this point I shall review some relevant literature in order both
to show what was and what is available for an adequate defense in
these two cases and any like them and to set a standard by which a
case can be judged.

A recent review of the SES-scholastic achievement relations by
White (1982) presents a meta-analysis of nearly 200 studies. He
classified the SES measures as "traditional"—referring to measures
of parental income, occupational status, education, source of income (for example, welfare), whether the home is owned or not,
number of appliances, books, or other possessions—or as "home
atmosphere"—including such dimensions as the intellectual aspirations and expectations of parents, the responsiveness and involvement of the mother as caretaker, the provision of appropriate
play materials, the avoidance of punishment, the language model
of the home, the number and variety of cultural and recreational
activities, academic guidance and support, and so on. Between
these two groups of factors—the less direct traditional and structural, and the more direct home environmental or process variables, respectively—are some that seem to fall in between: the
intactness and size of the family; its degree of participation,
through friends and social organizations, in the middle-class world;
the number of its generations in the middle class; and so on.

The traditional structural variables are typified by the Duncan
(1961) and Warner, Meeker, and Eels (1949) scales and tend to be
correlated with school achievement about $r = .30$ and somewhat
higher with IQ, as both Mercer and Humphreys testified. But
White's review showed that the more direct measures of home
environment yield a median correlation with school achievement
of .58.

Now, the data that needed to be shown at trial by the *Larry P.*

defense were those that one would adduce to make a plausible case that the IQ difference between races is caused by the same factors that cause the IQ differences between the socioeconomic strata within a race. Several approaches can be taken to make this case, which I will describe in order to illustrate the poverty of the state's attempt. One can try to show that when the races are matched on SES, there isn't much or any difference to worry about. For example, the report of IQs of the children who were subjects in the Collaborative Perinatal Project (Broman, Nichols, and Kennedy, 1975, p. 241) reported that in the eight (of twelve) hospitals serving a significant number of clinic patients of both races, the average SES difference of those children was only 5 points (a third of an S.D. unit). In a subset of these data, reported in Nichols (1970), the racial IQ differences were near zero in two hospitals where the subjects were almost perfectly matched in SES. However, data from elsewhere (Jensen and Figueroa, 1975; Kaufman and Doppelt, 1976; Shuey, 1966) dispute this approach.

Broadening the meaning of SES to include the process or psychosocial variables of family background and home environment is another way to show that SES, not culture, is the source of the race difference. One must avoid terming the process variables "cultural" since, for the most part, they are not. In the trial, Mercer termed a mixture of cultural, traditional SES and process variables "sociocultural," but since most are intended for use in various ethnic groups, they are clearly not "cultural" in the sense in which the term was used in the beginning of this chapter. The variables she testified to (RT 1629ff) were language spoken at home (English or other), crowdedness of home, parent education, parent aspiration for the child, and ownership or rental of home, and they were scored 1 or 0. Minority children of families scoring positively on all of these had average IQs (100 and 104 for black and Chicano children, respectively), while minority children whose parents scored zero had IQs of 83 and 84. Only one of the variables (language spoken) is cultural in the narrow sense of the term. "Sociocultural" could have been a sufficient opening through which to squeeze the broad definition of SES to show, if possible, that the same process measures that lead to low or high IQ in whites do so in the same way in blacks.[1]

The point is well made in a study by Trotman (1977). She showed that the families of black and white ninth grade girls who had nearly identical traditional SES scores using the Warner, Meeker, and Eels (1949) scale had very different scores (1 S.D. apart) on the home environmental process measures (Wolf, 1966), a fact that might explain, to a court if not to Jensen, the differences (again in S.D. units) of about 0.8 S.D. in IQ and achievement. There was even a correlation of .49 between number of generations the family was in the middle class and child's IQ performance. In fact, the families of the black children had been middle class for about one generation, while the white families had been in the middle class for about two. The aggregate of the process measures correlated .68 and .37 with IQ in blacks and whites, respectively, was more highly related to school achievement than IQ itself (correlations of about .75 versus .55) and was a far better predictor of IQ and achievement than structural SES.

A study by Bradley, Caldwell, and Elardo (1977) also showed that, for both blacks and whites, the process measures of home environment predicted three-year-old IQ substantially better than structural SES measures did, and the strength of the prediction was about the same (correlations of .62 and .58) for whites and blacks, respectively. The two samples were 20 points, or 1.3 S.D. units, apart in IQ and 1.3 S.D. units apart in the process measure (the structural SES scores were not given).

A recent study by Blau (1981) makes the point in a slightly different way. She studied black and white fifth and sixth grade children from both middle and working classes, as defined by the Duncan (1961) SES index. The IQs of the groups were 109 for white middle-class children, 100 for black middle-class and white working-class children, and 94 for black working-class children. The working class groups, though much alike on the structural SES measures, differed markedly in other respects, particularly in SES of family of origin and average education of mother's friends (see Table 2, which is adapted from Blau's Tables 2–2 and 2–4). Notice also that, though the occupation and education scores of black middle-class parents are far closer to those of the white middle class than to the white working class, the other scores, reflecting middle-class exposure or middle-class background of the parents, show the black middle class to be closer to the white working class than to the white middle class, just as are the IQs of their children.

The simple SES scores simply do not tell the whole story. In Blau's study the initial 10-point difference between her two samples of children was reduced to 6 points by various combinations of these tabulated variables, and it should be noted that they do not

Table 2. SES and Background Variables by Race and Social Class

	Means[a]			
	Middle Class		Working Class	
Variable	White	Black	White	Black
Duncan index	71.1	62.6	24.8	19.7
Mother education	6.2	5.6	4.4	4.2
Father education	6.7	5.6	4.3	4.1
Middle-class exposure[b]	2.2	1.7	1.2	1.1
Average education of mother's friends	3.4	2.7	2.1	1.3
SES origin of mother	51.7	23.7	26.2	15.2
SES origin of father	47.5	24.6	24.3	14.0
Number of mother's siblings	2.2	3.8	3.9	5.3
Number of father's siblings	2.4	3.8	4.7	5.7

[a]The scales and the standard deviations are not given.
[b]The middle classness of neighbors.

include the process variables. When family size and religion variables are controlled, the race difference reduces further to 3.5 points.

A third and related level of analysis of family background effects upon IQ goes to particular kinds of caretaker behavior that are carefully observed. That is, one wants to know in detail how the mother (usually) goes about fostering cognitive development and how strategies may vary with social class, regardless of race. Consider the language used in maternal instruction. Bernstein's (1971) work illustrates the different "language codes" typical of British upper-middle and working classes. The "elaborated code" stresses precision and analysis in language; the "restricted" code employs simpler phrases and more gestures in a more characteristically expressive function. The Bernstein sort of analysis has been done in the United States most notably by Hess and Shipman (1965). They repeated, in general, the British findings, looking at three groups of black mothers and children stratified by class. Again, the middle-class mothers, when helping their children in dealing with a problem, tended to offer support, suggestion, and general instruction; the lower-class mothers used more specific instruction, more commands, more negative comment, and less complex speech. Middle-class mothers tried to get their children to attend to basic features of the task, offered search strategies, and elicited responses from their children; lower-class mothers exhibited fewer or none of these behaviors. This pattern of results was repeated by Bee, Van Egeren, Streussguth, Nyman, and Leckie (1969), though their class comparison was confounded with race.

Class differences in child-rearing styles appear when the children are still younger than the preschoolers of Hess and Shipman or Bee et al. Tulkin and Kagan (1972), working with all-Caucasian samples, compared middle- and working-class mothers with respect to their interaction with 10-month-old infants (they did not measure IQ, but since it is known to correlate with SES, we might assume that the children of the working-class parents were lower in IQ). What they found was a number of reliable differences both in home environment and maternal behavior.

The working-class infants lived in more "noise": more TV, more people, fewer toys and objects to play with, and more restrictions. Their mothers were less responsive and entertaining, showed less interaction in general and less face-to-face proximity in particular, and, perhaps most important, showed less vocalization of all sorts to the infant. There were no significant differences in affectionate physical contact.

This line of research, from Bernstein through Hess and Shipman to Tulkin and Kagan, converges to show significant social class differences in stimulation, especially language stimulation, for cognitive development. Bereiter and Engelmann (1966), who worked closely with "culturally deprived" (read "cognitively disadvantaged") black children, recount in dramatic detail their children's inability to understand various autoclitics such as the difference between "and" and "or" and the use of plurals, negatives, vocal inflection and pause in exposition. They say (pp. 32–33):

> *Bernstein's theory has especially alarming implications for the lower-class child because it suggests that the child does not merely lack certain of the language skills that middle-class children have; he has learned a self-perpetuating language code that effectively bars him from acquiring these skills.*
>
> *Bernstein's theory and Hess' observations on the inability of lower-class mothers to teach combine to suggest a more fundamental reason for the deficiencies of lower-class children in school-relevant learning. When a cultural group possesses a distinctive body of knowledge and beliefs which the older generation feels obliged to pass on in some organized fashion to the younger generation, it is reasonable to suppose that the group will develop*

the language and teaching skills that are needed for such a purpose. Among disorganized and dispossessed minority groups, however, the culture appears to center around attitudes, interests, a style of life, and a scattering of unorganized beliefs and superstitions so unformalized that they may be transmitted without explanation, argument, or detailed exposition. Deliberate teaching is not a normal or necessary part of the adult role in such cultural groups, and neither the skills nor the language peculiar to teaching are developed and maintained. By contrast, in middle-class American society, as in most self-maintaining societies, nearly every adult can and does teach. It is a normal part of the adult role performed almost without awareness, particularly in the adult's relations with children.

Cultural deprivation, then, has a double edge. The lower-class child is not without culture, but he is deprived of that part of culture that can only be acquired through teaching—the knowledge, the meanings, the explanations, the structured beliefs that make up the conceptual furniture of culture. Beyond that, the child spends his early childhood in an environment where teaching does not take place and where the language with which teaching is carried out is not used; therefore, he may not even learn how to be taught, and when he is exposed to teaching, he may behave much as if he were mentally retarded or devoid of language altogether.

Note that if Bereiter and Englemann are correct, disadvantaged children do not come to school simply behind and needing only to be taught. If that were true, the white-black differences might be reduced quickly; we have seen they are not. Instead, they come to school with a developed set of modes of interaction that may make teaching unusually difficult.

These studies relating family background to IQ are very easy to criticize. After all, genes are part of family background, and perhaps smart parents create the stimulating environments that researchers see associated with smart children, or perhaps smart children stimulate their parents to reciprocate with more toys and chatter.[2] Furthermore, the individual studies are not without methodological difficulties. Trotman, for example, appears to have had but one interviewer, a circumstance that makes the possibility of experimenter bias less unlikely than it should be. And Blau, for example, finds that religious affiliation helps account for some of the IQ difference between races. But since very few whites and a large number of blacks are fundamentalist, religious affiliation becomes something of a proxy for race. The same remarks apply to Mercer's demonstration: More affluent blacks and Chicanos have children who score higher, but there are very few of them. This instance is one that Jensen calls the "sociologist's fallacy." Gordon, in fact, tried to explain it to the court without, I think, any success. In doing so, of course, he cast himself, under Condas's direction, as a critic of the SES theory, a theory vital to the state's case. (As we shall see, this was the least of his sins.)

How the SES Case Was Not Made

With this brief exposition of the sort of SES case that might have been made, we may now return to the consideration of the way the state handled the SES case. Mercer's data on the effect of "sociocultural" variables on IQ are an instance of a popular way of arguing that SES variables account for the racial difference in IQ. The method is simply to show that as socioeconomic conditions change for a group, the IQ goes up. The plaintiffs in *Larry P.* made this case repeatedly, citing the well-known studies of Klineberg (1935), Shodak and Skeels (1945, 1949), the Milwaukee Project (Garber and Heber, 1977, 1981), and Scarr and Weinberg (1976) to demonstrate that (to employ their terms) as a group gets closer to the Anglo core culture, they do better in the Anglo core culture's tests. In most texts on intelligence such studies would be described in sections about environmental and educational effects on IQ: not "Anglicization," but "middle-classization."

The state's experts were happy to accept such classics as Klineberg on change in IQ among blacks who moved to and lived in the North or Tuddenham (1948) on general secular changes in IQ from World War I or World War II in this country. But instead of accepting the plaintiffs' proffer of the effects of cross-race adoption of black children (Scarr and Weinberg, 1976) or of intensive and early educational intervention with black ghetto children in Milwaukee as a windfall, something to be embraced, they went out of their way to reject them.

These two studies fit themselves readily into the hopeful world view of environmentalists everywhere as powerful antidotes to the strong view of the dominance of heredity espoused by Jensen. They are, of course, easy to attack. The Milwaukee Project, in particular, suffers from never having been presented in any detail sufficient for real criticism (but see Page and Grandon, 1981, and Sommer and Sommer, 1983, for severe criticism anyhow). There are questions about sample selection and retention, about the durability of the very dramatic effects on IQ (increases in IQ to more than 120, more than 20 points better than controls, for the children given special instruction), and about the transfer of training to school achievement. Garber and Heber (1977, 1981) have stated recently that now that the children are back in mainly ghetto schools, their IQ and achievement scores have been falling (to about 105 with approximately normal grade equivalent achievement) even though they remain more than 1 S.D. unit better than their controls and siblings. This result is typical of intervention studies, often termed "fadeout," when the stimulating and attentive care is removed and children are returned to the very disadvantaged environment that may have caused the trouble in the first place.

The Scarr–Weinberg results showed that 130 black children, adopted at an average age of 18 months into middle-class white homes in Minnesota, averaged 106 in IQ when tested at some point between early childhood and adolescence, only 5 points below the mean of white children who had been adopted at 19 months. Of the subsets who had been adopted early (at less than a year old), the figures were 110 and 117, respectively. This study therefore supplements with cross-race data the famous showing by Skodak and Skeels (1945, 1949) that children of low-IQ mothers, adopted into middle-class homes, showed much higher IQs than would have been expected had they remained with their true mothers. But the Scarr–Weinberg study, too, is vulnerable to criticism. Over half of the black children had white mothers, and the IQ of these mixed-race children was 109, 12 points higher than that of the children of two black parents. Furthermore, many of the white mothers were students and so may not only have been genetically superior but may have attracted black fathers who were also more than usually intelligent.

Thus the environmentalist's case, like the hereditarian's, is ever open to competing interpretations. But if you are a lawyer representing the state and trying to prove that IQ is dependent on environment, at least to some substantial degree, and that environment, not race, is the culprit in the black–white difference, then you would bring out successively the evidence I have reviewed in its most environmentalist and nonracial light, whether or not plaintiffs categorized the SES and process variables as "cultural." You might start with standard SES structural variables, go through the home environment process variables, and finish by showing the similarity of social class effects within races. That is, you would show that the "cultural" effects were actually psychosocial and culture-free: class, not race, effects.

As will be seen, the state self-destructed on this issue, starting with what the judge termed its "flirtation" with the genetic hypothesis. Condas's whole SES case pretty well depended on the testimony of Dr. Herbert Grossman, a physician specializing in retardation, who recounted the several health-related ills that poor pregnant black mothers are heir to, along with a multitude of statistics on prenatality, birth weight, perinatal disorders, and so on. This testimony was met, and fairly destroyed, by the testimony of the plaintiffs' doctor, Gloria Powell, a UCLA pediatrician. She simply quoted two strong studies—the Collaborative Perinatal Project (Broman, Nichols, and Kennedy, 1975) and the "Kauai" study (Werner et al., 1968)—each of which concluded that such risk factors have little effect on IQ. (The judge had said in a pretrial conference that he wanted to hear from real doctors, and each side obligingly produced one.)

Plaintiffs, through Mercer, had introduced the SES variables, which she said accounted for 32 percent of the variance in IQ. The state, committed to a definition of intelligence as current performance (see subsequent discussion), was *not* officially committed to any theory about its ontogeny—it claimed, recall, "agnosticism" on the nature-nurture issue. The state ought, therefore, to have welcomed Mercer's testimony on cross-race adoption and the Milwaukee Project intervention. One need only to have had her reemphasize on cross-examination her testimony that most of her sociocultural variables (except language) applied to every ethnic group.

Dr. Powell herself gave SES variables, which she defined broadly to include process factors (not only more money and higher maternal education, but more time, fewer children, higher aspiration for children's education, more verbal interaction and stimulation, and provision of toys, books, and puzzles), credit for an astonishing 70 percent of the variance in IQ scores. One need only to have had her establish that middle-class black parents produced children with middle-class IQs, something she would have been happy to do.

Condas surprised me with the sophistication with which she met environmentalist arguments. She had clearly learned from her talks with Jensen. She knew, for example, just what was wrong with the Scarr–Weinberg adoption study, and she challenged me to explain the unusually high proportion of Chinese children (many of whose parents still spoke Chinese) in Lowell High (the prestigious magnet high school in San Francisco) and the unusually low proportion of blacks, nearly all of whose parents were native born. The example was intended to prove that the black claim of cultural difference militating against test-taking success was groundless. But she was using culture to refer to "true" culture, where the plaintiffs used it to refer to psychosocial variables. The real psychosocial differences are the Chinese reverence for education, their attention to their children, a tradition of family cohesiveness and personal industriousness, and, I think, a language model that, though foreign, is "elaborated." All of these factors are attenuated or missing in black ghettos. Half of all Chinese babies are not born out of wedlock, for example, or reared in households headed by women. Her response to this line of reply was polite but skeptical acknowledgment.

The state's first witness was Robert Thorndike, a reasonable, thoughtful, attractive witness. His chapter on standardized testing has a section (Thorndike and Hagen, 1977, pp. 331–334) on testing the culturally different. By culture he means general background, as his references to the secular changes in IQ in the white population (Tuddenham, 1948; Wheeler, 1942) make clear. He is concerned with persons who are members of minority groups, whose first language is not standard English, or who are in some way deprived early in their lives. He describes such deprivation with respect to the process variables we have already discussed and suggests that they will affect ability test scores of some minority groups to the extent that such facilitative processes are lacking. In his testimony he said he thought that a substantial portion of the black-white IQ difference was caused by such environmental influences on cognitive development and that it was not useful to ask questions that cannot be answered, such as how much innate potential the test is measuring. His testimony on SES effects was, in short, much like Powell's. But it was all brought out in cross-examination.

Nadine Lambert was similarly willing to affirm that sociocultural conditions affect test and school performance. She also mentioned, without prompting by her attorney, the article by Bradley et al. (1977), discussed earlier, concerning the greater power of home environmental process variables than SES to predict IQ. She referred again to it on cross-examination and caught the judge's attention: "This might cast some doubt upon the SES approach to this matter." He seemed ready to see the point made, but nobody was going to make it, for by this time the plaintiffs had begun to make a point of emphasizing the position of many defense experts that traditional SES could *not* explain the black-white difference.

Doppelt started this approach, understandably enough, since his own company's normative data for the WISC-R showed it (Kaufman and Doppelt, 1976). But Humphreys elaborated on the point and evoked the first instance that I noticed of plaintiffs echoing the point for emphasis. Humphreys was describing the massive Project Talent data bank and noted that when blacks and whites were matched on an "excellent" measure of SES (which did not, however, include any process variables), there were still large race differences in tests tapping general intelligence ("g"), while tests of simple motivation to work (the number of attempts made in a clerical checking task, say) did *not* yield large race differences and did not correlate with "g." Thus, he concluded, neither economic condition nor motivation could account for the race difference. Furthermore, he testified, SES itself may have a large genetic component. All of this, it should be noted, was evoked on direct examination by Condas.

On cross-examination of Humphreys by Mr. Madden the following interchange took place (RT 6294–6296):

> *Q:* Doctor, let me read to you a quotation from an article you prepared entitled race and sex differences and their implications for educational and occupational equality.
>
> "Although the conclusion will be unpalatable to many, and anathema to some, the surest and most effective social action the Negro community could take by itself to achieve equality in education and jobs would be to limit drastically the birth rate in those families providing the least effective environments for intellectual development."
>
> Have I correctly quoted your statement?
>
> *A:* You have.
>
> *Q:* Are those your views?
>
> *A:* Those are my views. May I expand on them?
>
> *The Court:* Yes.
>
> *The Witness:* The most recent data I have seen from the population reference bureau is that middle class blacks are having fewer children per family than their counterparts in the white groups, that

black women on AFDC are having more children than white women in the AFDC, and I am not at all concerned about a person's skin color. But when large numbers of children are being raised from the most extreme environmental conditions without regard to any possible genetic deprivation, which is problematical, but when large numbers of children are being raised under the most extreme environmental conditions I don't see how anyone can be but concerned, and a concerned environmentalist could have made that statement as readily as a confirmed hereditarian, and I am not either.

Q: Do you consider yourself a eugenicist?

A: No. I would consider myself—I would be willing to take social action to provide incentives for persons with inadequate environments and possibly inadequate genetic background to have fewer children, but I would do this because both the environmental and genetic causes for those differences point in precisely the same direction.

Shortly thereafter he dissociated himself somewhat from Thorndike—"I am not as certain as Thorndike apparently is that the differences are environmental"—and then plaintiffs' counsel highlighted the issue (RT 6304–6305, 6357):

Q: Doctor, when you were testifying regarding your article on race by sex interaction and also I think on the Project Talent article, you said, I believe, that when blacks and whites are of the same socioeconomic status that there was still a difference in the scores achieved by blacks on the cognitive abilities tests which had been administered; is that correct?

A: That's correct.

Q: And the blacks scored below the whites on these tests?

A: That is correct.

Q: And therefore the differences in performance cannot be accounted for by the measures of socioeconomic status that were used?

A: Correct.

Q: I take it, however, that this data does not tell us whether the differences were caused by genetics or by environmental factors which were not measured?

A: That is correct.

Q: Nor whether the test score differences were caused by differences—excuse me. Strike that.

Either of these factors, either the genetic factors or the environmental factors, in your view could make a contribution?

A: Correct.

I also added that the environmental factors, whatever they might be, were—one had to look beyond the economic deprivation, the obvious socioeconomic factors that have been discussed so thoroughly by many environmentalists.

Q: I wonder if you haven't fallen into something which I might call the statistician or psychometrist's fallacy when you say that you have held socioeconomic status equal and found blacks are lower than whites on their IQ scores, because you really can't hold all those things equal. There can still be cultural differences?

A: Yes. I said just a few minutes ago that the differences were undoubtedly more subtle than the objective indices of privilege.

The plaintiff's "cultural" is here equivalent to Humphrey's "subtle environmental factors," and there was still some opportunity (never taken) to establish such an equivalence. Lambert was yet to come, with her brief reference to Bradley et al. (1977), and Sattler actually brought up the Broman, Nichols, and Kennedy (1975) and the Nichols and Anderson (1973) findings about the near equivalence of black-white scores in samples having nearly the same SES and using the same clinics for prenatal care. This resulted in the following colloquy on cross-examination (RT 7089–7090):

Q: Doctor, you testified this morning referring to the Nichols and Anderson study. Do you have that one in mind? That you believe that this tended to show that blacks and whites [who] have the same socioeconomic status and background tended to achieve the same IQ scores.

A: I think that's what they concluded, that's correct.

Q: Now, we're interested in this because . . . your view seemed to be directly contrary to Dr. Humphreys, who testified that for blacks and whites of the same socioeconomic status, blacks had scored significantly poorer than whites for the same socioeconomic status on IQ scores?

A: I don't recall.

But remember in that study it was not only SES that was the variable, it was in the same hospital, the same perinatal care, and there were many, many variables that each group was matched on. It was not only SES.

So I do not see how it flagrantly contradicts Dr. Humphreys if he said SES, and they are saying SES, prenatal care, same hospital—highly limited, select sample. That's not SES.

Note, again, that this brief reference to the distinction between SES and a wider set of variables influencing mental ability came out on cross-examination and was never really clarified and elaborated.

As far as I can judge, the worst witness for the state's case was Gordon. He was brought on to rebut Mercer's testimony (see Gordon, 1975), which, since it ascribed the whole source of ethnic differences in IQ to "sociocultural" (read "environmental" or "psychosocial") variables, now brought out a fulsome attack on that position. He repeated the attacks on the Scarr–Weinberg study; asserted, quoting Jensen, that the black deficit could not be motivational because blacks are as good in simple tasks (for example, crossing out X's) as whites;[3] and cited the Jensen and Figueroa (1975) study, which showed that black and white groups matched on SES still differed substantially in IQ. His manner seemed to me condescending and pedantic—he even corrected the judge, who had referred to the 15-point difference, saying that the real difference was 16 or 17 points (RT 7274). He defended Cyril Burt[4] (he was the only witness to do so), and he introduced on direct examination some of the subtler evidence on race differences (for example, regression of offspring scores of IQ-matched parent samples to apparently different means). Finally, plaintiffs' counsel nailed the position down (RT 7433–7434):

Q: Isn't it true that this is one of the findings that Dr. Jensen has reported on a number of occasions, that is, if you hold socioeconomic status even, blacks score lower than whites?

A: If you hold socioeconomic status even, blacks score lower than whites. Yes, that is often the case.

Q: Now, if socioeconomic status doesn't account for the difference between blacks and whites on IQ scores, you will agree with me, will you not, that there are three possible explanations: first is a genetic explanation that blacks are inherently less intelligent than whites; second is a cultural explanation, black culture is different from white culture; third is some combination of those?

A: I guess that covers the possibilities.

Q: You testified here, did you not, that blacks and whites come from essentially the same culture?

A: In a number of important respects that would be major indices of similarity of culture, right.

Q: And you have also testified, have you not, that in your view IQ tests are not culturally biased?

A: Yes, within particular populations now. We are talking about blacks and whites.

If we gave an English IQ test to French-speaking people only, that would be a farcical demonstration of cultural bias, which is not the issue in this case.

So you always have to be specific when you talk about particular instances there, and we're very specific so far. So let's stay that way.

Q: Then you believe, Doctor, that the differences that are shown between blacks and whites on P–120 [Plaintiffs' Exhibit #120, the normal distributions of IQ scores for the two groups] are not explained by differences in culture between blacks and whites.

A: That's right.

The cross-examination and *voir dire* of Gordon were very aggressive, and Gordon was quite feisty himself. Consider the following exchange (RT 7451–7452):

Mr. Madden: Talking about genetics, you in your article talk about verbal ability genes. There is no such thing as a verbal ability gene, is there? No one could testify to that?

A: Well, Mr. Madden, you would have to consider what accounts for the difference in verbal ability between chimpanzees and Homo sapiens. Would you say that was due to culture?

Q: Doctor, the question to you is: Do you or do you not refer to verbal ability genes?

A: I refer to verbal ability genes as a hypothetical example to explain a very complex phenomena in my article. And you have picked up on that in my deposition and here to accuse me of believing in verbal ability genes.

And if you want to know, since you asked, I really do think that verbal ability is dependent on genes to some extent, because chimpanzees don't have it.

Q: And you think that blacks don't have as much of it as whites?

A: I didn't say that. That depends on the outcome of the heritability studies of the differences between race, which I maintain a totally agnostic position on at this point.

Q: We have an agnostic state and an agnostic witness.

It seems by way of summary that Condas did let her own beliefs and/or her need to rebut the testimony of Mercer blind her to making a good case about environment and IQ. Her witnesses, of course, were bound to say what they thought (see Chapter 10 for a discussion of the temptation affecting "experts"). But she is a lawyer and exempt from some of the ethical principles that may bind the scientist. She may suppress her own convictions in the zealous pursuit of her client's interest. There was simply no need to have Gordon there, for instance, even though he was one, with Thorndike, of her two favorite witnesses. His deposition could have tipped her off to his probable effect on the court. There are other critics of labeling theory and Mercer's views of testing and IQ. Sandra Scarr, in fact, would have been a fine state's witness and should not have been ignored or her work made the subject of criticism simply because Mercer cited her study as one of the three chief pieces of evidence supporting her own view.[5] As has been shown, there is a strong but not conclusive case to be made that the black-white difference in IQ is not "cultural" nor yet "racial" in any reasonably consensual sense of those words but is, rather, a function of the same kinds of influences that divide classes within races. Just because plaintiffs may term such influences "cultural" does not make them so. The state, as least, ought to have tried to identify these influences under their own label. Wilson Riles, the black defendant who was judged finally to have discriminated intentionally against black children, certainly would have agreed to such an approach.

PASE

In Chicago it was the defendants, not the plaintiffs, who introduced the Scarr and Weinberg (1976) paper and happily accepted testimony about the effects of educational intervention to effect improvement in the IQ scores of black children. This fact illustrates the great difference in approach. The other notable distinction is the vastly different reception given the testimony of Dr. Powell.

Early in the proceedings the plaintiffs produced Robert Williams, professor of psychology and black studies at Washington University and the author of the well-known BITCH test (see Chapter 6). He had testified that the culture of American blacks was a truly different culture in the narrow sense, with strong "Afrocentric" (as opposed to "Anglocentric") elements—for example, in kinship relations, or attitudes toward property (see RT 408ff). As a part of this testimony, he denied any intellectual deficit in blacks, asserting in its stead the cultural difference hypothesis; later (RT 597) he denied that poverty "might or could" increase the incidence of school failure in blacks.

Nevertheless, other plaintiffs' witnesses pointed to various features of the environment, especially common among poor blacks, that affected school success. Albee talked of residential stability and intactness of family and brought out the results of the Milwaukee Project (Garber and Heber, 1981) and Scarr and Weinberg (1976). Stoner talked of "cultural disadvantages," exemplified by welfare, uneducated mothers, broken homes, and lack of motivation. These, of course, are a mix of the traditional SES and psychosocial process variables.

It was not until the final three witnesses, however, that the issues were clearly drawn and such clarity was more often demanded by the judge than by the attorneys. Dr. Powell had been unable to arrive for the plaintiffs in time to testify before the defense had begun its case-in-chief. Its penultimate defense witness was Alice Zimmerman, director of the Mentally Handicapped Development Program for the CBE. She testified primarily about the EMH program but along the way introduced the notion that there were "pockets of poverty" (RT 1540ff) where Headstart and Title I compensatory education programs were chiefly located and where EMH rates were highest.[6] She went on to spell out what she thought was wrong: " . . . the problems that preclude a child from benefitting from the instructional program . . . [are] the poverty, housing, the psychological, you know, the love and respect and affection and the childhood security, all of these things are missing. There is a lack of early stimulation" (RT 1541).

Later, Judge Grady asked what the racial composition of such poverty pockets was ("black and Latino" was the answer) and what early stimulation was, what role it played, and whether there were certain ages at which a child was best able to learn things (RT 1578–1581). Zimmerman's answers were not sophisticated ("sitting in front of a television set is not really stimulation . . ."), but the existence of psychological home environment factors was clearly at issue. Judge Grady did something finally that Judge Peckham had never done, which was to see the SES case as more than a matter of physical or physiological deficits attendant upon poverty. Attorney Winters, cross-examining Zimmerman, introduced the data of the Collaborative Perinatal Project (Broman, Nichols, and Kennedy, 1975) to show that there was little relation between health and nutritional factors and IQ. Judge Grady queried him:

> *I still don't understand your question. There is one factor we could call nutrition and prenatal care, and then there is another whole set of matters that she discussed in terms of educational deficit during the early learning years.*

Then it was Powell's turn in what seems, to me, to be the climax of the lawsuit. As she had done in *Larry P.*, she pointed to several psychosocial causes of retarded intellectual function, including lack of mother-child, especially verbal, interaction, of "synchrony," and of general early stimulation. She even drew attention to the strongest correlates of 4-year-old childhood IQ in the Collaborative Perinatal Project, namely, maternal education and maternal IQ.

But Powell was unwilling to say that such deficits occurred more among poor blacks in Chicago (or anywhere else) than among advantaged whites or blacks. Had she done so, the plaintiffs' case would be gone. The following shows the bind she was in and the judge's reaction to it (RT 1658–1663):

> *The Court:* Let me ask you this on another subject. You indicated that there is no correlation between being black and being poor on the one hand, and the occurrence of some of these deficits on the other. Do you mean to include in that the lack of early stimulation? Specifically, are you saying that there is just as much intellectual stimulation in the environment of a child in a poor black household as there is in, say, an average white household?
>
> *The Witness:* Okay. Although studies show, and most notably Kathryn Chillman's study on child-rearing techniques of poor families and middle-class families, and one of the predominant child-bearing techniques of middle-class families, is to talk to the child a great deal straight from birth, and if you have children of your own you know how you just go on cooing and laughing and saying, and they start to imitate us, and that seems to be characteristic of parents who are educated, and very verbal themselves, and so the children imitate them.
>
> It is not correct to say that that kind of verbal interaction will not occur in a lower socioeconomic status family. I, myself, come from a family that received aid to families with dependent children. My

father died when I was 3. My mother had only an educational level of a sixth grade education, which she got in evening school at Cambridge High in Latin, but her verbal capacities were just extraordinary, and I'm certain that's why I talked so early.

The Court: Well, there isn't any question that in every statement you make there are thousands of exceptions, and we are not dealing here with every last family.

The Witness: But, in the Caribbean study, we showed that when we looked at maternal-child teaching styles, that they predicted better performance on a perceptual cognitive test than did socioeconomic status. That is to say, the children from the lower socioeconomic status homes who had mothers who were very verbal in their interactions did as well as middle-class children who had the similar kind of stimulation from their parents.

The Court: Well, that isn't my question. Actually, that sounds like an answer of a different kind than the one I understood you to give.

What I want to know is, do black children in an urban society, and specifically in Chicago is what we are dealing with, in what has been referred to as pockets of poverty, get as much early stimulation as white children of the same age? And if the answer is yes, they do, then the next question I have is what are these children learning in Headstart then that they don't get at home? What is the whole purpose of Headstart for children if they don't have any needs that are being met?

The Witness: First of all, let me respond by saying that you cannot categorically classify all of urban black families as being homes in which stimulation does not occur. It really depends on the individual family. You may find, in an urban ghetto situation, some black parents who provide a great deal of stimulation and the children do well in school, and some black families who do not provide that, and they do not do well in school.

The Court: Well, all right. Let's just take two children who, as you suggested, one who does well in school, one doesn't. You know nothing at all about the home. All you have is this, again, that one's going like a house on fire and the other one's not doing well at all. What would you expect to find in the respective homes?

The Witness: Okay. Based on the data that I have just stated to you, I would say that if it's a low socioeconomic child, it may well be that there are certain lacks of attention to learning paths in that home which predict his low performance, that that would predict it more so than the fact that he had a low birth weight or any other kind of medical or organic problem, that the results are probably environmental, that he hasn't gotten enough stimulation from his home environment, has not been helped to be prepared for the test in school.

The Court: Would you expect a higher incidence of that kind of thing in the case of poor black children than you would in the case of white children?

The Witness: By and large, the culture of the public school is a middle-class white culture, and the expectations are that one has been trained in that way.

Kenneth Clark, who is one of our most outstanding psychologists, has talked about school problems that occur because of the class of culture in the classroom, which is to say that because some teachers in the educational systems may not, do not, understand the home environment of which the child comes, the cultural differences, and the way of interacting in the world, that school curriculum is not geared to meet their needs, and then produces iatrogenic school failure.

In other words, what I am really trying to convey to you is that although on paper it may look like that many more poor black children do not get the kind of stimulation that they need, the kind of environment that they come from produces the adaptive intellectual function that is necessary for them to survive in the world and is socially competent, vis-à-vis what is expected of them in the environment, in their community and in their home, but inasmuch as they have not been instructed in terms of tasks that are more school related, they are then felt to be mentally retarded, mentally deficient, etc. But, what the Headstart studies clearly show, first of all, it's those children who have had a great deal of stimulation, be it from the nursery school environment that Headstart provides, or either from the home itself, do better than those children who come from situations in which that kind of environment is not given, and they move immediately into the public school classroom.

To make the statement that because black children are poor, that they will not have academic achievement, is to contravene the longitudinal studies that I quoted in terms of patterns of black excellence which indicates that for black students, and all black schools in the South, and elsewhere, that when the school environment is such that it provides the kind of learning environment for the child in terms of expectations of his succeeding, the children do do well.

The Court: All right. Your testimony is the same as that of a black psychologist [Williams] who testified earlier in the trial, which, in substance, was there is nothing deficient about the stimulation that a black child receives early in his life, rather it's a different kind of stimulation.

The Witness: Exactly.

The Court: So that whether or not the plaintiffs have a case here really gets down to the question of whether it is that different, which is a different kind of case than I would try to present, frankly, if I were running it, but I'm not running it. So, go ahead.

Powell dealt with the issue of black school deficit in familiar ways: highlighting exceptions, telling anecdotes, attributing failure to schools and teachers. The judge was very plainly skeptical. She had already insisted that the *only* reason for the disproportionately high representation of black children in EMH was "misassessment."

The plaintiffs' case was now in trouble, and lead defense attorney Halligan knew it. To the judge's inquiry he said he would have a long cross-examination of Powell. A lunch recess was thereupon called, after which Halligan returned to say he had decided to excuse the witness. But Judge Grady had much still to ask. He started with what he described as a "summing up" question: "Are you saying that the only reasonable explanation of the fact that more black children than white are placed in EMH classes in Chicago is that they get lower IQ scores than white children?" (RT 1677). Powell adverted to other parts of the typical multiple assessment, especially Adaptive Behavior (AB) scales. "Is there anything in [such an] assessment . . . that would indicate to the evaluator that this is a retarded child other than the fact that this child got a low IQ score?" asked the judge. The colloquy ended as follows:

> *Dr. Powell:* You give the same scale to everybody. The adaptive scales more nearly approximate the measurement of innate capabilities. The IQ tests more nearly tell you that this child's culture from whence he comes prepares him for the culture of the classroom, or that is to say, that this child has had learning experiences outside of school that will help him in the school classroom in terms of what is expected of him, in terms of performance in the classroom, but it does not, and cannot, tell you what is the definitive innate capabilities of the child.
>
> *The Court:* Well, again, it's an apple and orange situation. I am putting it right over the plate here, and I just don't think I can do it any better. I understand why the defendant has waived cross-examination.
>
> If you are going to try your case along political lines, you might get

a political result. What was it somebody said earlier? Garbage in, garbage out?

Ms. Lipton: Well, if I may respond, Your Honor?

The Court: I can only work with what I have. I am not indicating that I am leaning one way or the other. I do think that there are ideological and philosophical predilections that are handicapping, if you don't mind the use of that word, the presentation of the plaintiffs' case.

Then, after a brief exchange with plaintiffs' attorney, he elaborated in what seems, on reading it, a sort of judicial outburst (RT 1681–1684):

You can't really assume in this day and age that any judge in the United States is a complete tabula rasa on the subject matters that are being presented here.

First of all, most of us have gone to college, and in college we have been exposed to the classes in psychology, sociology, all sorts of things that bear upon the issues presented here. Now, that's ancient history and time marches on. We don't stop reading when we leave college either. We don't even stop reading when we leave law school. Once in a while we read a book that pertains to something other than the rule against perpetuity, and anyone who is a knowledgeable citizen in the state of Illinois knows that there are certain statistical data which characterize so-called black families, or so-called ghetto families, in the black community.

One knows, for instance, statistically that in the city of Chicago last year more black children were born out of wedlock than were born in wedlock. One knows that the average age of black mothers is far lower than the average age of white mothers. One knows that there are disruptive factors that intervene in the relationship between any parent and these young children.

Now, I cannot create evidence, and this is the last time I am going to say anything like this, but it would not take a superhuman feat of cognition to see a relationship between the kinds of factors that I have just mentioned and poor performance on an IQ test.

Now, what is happening here is that, as a matter of ideology, no one is willing to say that there is anything deficient about the black culture. It's wonderful. It's just that it's different, and the reason that a black kid doesn't deal with the information on the IQ test as well as the white kid is solely because he comes from a different stimulating learning experience. It's not that he has lacked stimulation. It's not that he lacks motivation. It's simply that his stimulation has been along different lines, his motivation has been along different lines.

Now, if you want to narrow the case down to the question of whether these IQ tests cannot be dealt with adequately by a black child in the year 1980 who comes out of a very good and stimulating, and, in all respects, adequate environment in the city of Chicago, then that's the way I've got to decide the case. That's the issue I will have to answer.

I haven't read the IQ test yet. I have read some of the questions. At first blush some of them seemed to me to be difficult for such a child to answer, but it doesn't have anything to do with whether they are white or black. It has to do with what their storehouse of information is, and you can have a white child who is as ignorant as a black child, depending on what his opportunities have been. There may be other questions that I will conclude can be answered by anyone who has had an adequate diet of culturally relevant information. I don't care what subculture you are talking about. These people are not living on a different planet, and I am not going to accept something as true simply because somebody says it is.

So, I am pointing out to you that you are taking a risk in letting everything ride on the IQ tests. Now, that may be a deliberate decision. You may want to gamble, and put all your eggs in that one basket. If that has been your calculated decision, so be it.

Ordinarily, I don't get into the trial of the lawsuits to the extent I have just done. I stopped trying lawsuits four years ago. My role now is to try to reach an intelligent judgment on the basis of what other people do in the trial of their lawsuits, but there is more at stake here than the vindication of some political ideology. What is at stake here is the welfare of thousands of children who are residing today in the city of Chicago, and who will reside here long after this case is over, and for that reason I thought it appropriate to make these remarks.

As I say, it's the last intervention you will get from me, and if it's bad advice, ignore it.

All right, I have completed my questions of Dr. Powell and I am satisfied that her view is that the whole thing rests on the IQ tests.

After that, the final defense witness, Elmer Smith, was a bit of an anticlimax. He was the administrator of the child study programs for the Bureau of Child Study of the CBE, and he introduced, with Defense Exhibit 8A, a body of statistical evidence that showed, on sixty-five different social indicators such as rates of welfare, unemployment, victimization, illiteracy, mobility, crowdedness of homes, death, blacks to be far behind whites. Smith added that the middle class of all races were alike on their indices, that he would expect Appalachian whites to be comparable to poor blacks on them, and that they were associated with EMH placement.

Finally, with respect to the SES argument, the defense introduced through Smith's affidavit the dissertation of Nichols (1970), that most striking of demonstrations of black-white equality of IQ with equality of SES—the very data so briefly alluded to by Sattler during his cross-examination in *Larry P.*

With no experts of national prominence, Halligan managed to make a convincing SES case. He did it partly by not being burdened by any association with the Jensen hypothesis. But he did it mainly by concentrating on it, and less on the health and nutrition aspect of it than on the crucial psychosocial, mother-child interactive aspects of the hypothesis. One great advantage of the defense lay in something it did not do, namely, deal with the issue of heritability. Although the defense did offer one paper by Jensen (1976, on test bias) as an exhibit, his name, and the associated genetic hypothesis, scarcely came up. The city had nothing to do with it.

Finally, he was lucky in his setting. Chicago has a sufficiently large black middle class (some members of which were testifying for the defense) that it was plausible to claim that it was poverty, not race, that caused high EMH rates. In California, data had to cover the whole state, and the correlation (introduced then by *plaintiffs*) between income of a district and EMR rates was low, about .30. The difference may have been caused by the fact that Hispanic EMH rates were quota-controlled and low, even though several Hispanic-dominated areas were poor.

Though the *PASE* defense introduced many scholarly papers, none concerned psychosocial factors in the home. The defense relied entirely on statements by various witnesses that education, language models, aspiration levels, mother-child interaction styles, and so on were affected by poverty to the detriment of black children. It is a plausible case, and the judge was ready, as his quoted outburst shows, to believe it.

That brings us to a final set of factors, of unknown influence, that are extra-procedural and unsystematic—they have to do with the particular personality, knowledge, and intellectual style of the judge. The defense in *PASE* was especially lucky in having Judge Grady as the fact-finder. He probably had, as his extended remarks would seem to indicate, unusual familiarity with the conditions of ghetto life in Chicago. Such familiarity might make it especially difficult to reject the notion of deficit in favor of the Williams–Powell idea of cultural difference. It is also likely that those two witnesses had been received with greater respect in the several other lawsuits in which they had participated than they got from

Judge Grady. Williams was, on my reading, both too confident and too argumentative to be convincing, and Judge Grady clearly did not believe much of what he had to say—the opinion is instinct with skepticism of his testimony. The reader has just seen his reactions to Powell. Her reaction to him, in turn, was negative. During the recess in her appearance, she said to Winters that in her opinion the judge was a racist, a pronouncement that was duly reported (before final argument) by a journalist standing within earshot.

Summary

Had Halligan led the defense in *Larry P.*, he would, I think, still have had more trouble than he had in *PASE*. But he would not have been burdened with the Jensen hypothesis or with an SES case too impoverished to supply a reasonable alternative to it. Conversely, Condas could have lost in Chicago with the arguments and witnesses she used in California. Given Judge Grady's view of the major issue in *PASE*, however (whether the items that make up the tests were biased), it is unlikely that any reasonable defense would have lost in Chicago.

Endnotes

1. Mercer herself (RT 1584) also used the more traditional and narrower sense of "culture" and defined it with respect to language, values in the home, the history of the group, and the "lifestyle" of the group.
2. For a recent debate on this point, see Longstreth et al. (1978) indicating that maternal IQ, not home environment, is the critical variable, and Yeates et al. (1983), arguing that home environment becomes an even more important independent factor in child IQ with the child's age.
3. This reasoning about motivation is not self-evident. Surely, the fact that one is motivated on one test (which one can succeed in) does not mean that one will be equally motivated on others (which may be similar to previous occasions for failure). The psychological notes about some of the plaintiff children made that very point: On some tests, but not others, they would simply turn off.
4. Cyril Burt was an English psychologist exposed by Leon Kamin as having made up data supporting the hypothesis of strong heritability of IQ.
5. Consider the following from Scarr (1978, p. 340), written probably before the trial was over and certainly before the decision came down: "Other less objective assessments will be found and used as long as the bias in the criteria

remains. Halting the use of the tests will not solve the problem. Nor will adding points to the scores of those who come from disadvantaged and culturally different backgrounds. They will still fail at the criterion, just as the tests would predict, for the aforementioned reasons of shared cultural loading." She would, she told me, have been happy to be a defense expert, but she was never asked.

6. For the 1980–1981 school year there was, in fact, a rank order correlation of .72 between EMH placement rates for black students and percentage of low-income students in the districts (Designs for Change, 1982, p. 22, Table 9; calculated by me from the figures given in Table 9).

Chapter 4

THE NATURE OF INTELLIGENCE

"What is intelligence?" asked Judge Peckham, and he did stay for an answer. He got several, not less various than any textbook compilation (see, for example, Sattler, 1982, p. 37). The question has point. If intelligence tests are biased, they are unfair or inaccurate in their measures of one or more persons or groups—that is, they are invalid. But to know when a measure is invalid, we must know when it is valid, when it measures correctly that which it is supposed to measure. We must know, in short, what the construct is. Questions about the construct were a very large feature of *Larry P.*, where several witnesses delivered formal definitions; those questions were far less evident in *PASE*.

Larry P.

Differences in Definitions

In *Larry P.* there were pretty clearly three broad ideas of what intelligence is: first, what the plaintiffs thought it was; second, what the defendants thought it was; and third, what the plaintiffs thought the public, and probably the defendants, *really* thought it was (which is also what the plaintiffs and the judge really thought it was). Humphreys claimed that there is a consensus among psychologists, except for a few dissenting psychologists, that the WISC and Stanford–Binet represent the kinds of intellectual skills they refer to when they speak of intelligence.

72

Among the dissenting black psychologists were, presumably, Hilliard and Dent. Of the better-known definitions, they subscribed to Wechsler's (1975, p. 139):

> *What we measure with tests is not what tests measure—not information, not spatial perception, not reasoning ability. These are only a means to an end. What intelligence tests measure, what we hope they measure, is something much more important: the capacity of an individual to understand the world about him and his resourcefulness to cope with its challenges.*

The definition, also cited by Doppelt (RT 5520), who worked for Wechsler's publisher, is broad, and it is capacious enough to permit an "adaptiveness to the environment" interpretation that diminishes the importance of strictly cognitive skills. Thus it suits defenders of the "intelligence" of children who are failing in a strongly cognitive domain (school) but who are coping with the rest of the world about them. Hilliard simplified it (RT 105) as the ability to adapt to the environment in which you live. Kamin produced a masterpiece of S-R empiricism: Intelligence tests measure "the degree to which a particular individual who takes the test has experience with a particular piece of information, the particular bits of knowledge, the particular habits and approaches that are tested" (RT 880). The addition of "habits and approaches" could be taken to allude to higher-level cognitive strategies, but the modifier "particular" makes such a view hard to impute.

Neither these nor any other of plaintiffs' witnesses saw any use at all for the IQ. According to them, IQ scores did not really add to grades and achievement tests as predictors of future achievement; nor did they consider the Stanford–Binet or WISC very efficient as diagnostic tests for use in guiding a teacher's instruction. Hilliard added several criticisms that in their extremity serve to underline the hostility of the black psychologists; for example, if a psychologist is respectable enough, he can make up the test in his living room (RT 302); that the test favors obsessives (RT 328); and that differences among siblings in the family are just a matter of style (RT 747).

But the most severe and radical critic of the tests was Mercer. Her characterization of what the test measures was utterly dismissive: It is a measure of conformity of middle-class expectations for the typical child in the typical public school in the United States (RT 1489)[1] and just another adaptive behavior (RT 1587). For her, the criteria of intelligence should be multiple, including success with peers, in community activities, and so on (RT 1621). She contrasted her view with that of Cleary et al. (1975), saying that they are opting for a single, "Anglo" core culture and "mono-cultural" schools that turn out a mass-produced product, a process she likened to the Ford Motor Company operation (RT 1624). Not only achievement tests but tests of reading and math as well were said to be a part of this Anglo monocultural hegemony. As Gordon pointed out at the trial and in print (1980), she could as easily have characterized the culture and its schools as Japanese, or Jewish, or Chinese—indeed, as any culture that puts high value on education as it is known in industrialized and highly complex societies.

Mercer appears to be among the radical revisionists interpreting the American public schools as instruments by which the ruling class perpetuates its status, ensures an adequate supply of rela-tively uneducated labor, and discovers and co-opts the bright and potentially rebellious children of the lower class. This vision is, of course, diametrically (and dialectically) opposed to the view of public schools as the instrument of social mobility for the meritori-ous, who are discovered by standardized tests that do not give points to being wealthy or established. It was also a little strong for the judge (RT 2188):

> It is well enough to say we should have a pluralistic society, but we need to function in the monocultural society described. If you are a minority person and you want to work for Standard Oil or in the federal courthouse it serves no purpose to turn out people who aren't educated to function in society as it is.

At any rate, Mercer's line of argument, extending the role of intelligence to every sort of adaptive behavior, and categorizing school learning as not merely one of many equally important areas of adaptation but as a narrow, middle class, monocultural one at that, surely does make IQ seem less important, even if it is predictive of school grades, which, Mercer added, it is in fact not.

In Mercer's view, as in that of all the plaintiffs' witnesses, there are no differences in intelligence among ethnic groups, despite differences in test scores. That is, their view of intelligence is that it is innate potential, and not current performance. Their concern, after all, was for children who did badly in school (and on tests), who *might* have done well if only they had had reasonable environ-mental support. Thus, as we have seen, Mercer showed (RT 1629ff) that if Chicano and black families are scored dichotomously on five "sociocultural" variables, children of families scoring positively on all five factors have average IQ scores whereas children of families scoring zero had IQs about 1 standard deviation lower.

On the assumption of group equality in "intelligence," Mercer had constructed a system (System of Multicultural Pluralistic Assessment, 1979, termed SOMPA, for short) in which points are added to the WISC-R score in proportion as the child's sociocultural scores are low. Her example (RT 1977ff) was a black girl of WISC-R Full Score IQ 109, whose father is a painter born in rural Louisiana, did not graduate from high school, and lives with his wife and seven children in a rented apartment in Los Angeles. Such a girl, when compared with other children of similar sociocultural circumstances, has a "true" IQ of 130 to 133, according to Mercer, whose system supplies tables by which one can determine this "ELP" (estimated learning potential). Note the inference to innate capacity involved here, along with the assumption that unadjusted scores should underpredict the school performance of disadvantaged minority children, unless the middle-class bias of the school discourages or undervalues their performance.

Intelligence A and Intelligence B

This casting of adjusted IQ as innate potential is peculiar because plaintiffs' witnesses gave every indication that they were sure that both the public at large and the older testers thought of IQ as fixed and innate and that such a view was mistaken. The trial would, I think, have profited from the use of Hebb's (1949) terms, Intelligence A and Intelligence B.[2] Intelligence A is the unknown potential; Intelligence B is the average of a person's actual current performance in a variety of cognitive, intellectual, and school-related tasks. Mercer's ELP, being a "what might have been under ideal environmental conditions," is Intelligence A, and not measurable. The judge, I think, believed those witnesses who claimed that the public, teachers, and parents thought of IQ as Intelligence A. He could not understand why publishers would not rename their tests, as Mercer did for the WISC-R score (as "School Functioning Level") or as Thorndike did with the Lorge-Thorndike Intelligence Test (as the Cognitive Abilities Test), to something with less surplus meaning. Condas certainly would have been happy with terms bearing less weight, but it is clear that such witnesses as Humphreys and Gordon thought of Intelligence B as something, however phenotypic and whatever its ontogeny, like

the famous Spearman "g"; a trait of great penetration and general-
ity, properly to be called "intelligence."

The judge himself thought of intelligence as Intelligence A.
Consider the following comments of the judge to Condas, during
her cross examination of Dent on the scoring of comprehension
and information items of the WISC (RT 3960):

> _Well, you know what strikes me is this: with respect to socialization,
> I suppose possibly you could have somebody who really is poten-
> tially a genius who would do poorly because of lack of proper
> exposure . . . you know, what color is a ruby? Obviously you could
> be terribly bright and not know that. I mean that's not something
> that—you are not born with that knowledge._

The state's experts, of course, took both a more traditionally
restricted view of intelligence as mental ability and a more modern
one—that Intelligence B is all we can know. Just as the plaintiffs'
view of it was as something global but not too important except in
school, the state's view was that it was very important even though
restricted to abilities best evoked in schools and increasingly
important in modern technological societies outside of school. The
Cleary et al. (1975) report set the standard. It was heavily influenced by Humphreys, its initial definition of intelligence being
precisely the one he gave in 1971 (p. 19):

> _Intelligence is defined as the entire repertoire of acquired skills,
> knowledge, learning sets, and generalization tendencies considered
> intellectual in nature that are available at any one period in time.
> An intelligence test contains items that sample such acquisitions.
> Intelligence so defined is not any entity such as Spearman's "mental
> energy." Instead, the definition suggests the Thomson "multiple
> bonds" approach. Nevertheless, for the sake of convenience, intelli-
> gence will be discussed as if it were a unitary disposition to solve
> intellectual problems._
>
> _The definition of intelligence proposed here would be circular as a
> function of the use of "intellectual" if it were not for the fact that
> there is a consensus among psychologists as to the kinds of behav-
> iors that are labeled intellectual. The Stanford–Binet and the
> Wechsler tests both exemplify and define the consensus._

Note that the definition specifies current performance—it
clearly refers to a phenotypic trait. It does not refer to any theory
of causality. All the state's experts asserted that there was simply
no way to sort out nature from nurture as the cause of what was
observed and no way to tap innate potential.

The Cleary et al. (1975) definition does not say anything about how easy it is to change a score, though later in their paper they are very guarded about the ease with which intellectual levels are raised (p. 23):

> *It is also a very reasonable hypothesis that the level of a particular subgroup could be raised. The amount and specific kinds of effort required, however, are unknown. The following recommendation is justified: It is undesirable to underestimate the amount of effort required or to view narrowly the kind required. An effective compensatory program may take years and involve the family, the neighborhood, the peer group, and the schools.*

Thus, for the state's experts, a score of 70 in a black child is not a score of 90 in sociocultural disguise—it is a 70 (± 4), and has roughly the same predictive meaning whoever gets it. That is perhaps too strongly stated. Thorndike, for one, was willing to say that a score of 90 for a white banker's son had a different meaning from the same score earned by the son of a black sharecropper. What he appears to have meant is that there might be a difference in Intelligence A: That is, the black child might respond positively to improved educationally relevant environments because there was considerable room for improvement; while the white child would be already near the top of the scale of environmental quality and so would probably not improve. In his book (Thorndike and Hagen, 1977) he spells this out; the prognosis for a minority child is not likely to improve beyond the level indicated by test scores unless the environment changes. That, of course, was Humphreys's view: In the short run, at least, the prediction from a score is about the same no matter who gets it.

This view of intelligence as being current performance led to what Menocal considered one of the two big turning points in the case. He told me that the judge had seemed very well impressed with both the credentials and the testimony of Humphreys, which indeed reads as a set of knowledgeable, forceful but properly qualified statements. At the end of his direct examination, there was some time left in the afternoon session, but little enough that the cross-examination could with propriety have been postponed until the next court day. However, plaintiffs decided to start the cross-examination, which began as follows (RT 6291–6292):

> *Q:* Doctor, it is your view, is it not, that black people have less intelligence than white people?
>
> *A:* By my definition at the current point in history, the answer is yes.

Q: And you will agree with me that your definition is going against 2000 years of tradition?

A: Yes.

The Court: What was that?

Mr. Madden: He testified earlier that we have a common definition of what intelligence means that I believe he stretched back to Aristotle, which is that intelligence is essentially a capacity. And the definition that Dr. Humphreys offers is substantially different from that.

The Court: Yes, I understand. I didn't hear you.

Mr. Madden: Doctor, it is true, is it not, that many, many people believe that intelligence is an innate capacity?

Ms. Condas: I object. I don't believe the witness has been qualified as a public opinion expert.

The Court: Overruled.

The Witness: I expect that is true. I have no numbers to give you.

Humphreys's answer is certainly consistent with his definition, but it might have been softened by explaining that he did not refer to innate potential. In any case, Menocal thought it had a strong effect on the judge.

Sattler was later trapped by the same ambiguity about "intelligence." He said (1) he thought blacks and whites were equal in intelligence, (2) he thought that a given score meant the same thing, regardless of race, (3) he granted the large score difference between the races, (4) he thought that scores are valid indicators of intelligence. Without distinguishing Intelligences A and B, this sort of testimony is likely to make experts look silly or deliberately obfuscatory. But it is hard to assert publicly that one group is less intelligent than another, even when you have nonracist reasons to do so. Munday handled the question best, perhaps. Consider the following from his cross-examination (RT 5200–5202):

Q: All right. Well, let me ask you this: David Wechsler, you are familiar with him, aren't you?

A: Yes, I am, Mr. Miller.

Q: Okay. He defines intelligence as the overall capacity of an individual to understand and cope with the world around him.

A: Yes.

Q: Taking that as a definition of intelligence, do you believe that blacks are as intelligent as whites?

A: Mr. Miller, I have to have more than that in order to answer the question because I have to know whether—if one is talking about observed test scores, then I would say the answer is no. If you say, "Well, those observed test scores really don't measure blacks accurately," I would say to you that they do predict subsequent school achievement accurately for the blacks.

Now, if you say to me, "What about the innate capacity of blacks? Is it the same as for whites?" I would say to you that I don't know whether it is or not since I have never seen a test of innate capacity. I guess I would add to that that it is the working hypothesis that I think everybody in America has that all groups are equal. That's a working hypothesis . . . that everybody has.

At the same time, I am not going to give a slow learner an advanced reading book in school. See, there are so many things that we're dealing with here. I don't know whether that's helpful or not.

Q: So are you saying that without the ability to measure innate capacity, you can't say whether blacks and whites are of equal intelligence?

A: Yes.

Q: Would you say that just because someone doesn't do well in school, that means he is not intelligent?

A: Well, again, Mr. Miller, I think you are using the word "intelligence" as synonymous with innate capacity and I say if a youngster is not doing well in school, I don't know what the youngster's innate capacity is.

Now, if you say, "Does that mean that he is not intelligent?" I would interpret that to mean, "Does that mean that he doesn't have much academic ability if he is not doing well in school?" And I say that's one of the reasons that Stanford–Binet was devised, to administer the test to the youngster and see if one of the reasons that he is not doing well in school is that the child is low in academic ability.

The state's experts offered some highly abstract views of intelligence in addition to their ostensive definition (the WISC-R was in evidence). Thus, Humphreys (RT 6191) offered a close paraphrase of the definition he had given more precisely in 1979: "Intelligence as the resultant of the processes of acquiring, storing in memory, retrieving, combining, comparing, and using in a new context information and conceptual skills; it is an abstraction." Sattler (RT 6793) said that intelligence was a "set of strategies for processing information and for problem solving which has crystallized out of a complex interaction of individual variables, family interaction, and schooling." Gordon (RT 7282) was brief (especially for him): Intelligence is the manipulation of abstractions of increasing complexity.

And, finally, Thorndike (RT 4972) defined it as the "general tendency to consistently display effective responses to problems of an abstract or symbolic nature." Thorndike was the most thoughtful definer and worked to spell his view out—abstractions about abstractions are not, after all, very vivid as evidence. He talked about perceiving relationships as in analogies, forming concepts by classification and discrimination, recognizing problems, dimensionalizing their relevant features, and organizing and using relevant information in their solution. And he did it with reference mainly to items from his own Cognitive Abilities Test.

Clearly these kinds of definitions are different, first, from those including general adaptation to one's environment (nearly all extant species are by definition good adapters), and, second, from the sort of bits-and-pieces-of-experience notion of Kamin. What the state's experts conceived of intelligence as being is ability to work on the experience, so it is not so much storage as the power of the programs and the programming capability to make use of stored material. Chess-playing computers are the computer paradigms; philosophers, mathematicians, and theoretical scientists are familiar exemplars. And the most illustrative tests tend not to be assessments of information or vocabulary (though the latter is probably the single best practical test) but the so-called nonverbal, or culture-reduced tests, like the Ravens Matrices.

Intelligence as What Tests Test in School

Much of the argument about intelligence turned on the degree to which it is a trait almost entirely associated with schools. Thus, for the plaintiffs, items on IQ tests, on achievement tests, and on teacher-made subject matter examinations are all drawn from essentially the same item pool. For the defendants, the IQ items represent a population of items broader than, though overlapping, school-based items.

We may consider the WISC-R's subtests for illustration, especially with respect to Mercer's claim that IQ and achievement tests are made up from the same item pool, and thus "autocorrelate," or automatically validate, one another. The Performance subtests, in particular, are rarely if ever the subject of deliberate teaching in the school—no school teaches, for example, that the mirror image of a girl holding a doll should itself have a doll (Picture Completion), or, as a matter of formal curriculum, how to put pictures of objects together from a set of pieces (Object Assembly), or copy geometric designs with blocks (Block Design), or do mazes (Mazes), or write the correct nonsense symbol under the number it is said to be associated with (Coding), or put a series of mixed-up comic-strip-like panels in the order that tells a meaningful story (Picture Arrangement).

Nor, in the case of Verbal Scale subtests, do schools deliberately teach the abstraction necessary to see and say how, for example, a yard and a pound are alike (Similarities), or provide practice in memorizing a series of spoken digits and repeating them, forward or backward (Digit Span). Only the remaining four Verbal Scale Subtests are made up of the sort of material explicit in the primary school curriculum: Vocabulary, word problems in Arithmetic, and general information about the world we live in (the Information and Comprehension subtests).

On the other hand, achievement tests, especially in the early grades, contain items very closely tied to what is taught in the standard American curriculum. For example, the reading tests of the Metropolitan Achievement Tests, Primary Level II (second and third grade), include the following: sight vocabulary, phoneme-grapheme correspondence, vocabulary in context, use of affixes and suffixes as clues to meaning, and reading comprehension. Apart from the vocabulary tests, these items are not found on the WISC-R. And, of course, unlike the WISC-R tests, achievement tests require that the child has had formal education and usually require, at least after first grade, that he or she can read.

It is thus possible, obviously, to differentiate test-based from school-based items. That the plaintiffs lumped them into an undiscriminated mass is consistent with their view of general school-related intellectual activity as merely one of many adaptations that represent intelligence. It concedes little importance to the different varieties of intellectual behavior or mental abilities that are the focus of study of such scholars as Thorndike, Humphreys, and Sattler. In their view, there are real differences between achievement and IQ tests, despite their obvious relation. The exposition is that found in Cleary et al. (1975): Achievement tests are narrower than IQ tests, more tightly tied to a curriculum, and more geared to evaluation of what has recently been learned than to prediction or diagnosis.

The argument about whether achievement tests were just another form of IQ tests or were reasonable criteria of school performance against which the predictive validity of the IQ test could be assessed pervaded the trial, because IQ test validity was a pivotal issue. Plaintiffs insisted that grades given by teachers in the elementary grades were the *only* valid criterion to be predicted, and these included grades in the less academic areas of music, health, art, and physical education. Such a definition emphasizes the Mercer view that being in school is a social role, one among very many, with the teacher being the designated judge of the student's success in that role. Hence, if teachers use effort, politeness, cleanliness, or niceness as components of their grades, those are legitimate components.

The defense experts were uniform in citing as flaws in the grading system the very factors that Mercer supported. To Thorndike, Munday, Doppelt, Humphreys, Sattler, Lambert, and Gordon, school performance was most properly measured by the attainment of curricular academic goals. Subjective elements, within- and between-school differences in standards and criteria, and nonintellectual characteristics of the pupil are minimized when standard achievement tests are used, so that that criterion is purer than grades. The difference, again, is one of breadth of focus: Is the matter at issue a narrowly defined and testable set of intellectual skills, or is it a broadly defined adjustment to one of many social roles? As we have seen, this difference in emphasis was reflected in the differing conceptions of intelligence. These different views about intelligence had many consequences. They concerned the utility of the IQ test for instruction and diagnostic evaluation, its role in placement, and the definition of educable mental retardation.

Proposed Alternative Measures of Intelligence

At the beginning of the trial the plaintiffs' response to a court order requiring them to summarize the views of their experts on alternatives to the basic tests gave, in part, the following list:

> *(1) tests that assess the learning style of the child that can inform the teacher which curriculum is appropriate; (2) tests that are used by clinical psychologists to determine the incidence of retardation that involve observation of the child within a variety of settings; (3) Doctor Mercer's SOMPA system; (4) tests based on Piaget's models*

that appear to offer unbiased assessment devices; (5) culturally
specific tests; and (6) tests that measure a child's learning rate.

Of these, number 1 refers probably to diagnostic tests and is
relatively noncontroversial, except concerning the extent to which
such an alternative would actually include the use of standardized
IQ tests. Number 3 has already been discussed as a manifestation
of a view of intelligence, and we postpone a discussion of number 5
for the section on test bias. But there was considerable testimony
about numbers 4, 6, and 2: the status of Piagetian tests, learning
rate, and use of observation as alternative measures of intelligence.

The black psychologists had their own agenda, and it did not
necessarily include even the use of the WISC-R as employed and
renamed by Mercer. Hilliard was opposed to psychometric testing
(see also Hilliard, 1979) as being irrelevant to issues of instruction.
Dent, when asked whether there was any instance in which the
intellectual functioning of the black child needs to be assessed,
answered, "Not in the educational situation," an answer which I
assume must refer to the use of standardized IQ and achievement
tests, because all the black psychologists were willing to accept
criterion-referenced tests, preferably teacher-made, and individu-
alized teaching based upon the information given by such tests.
Their ideas about these matters were not well detailed, since they
were not primarily either school psychologists or teachers in their
training or experience. Nevertheless, it is clear that they wanted
black children to be able to move ahead through a curriculum at
their own pace without being pejoratively labeled even though the
pace might be slow.

This desideratum is represented in the well-known "IEP" (indi-
vidualized educational program) required by many statutes for the
education of the handicapped. It is not required, however, for
unlabeled students in regular classes. Plaintiffs' proposed Remedy
Memorandum, filed March 8, 1978, asked the court to direct
school districts to provide *all* disadvantaged black children,
whether or not they had been labeled EMR, with individual
assistance. This remedy would have taken care of disadvantaged
students not in districts that funded compensatory education
programs.

The state's experts did, predictably, see tests as useful not so
much in designing a curriculum as in finding out something about
the appropriate form and tempo of instruction. Sattler added that

the subtest variation may also be useful to psychologists in diagnosing learning disabilities. It is hard to show convincingly, however, that there is anything uniquely useful about IQ tests with respect to prescriptions for teaching, and it was not convincingly done at trial.

To Mercer and the black psychologists, learning rate was the real measure and validator of intelligence. Again, this is a view of intelligence as Intelligence A because they specified a task that was novel, one with which all groups and persons would have had a similar (lack of) experience. Strictly speaking, there is no completely novel task, so this requirement must be softened. Still, Hilliard at various points suggested both Piagetian tests and Ravens Matrices as adequate, or at least relatively unbiased measures. In fact, race differences, in standard deviation units, are about as great on these measures as on any other ability tests (Tuddenham, 1970; Gaudia, 1972; Jensen, 1974b, 1980). Humphreys was particularly emphatic on the point about Piagetian tests, testifying to a correlation of .88 between them and conventional ability tests (RT 6279). Lambert was ready to accede to learning rate as a criterion of intelligence (A or B) provided the tasks to be learned were complex.

The fact is that the rate of learning of well-programmed academic material does vary from student to student, even when they all finally arrive at a common final performance (Resnick, Wang, and Kaplan, 1973) and differences in such rates are correlated with conventional IQ tests. Gettinger and White (1979) found that trials to criterion in attaining mastery of school materials correlated about .60 with the Lorge–Thorndike IQ in both middle- and lower-middle-class elementary class students. The same authors (1980) have repeated this result among children of average IQ with both WISC-R and a group test of intelligence. Correlations between time-to-learn and standardized achievement test scores are higher still, a fact that implies that individually paced mastery learning systems will tend to magnify initial differences if left uncontrolled.

This implication has been examined by Arlin (1984a, 1984b) and Arlin and Webster (1983), who found that individual differences in learning rate are stable over periods as long as four years. If slower students are to catch up, faster students must wait, or give up instructional resources, or both. A society might regard such truly compensatory arrangements as just, but if it allowed equal time and resources to all students, initial achievement differences would surely magnify as a function of an intelligence-related rate-of-learning variable.

Plaintiffs' witnesses, when asked how they would assess children without tests, offered observation as the technique of choice. They did not specify any kind of observation scale or what the dimensions of observations would be. Clearly, adaptive behavior (AB) in various settings would be assessed, but the two most common AB scales, Mercer's Adaptive Behavior Inventory for Children (ABIC) and the public school version of the American Association on Mental Deficiency Adaptive Behavior Scale (ABS-PSV), are filled out by reference to reports of teachers and parents (Lambert, Windmiller, Cole, and Figueroa, 1975), not by observation. The teachers, of course, observe the intellectual and other behavior of the children, but the evidence, misunderstood or ignored by the judge, showed that it is the teachers who are the source of ethnic disproportions. (See Chapter 6.) There is some irony in plaintiffs' stress on observation as a substitute for testing, since testing arose partly from the need for and the development of systematic observation.

So it is that three of the plaintiffs' alternatives to IQ tests either perpetuate the observed disproportions (learning rate tests or Piagetian tests) or require the development of some scale of systematic observations that is likely to do so. Of the two yet to be discussed in Chapter 5, Mercer's SOMPA system is a poorer predictor of teacher-rated academic competence and achievement scores than the WISC-R; and no culturally specific test has been developed, nor were any items offered, that predict school performance in *any* ethnic group better than do the items and scales of the tests under attack.

At the end, the judge, after hearing all the testimony on intelligence, came to one correct and one probably wrong conclusion (1979, p. 952). ". . . we cannot truly define, much less measure, intelligence. We can measure certain skills but not native intelligence." The last sentence is true. But there *is* a consensus definition and a set of consensus measures. He meant that lack of opportunity to learn invalidates a test for the disadvantaged. But it does not do so when Intelligence B is at issue. In fairness, he had plenty of help in his confusion, and he resolved his uncertainty by going back to his views earlier expressed (Peckham, 1972) and to Judge Wright's views in *Hobson*.

PASE

Plaintiffs opened with Kamin, who repeated his *Larry P.* "bits and pieces of information" definition to a close approximation. Judge Grady asked him about it during cross examination: "You would say that what is being measured there is simply this child's storehouse of information?" (RT 124). The answer, in part, emphasized the aspect that was not emphasized in *Larry P.*: "Yes. . . . It is not only specific items of information, but also training in methods of approach or habits of regard, I might say."

Judge Grady had just asked him how he might account for a black ghetto child who "to all appearances had no source of information superior to that of other people in his tenement building, who turned up with an IQ of 145?" (RT 123–124). Kamin answered that he "would assume that there were experiences that led the child to be more interested in and thus exposed himself more to the kinds of items that are measured in the test." Judge Grady pressed on: "Do you believe there are differences in innate capacity as between individuals?" (RT 125). Kamin, very consistently, answered that, as there was no means of assessing innate intelligence, "it is futile speculation to wonder whether people may or may not differ with respect to it." He then cited with approval the Cleary et al. (1975) definition.

Kamin did not say that the impossibility of measuring Intelligence A does not imply that researchers cannot study the heritability of Intelligence B. The judge clearly thought, as is implied by his questions about IQ differences among children in similar environments, that much of the difference might be heritable, as his decision makes clear (Grady, 1980, p. 877):

> The IQ tests do not purport to measure innate intelligence. The test authors expressly disavow any such purpose. Both sides agree that no test has been or probably can be devised which will do that. What the tests appear to measure is the extent to which one utilizes his innate abilities in the performance of certain general categories of learned intellectual tasks. Performance on the tests reflects, for instance, the extent to which one has learned to observe, to see similarities and differences, to notice causal relationships, to remember, to draw inferences, to generalize, and to concentrate. The tests also indicate how well one has used those abilities to acquire certain specific knowledge, such as language and arithmetical concepts.

That the judge saw it that way had little to do with the testimony. The defense attorney foreswore any interest in genetics or heritability. But several plaintiffs' witnesses, like those in *Larry P.*, clearly disagreed both with Kamin and the judge as to the role of the genome. Like Mercer, their view of "true" intelligence was that it was Intelligence A, and they criticized the test for failing to measure it. Also, like Mercer, they equated IQ tests with school achievement tests, both being measures of exposure to white middle-class culture (Kamin gave the correlation between IQ and school achievement as .50, but there seems to have been an implicit stipulation in the trial that it was .40). Williams (RT 539) went so far as to say that the quality of a child's work in school says nothing about his intelligence.

Albee said that the IQ score was not a "biologically observed fact" (RT 143), which seems to imply that he rules phenotypic behavior out of biology. He later said (RT 155) that the score was the *minimum* estimate of "true" capability. For Williams (RT 508), learning rate was a truer measure of intelligence, and for Powell, adaptive behavior scales provided the appropriate measures of innate ability (RT 1664).

These views clearly share the notion of potentially measurable innate capacity, as Judge Grady saw. He pushed Albee (RT 226–227), asking how he accounted for middle-class white children who scored poorly in IQ tests. Albee answered that there were all kinds of potential emotional and/or organic factors that can have profound or subtle influence on performance, and he said that even such psychologists as McNemar or Thorndike would disagree that the IQ test was measuring something innate. It was a relatively ambiguous way to put it, since intelligent behavior is as innate as any other and, at least according to those two psychologists, heritable to some degree.

The plaintiffs again took up the broadest possible definition of intelligence, and in this case they met strong judicial challenge. The clearest example came during Albee's direct examination, when he was discussing the role of adaptive behavior in defining intelligence. After he described the sorts of behaviors that AB scales are concerned with (for example, getting along with others, knowing one's way around the community), the following colloquy ensued (RT 157–159):

The Court: Do you equate that with what we commonly call intelligence?

The Witness: Certainly what is commonly called intelligence is, in

Wechsler's definition, the ability to adapt to the social environment, so that would be a major component of what even David Wechsler considers to be part of intelligence.

The Court: Is it true that there are some children who do extremely well with what we might narrowly call intellectual problems in school and who are maladroit on the playground and vice versa?

The Witness: Yes.

The Court: Let's take the child who is the star athlete, but who just does not seem to be able to get his studies . . . which parenthetically, I guess, is not altogether uncommon. How do you account for that? Are we measuring the same kind of thing; that is, the ability to stuff a basketball or run a football and baseball, or the ability to get along well with people? Is that the same sort of thing we are measuring when we measure the ability to master the multiplication tables?

The Witness: I think that most intelligence tests stress cognitive abilities, the ability to manipulate, assemble, and to learn and to remember. But there are other components of intelligence that are fairly generally agreed on that include these other things as well. Binet and Wechsler in their writings both stressed that the measurement of cognitive ability is not the sole measure of intelligence.

The Court: I don't think anybody today, at least, would say that it is. I just want to steer us away from any false issue here. I don't think anybody is saying that an IQ test measures the entire spectrum of human achievement or human capacity.

I think what we are concerned with is, does it do anything worthwhile?

Later Williams also cited his version of the adaptability definition: "One's ability to cope with one's environment, whatever that environment is" (RT 406). And, as we have seen, Powell thought of AB as the true measure of innate capacity. The judge's response to these views appears in his opinion (1980, p. 851): "We believe Dr. Williams interprets too literally Wechsler's definition of intelligence as an ability to cope with one's 'environment.' The word 'environment' in this context does not denote only one's immediate physical surroundings. It means the milieu one is called upon to deal with, which, in the case of a school child, includes the demands of the classroom as well as those of the playground and the home neighborhood."

As in *Larry P.*, plaintiffs here generally took the view that if any test might be relevant educationally, it was a criterion-referenced test to assess gain in self-paced mastery programs. (Stoner, the plaintiffs' school psychologist, was something of an exception, since he found IQ tests useful, though culturally biased, especially in the diagnosis of learning disability.) This view lends itself to the use of cutoff scores for mastery and, generally, a pass–fail function of testing (see Glass, 1978, on the relation between "mastery" and "minimum competence").

The view is also broadly dismissive of differences above the cut-off score for mastery of competence: All who pass are considered equally qualified for whatever resource passing makes available. Thus Williams attacked the SATs by saying that blacks who score in the 300s still graduate from college, and if they can do that, there must be something wrong with the SATs (RT 584). Along with the depreciation of the importance of mental ability scores above some low level, Williams adopted the expansive Guilford view of intelligence as something that includes such abilities as music, dance, and so on.

It must be said that neither the plaintiffs' nor the defendant's case was worked out to any thing like the degree that was obtained in *Larry P.*—there was no Jane Mercer, elaborating a set of views for nearly a week on the stand. (She was represented, however, in Plaintiffs' Exhibit 55C, a copy of her 1978 paper analyzing facts from the perspective of the "sociology of knowledge.") Nor was there a Thorndike, Humphreys, Sattler, Munday, or Gordon for the defense. The defense was happy to concede that IQ tests did not measure anything innate, that there was no genetic difference between the races in basic capacity, and that tests and schools were both features of the dominant Chicago and American culture. The defense claimed only that the tests, even if imperfect, were useful, and as useful for one race as for another. It was a simple defense, and it simply ignored several large theoretical issues. The possibilities of confusion between Intelligence A and Intelligence B were never allowed to arise; certainly no defense witness was going to say, as Humphreys had, that blacks were less intelligent than whites (recall that two of the four defense witnesses were themselves black).

All this circumspection at last annoyed Judge Grady. During closing defense argument, Ms. Cheatom was defending the information value of the WISC (Closing Arguments, 189–190):

Ms. Cheatom: Those are some of the kinds of information that the witnesses have testified psychologists—trained psychologists—are able to glean from the IQ test alone, but this is still not to say that we use the IQ test in order to try to determine whether or not a condition known as mental retardation exists, but with it being able to give us this information, we are able to try to discern what is causing the child's particular problem at that point.

The Court: I don't know why you people are so skittish on that subject.

Ms. Cheatom: Well, Your Honor, I don't think we are. We became very concerned when you indicated that.

The Court: As long as everybody concedes that the so-called intelligence that this test purports to measure is subject to increase and is not something innate, which nobody claims it is, why all this timorousness, which is the only way I can characterize Mr. Halligan's argument, anyway. Now you are facing up to it with considerably more candor than Mr. Halligan did. It is ridiculous to go through that mound of documents here, which I have gone through, and say that the defendant does not use these tests for the purpose of measuring something called intelligence. Now that does not mean that the defendant says intelligence is something immutably set in concrete or that it is necessarily something that is genetic. But talk about the inability to distinguish apples from oranges, I think the defendant has been afflicted with that disease during at least a portion of its presentation here.

Ms. Cheatom: Well, Your Honor, we did not feel though that—

The Court: That, incidentally, is what I referred to as the political flavor of the trial of this case from both sides. You are both bending over backwards not to offend anybody, and you would have a great deal more success with me, quite frankly, if you would just simply let the chips fall where they may and let me worry about what it means. I am the one who is going to make the decision.

Summary

Suppose there were, as in pre-Binet days, no IQ tests. These cases could have still been brought against disproportionate placement in EMR (EMH) classes, since the stigma associated with placement and the separate curriculum would still have existed. But what would plaintiffs attack? One imagines they would have to go after the curriculum, the measures of achievement, or the cultural inappropriateness of teacher behavior with respect to instruction. Cronbach (1969, pp. 340–341) put the issue nicely:

> *If we are to bring these children to a self-respecting adulthood, we must define for them a prospective role that has at least as great a value, to the individual and to society, as the middle-class model of industry, articulateness, social and cultural concern, and self-regulation. No one protesting against middle-classness has gone on to describe a possible, viable society in which large subsegments of society have radically different orientations and functions.*

In these lawsuits, however, no one save Mercer really challenged the appropriateness of the basic curriculum—schools arose in the modern world just because they teach skills thought to be essential but not easily taught at home, like reading and calculating. Williams's suggestion (RT 614) that more ethnic studies courses ought to be included might be a good one but doesn't go to the basic skills curriculum and the development of reasoning and logical operations. Certainly, some suggested that individuality of learning styles and paces be respected, and no one really argued with the notion. Teacher behavior came up in discussions of teacher expectancy on learning, and that argument will be reviewed in the next chapter, where the effect of labeling a child "retarded" was an issue.

That leaves measures of achievement as a focus of attack. They are important because low achievement is the chief determinant of teacher referral. But it is hard to make a claim that an arithmetic or a reading test is biased against black children. To equate IQ and achievement tests (as plaintiffs did) but sue to enjoin the use of the IQ test only therefore appears to be inconsistent. Only the IQ test, however, made children officially eligible for the "retarded" label, and it was the IQ difference between races from which notorious genetic inferences were most often drawn. Achievement is tied to school and can be affected by disparities in access to quality education; but IQ, which is often measured before school starts, seems more easily attributable to persons than to institutions.

The other reason for plaintiffs not suing to enjoin achievement tests was probably that they really are closely tied to curriculum. When one impugns tests of reading comprehension or number facts as culturally biased and unlawful, one is attacking the school system, the curriculum, and the teachers—a very formidable collective opponent. The evaluation of educational programs can do without IQ tests far more easily than without achievement tests.

Nearly everyone in these trials agreed that IQ scores and achievement test scores had something substantial to do with each other. Where the parties disagreed was on the question whether those two measures had much of anything to do with intelligence. The Mercer–Williams view was that they were an alternate test form of school performance but had little to do with intelligence, which they saw as adaptation to *all* of one's environments. The *Larry P.* defendants saw intelligence as a relatively stable trait involving certain kinds of higher mental processes very commonly evoked in school and of varying importance in other environments. The *PASE* defense was unconcerned about such definitions—it was willing to rest its case on test utility.

We have seen that the plaintiffs' view also sees the various academic skills and IQ scores as largely nonheritable and, therefore, potentially more easily affected by environmental manipulations than would be any trait that was at least moderately heritable.

Combine these two plaintiffs' views and two conclusions follow: First, a child who is an A student of IQ 130 but has only average social skills and a child who is a C+ student with outstanding social skills are equally intelligent; second, appropriate school programs can fairly readily improve whatever academic disabilities they encounter in their clientele.

The plaintiffs were sanguine about the power of schools to remedy academic deficiencies, in the tradition of Judge Wright (1967, p. 485) in *Hobson* when he was so taken with the "Lorton Study," wherein criminals in jail were reported (in a study not published) to make remarkable academic progress in a relatively short period. Hilliard similarly told (RT 764) of a study in which high school students gained three years in only thirty-two hours of instruction. In general, the view was that schools could, if they would, bring low-achieving students up to a considerable degree of achievement.

Not all plaintiffs' witnesses were equal in the extent of their environmentalism. Albee cited (RT 147) with approval the view that, above IQ 50, all persons are "normal," and the environmentalist implication is that given similar environments, all would have about the same IQs. Kamin, we have seen, went quickly to an environmentalist account in explaining how children reared in "similar" environments could differ considerably in IQ. Mercer, on the other hand, obviously has cases where children with the same "sociocultural" scores differ widely in "estimated learning potential," which sounds like innate capacity.

Any discussion of intelligence implies a consideration of low

intelligence. The *Larry P.* opinion (Peckham, 1979, p. 954) includes Figure 1 in Chapter 1. It was introduced during Mercer's
testimony to show three normal curves approximating the distribution of WISC-R scores in her samples of California blacks, Chicanos, and Anglos. Note that, despite the black-white difference,
there is substantial overlap and many blacks score in the upper
part of the white range.

The plaintiffs were interested neither in the upper parts of the
distributions nor in palliating the stark implications of the black-
white differences at the lower end, which imply that 11.5 percent
of black children (compared with 1.4 percent of white children) are
below the cutoff for a finding of retardation—that is, below IQ 70.
To witness after witness they would produce the normal curves
showing the IQ distributions and ask whether the witness really
thought that that many black children were intellectually retarded.
Witnesses could either try to evade by recourse to the fact that the
definition of retardation requires deficient adaptive behavior as
well as low IQ, or, like one state EMR consultant, Fred Hanson,
say, yes, he *did* think there were that many. Part of the colloquy
appears in the opinion (Peckham, 1979, p. 947), but, since Menocal identified it to me as the second of the two most significant
points in the trial, and since it leads us naturally to the next
chapter, it is worth quoting (RT 3798-99):

> *The Court:* Mr. Hanson, do you think that these tests on the list are
> culturally or racially biased?
>
> *The Witness:* They are no more biased than our school system, our
> equating of whether or not an individual is responsive in terms of a
> quote standard.
>
> The individual intelligence tests presumably are attempting to
> measure what is the accepted, you know, mode of behavior, ac-
> cepted responses to whether—in terms of intelligence or other
> kinds—cognitive, reasonable ways in which—reasonable in
> quotes—as reflected in the majority culture. Those individuals who
> do not, of course—are not able to cope with that, or have not had
> either the exposure to or are having some difficulty, for whatever
> reason or other, are indeed, in jeopardy as far as making their
> particular performance in keeping with the majority culture.
>
> *The Court:* Is it fair, just because they haven't been exposed to the
> majority culture, to put them in a special class where they get an
> education different from the mainstream?
>
> *The Witness:* Yes, I contend that it is; that an individual who has—

just as we have opportunity classes, we have compensatory education for individuals that have some differences—some distinction—

The Court: We are not talking about compensatory. Everyone in this courtroom agrees that people that have been deprived perhaps need compensatory education.

. . . Do you feel that some of these districts use these EMR classes really as a substitute for compensatory education classes?

The Witness: No. I think they are responding in terms of a continuum of abilities within their responsibilities as far as the school district.

The Court: You really think that there were, back before the drop, that many mildly mentally retarded people among the Spanish surnamed people?

The Witness: Absolutely.

The Court: You do?

And you think there were that many among the blacks?

The Witness: Absolutely.

Menocal wisely moved to another topic, letting the impact remain undiffused by further discussion. We, too, move to the topic of the low end of the distribution, the topic of mental retardation.

Endnotes

1. She constructed a seeming dilemma for the IQ test advocate who would validate the test by equal prediction of school performance for blacks as for whites. If the test does *not* predict as well for blacks, it is ipso facto biased, and if it does, it is because the same cultural bias that makes blacks do badly in tests also makes them do badly in school.
2. Vernon (1979) has added Intelligence C—the specific test score, as distinct from the population of cognitive skills it samples. I don't think we need that much refinement here; we shall simply assume that C represents phenotypic (B) intelligence reasonably well.

Chapter 5

MILD AND EDUCABLE MENTAL RETARDATION

The two lawsuits differed in two areas not so much in how plaintiffs made an argument as in the extent to which they made it. One concerned mild mental retardation; the other concerned the role of the state (see Chapter 7). In both cases *Larry P.* was by far the more complete and emphatic; it was also the better represented by experts: Powell, Jones, Albee, and Whitenach for plaintiffs, and Lambert, Meyers, Goldstein, and several teachers, a supervisor, and a school psychologist for the defense. In *PASE*, plaintiffs put on Albee and Layman, and defendants had no experts save CBE administrators and a school psychologist. The great difference is that Judge Peckham came to believe that EMR classrooms were bad, perhaps for anyone. Judge Grady, having framed the main issue as test bias, had little to say about the nature of EMR once he found no substantial bias. He did, however, get very interested in the learning disabilities (LD) category, which is what plaintiffs argued they ought properly to have been diagnosed; in *Larry P.* that issue scarcely arose.

Larry P.

Definitions

"Mental Retardation refers to significantly subaverage general intellectual functioning existing concurrently with deficits in adaptive behavior, and manifested during the developmental period"

(Grossman, 1973, 1977). "Significantly subaverage" was translated in California in 1970 to forbid placement into EMR of pupils who scored higher than two standard deviations below the norm of the test used (Ed. Code Sections 56505, 56506). Furthermore, the adaptive behavior (AB) branch of the definition was translated by the legislature in 1971 to a requirement that retarded intellectual development indicated by test scores be substantiated by estimates informed by a home visit, developmental history, cultural background, and school achievement (Ed. Code Section 56504). California defined EMR pupils as those "who because of retarded intellectual development as determined by individual psychological examination are incapable of being educated efficiently and profitably through ordinary classroom instruction" (Ed. Code Section 56500).

The state came to regret the word "incapable," which seems pretty clearly to refer to Intelligence A. The definition was put into the code in 1947, but by 1977 the state wanted to argue that the important and operative part of the definition concerned repeated, serious failure to profit by ordinary classroom instruction.

The state was, of course, bound by its legislature. But, though the 2 standard deviation IQ cutoff was clear enough, adaptive behavior is not easy to define, nor is the meaning of "deficit" in AB a matter of consensus, since there were no scales for use with EMR children at the time the statute was proposed. The state's expert Ashurst used the following definition, which he took from Filler et al. (1975, p. 207):

> General intellectual functioning below the average of the general population; predicted or demonstrated inability to cope with the school curriculum designed for others of his chronological age; potential for achieving a third- or fourth-grade level in basic academic skills, if provided with the appropriate curriculum; and potential for developing social and occupational skills necessary for independent adult living.

Note that this definition, while compatible with that previously quoted from Grossman, emphasizes intellectual and school achievement in three of its four tests.

In the severer forms of retardation (IQs of 50 and below), the retardation is comprehensive and permanent and is commonly associated with biological impairment. But the milder forms, "mild" or "educable" (IQs 50–70) and "borderline" (IQs 70–85), are rarely associated with clear organic involvement. The witnesses

Albee and Goldstein agreed that not more than about 15 percent of the EMR population in the IQ range 50–70 show serious biological impairment. Rather, the group seems to be the normal tail of a normal distribution. Persons in this range very often go unnoticed except during the school years; Mercer's (1975) data, and those of many others, showed that the vast majority hold jobs, marry, and so on after schooling is over.

Prevalence levels have been reviewed by Shonkoff (1982). Definitions that emphasize school and psychometric test performance yield rates of about 2.0 percent. The theoretically expected rate, using Mercer's data given in Chapter 1 (Figure 1), would be about 2.28 percent, assuming a population of 91 percent white and 9 percent black. The rates when nonacademic adaptive behavior is taken into account are lower, nearer to 1 percent.

The plaintiffs' view was that since many of the EMR children were adapting to their environments outside school hours, and since intelligence was a global adaptation, they were not retarded and should not have been classified as such. They may have been ignorant of middle-class scholastic knowledge, but they were not stupid. They were "six-hour retardates." The state's witnesses focused on the failure in school, a view also consistent with *their* definition of intelligence as a well-discriminated, relatively narrow set of intellectual skills. All the arguments about intelligence were thus recapitulated in the context of mild retardation.

For example, the black psychologists Hilliard and Pierce viewed retardation, as they in fact viewed intelligence, as something relatively biological and structural. Thus Hilliard: "Mental retardation is specific trauma-induced impairment" (RT 120). And for Pierce, mental retardation was "a chronic, irreversible state of affairs in terms of one's ability to function" (RT 2929); and later, after being asked how he knew one of the plaintiff children was not retarded: "You can tell if someone was walking funny or talking funny or acting atypical right out" (RT 3086). And Mercer allowed a prevalence figure of about 1 percent as proper (RT 1925)—that figure would make a substantial proportion of the retarded population to be "true" (organically impaired, comprehensive, and permanent) retardates.

The *American Association on Mental Deficiency* (AAMD) *Manual* stresses that retardation is a current performance and subject to change, and it takes no position about etiology—as Goldstein pointed out, slow is slow, no matter what the cause. This sort of view is an exact equivalent of Humphreys' view of intelligence.[1] The view of the plaintiffs, on the other hand, implies that if you are physically normal, and functioning reasonably well outside school, you cannot be retarded. Since school performance mattered relatively little in their conception of intelligence, school failure plays but a small role in the judgment of retardation. In cross-examining Mercer, Condas at one point protested that it was schools, not society, on trial in the case. But if, as plaintiffs would have it, retardation is defined with reference to most of life's social roles, then it *was* society on trial, at least insofar as it goes about making classifications of retardation.

Measures of Adaptive Behavior and Their Effects

In the history of such classifications, poor adaptive behavior had played a great role in establishing the comprehensiveness of the retardation and was nearly always at low levels among the severely retarded. For the mildly retarded, however, serious school and intellectual failure were virtually the only required signs. According to Reschly (1982), whose excellent treatment I rely on here, the first noticeable departure from this standard came with Heber's (1961) manual on terminology, which, however, still emphasized academic performance for children of school age. But the "normalization" and "deinstitutionalization" movements of mental health law, and the protests of minorities about bias in testing and overrepresentation in the EMR classrooms, combined to help effect a change in the standard, toward ever more emphasis on adaptive behavior. The *AAMD Manual* today, as we have seen, suggests a two-part test, with academic performance perhaps being first among equals. Mercer would have school behavior a good deal less important than that.

As it happens, these two points of view each resulted in AB scales, each developed by a witness at trial. Mercer and Lewis (1978) have developed the Adaptive Behavior Inventory for Children (ABIC), a 242-item scale that is filled out in an interview with the child's caretaker, usually the mother, and covers behavior in the family and community and with peers with respect to nonacademic aspects of school, earning and consuming, and self-maintenance. A typical item is No. 132: "How often does _____ take his/her school supplies and books to school without being reminded? Occasionally (1), Seldom (0), or Regularly (2)."

The validity criterion, to Mercer, is the degree to which scores accurately reflect how well the child meets the expectations of the social system he or she lives in. Different mothers, of course, may have different standards, be more or less accurate and knowledgeable, and so on, so that the criterion may itself be quite unreliable. Gordon, Goldstein, Humphreys, and Lambert all testified that mothers are a poor source of objective information, with Goldstein and Gordon adding that mothers of low-IQ children may have accommodated their expectations downward.[2] Whatever the truth, there is no evidence that ABIC relates well to any other measures of competence. The school behavior item is deliberately nonintellectual and, in fact, does not correlate with any teacher rating of competence in minority groups (Kazimour and Reschly, 1981).

Correlations of ABIC with standard IQ and achievement tests tend to run from near zero to about .30 (Kazimour and Reschly, 1981; Oakland, 1979, 1983; Sapp, Horton, McElroy, and Ray, 1979). Not by accident, Mercer has succeeded in dimensionalizing AB so that it is nearly orthogonal to academic performance, partly by not consulting teachers for any competence-related information (or any information at all—the school is pretty well ignored) and partly by typically asking "How often?" rather than "How well?" a child does something, making the inference of competence less direct than it might be.

Lambert (Lambert, Windmiller, Cole, and Figueroa, 1975) headed the development of the public school version of the AAMD Adaptive Behavior Scale (ABS-PSV), and, by contrast, the usual interviewee is in this case the teacher, though parent respondents are also desired. Lambert testified that it seemed unnecessary to duplicate Mercer's efforts, which were going forward at the same time. Her scale covers nine of the ten "Behavior Domains" of the AAMD AB scale on which it was based, and these include language development, number and time concepts, and, as part of economic activity, money handling and budgeting. These scales correlate with intelligence quite strongly, about .60 (Lambert, 1978a), partly because, we may suppose, they concern academic concepts and partly because teachers will be unlikely to rate some child as competent in AB who they think is not competent in intelligence. But Lambert (1978b) testified on some findings reported later to the effect that parents and teachers of white and Chicano EMR children do agree about their adaptive behavior as being low, the implication being that retardation, even in school children, manifests itself for more than the six hours they are in school.

As it stood recently in California, as in forty-one other states (Patrick and Reschly, 1982), AB is part of the definition of EMR, though there is (typically) little guidance about how much AB is enough to forestall placement. Where AB is really independent of intellectual performance, as it is in Mercer's system, its use will cut down drastically the number of pupils otherwise eligible by virtue of IQs in the 50–70 range and referral from a teacher after demonstrated failures. Thus Talley (1979), reporting from the Pueblo, Colorado, school system (itself under pressure to reduce excessive minority EMR enrollment), said that of 300 referrals, 48 were found IQ eligible (<70), but use of the ABIC made them ineligible. In Corpus Christi, Texas, Fisher (1978) and Scott (1979) showed that over half of all EMR whites, and 60 percent to 70 percent of the EMR Hispanics and blacks were declassified by use of the ABIC. Of those declassified, only half could be placed in other special education programs. Reschly (1981), working with a random sample of 524 children in Pima Co., Arizona, showed that combined use of a -2 S.D. cutoff level on both AB and IQ would cut the number of potentially eligible students from forty-seven, on an IQ basis alone, to two. There was certainly no disproportion between the two students, though there would have been among the forty-seven, with blacks and Hispanics appearing about four times as often as whites in that low range.

Thus use of Mercer's ABIC, on which there are no black-white differences, would achieve the plaintiffs' goal. So would the quota that was imposed by Judge Peckham. It would reduce the number of black children in California labeled EMR to about 1600, for a rate of 0.4 percent, with the state rate being 0.36 percent.[3] These rates are to be compared with an average national prevalence rate of 1.6 percent (Patrick and Reschly, 1982) and the 1968–1969 California rates of 3.2 percent for blacks and 1.3 percent for all pupils in the state. This new, very small rate is close to the rate very commonly associated with "true" retardation of the biological, comprehensive kind. The quota, and the use of ABIC, in other words, had the potential to make the plaintiffs' definition of retardation come true, but at the expense of virtually eliminating the mild mental retardation category. (The "borderline" category of retardation was more or less abolished earlier by the *AAMD Manual* change from -1 S.D. to -2 S.D. or from IQ 85 to IQ 70, as the threshold.) Such a reduction in the mild MR category would also achieve ethnic parity, in that it has long been known that there is little ethnic disproportion among the severer forms of retardation.

It might be cause for rejoicing in Pueblo, Corpus Christi, and California that EMR classes have been cut by well over half. The question was, Were the declassified (in California the term is "decertified"—I will use D) children being relieved of a burden or deprived of a benefit? The two sides agreed on two issues: The EMR classes were small, and that was an advantage; and the label "mentally retarded" was stigmatizing. They disagreed about the usefulness and character of the EMR curriculum.

Is EMR Placement a Benefit?

Plaintiffs alleged that, having been misclassified and put into EMR, they then suffered irreparable harm because the curriculum was totally different from the regular class program. They quoted SDE bulletins and elicited testimony from state and city officials to that effect—the curriculum stressed social and vocational skills and was not intended to be a remedial, compensatory, or "catch-up" curriculum that would equip the children for reentry into the mainstream. The plaintiffs' original complaint (p. 4) had painted a dim picture indeed, describing the EMR derisively as providing minimal training in reading, spelling, and math and concentrating instead on such matters as bodily care and cleanliness, how to slice meat, how to fold a piece of paper diagonally, and how to chew and swallow food. This line of argument obviously persuaded the judge, who referred continually in his opinion to "dead-end, isolated, and stigmatizing classes," or words to that effect (Peckham, 1979, pp. 933, 945, 965, 971, 979, 986, 980; and elsewhere: Reschly, 1980, counted twenty-seven such derogatory references).

The notion of a "catch-up" curriculum for pupils such as the plaintiff children warrants some scrutiny. The judge seemed offended that EMR children fall ever further behind their regular class age peers. But, of course, so do most minority students, labeled or not, relative to white children. Time and again he asked the question he had put in the pretrial conference: How does the EMR curriculum differ from a compensatory education or a slow learner curriculum, which everyone agreed was the regular curriculum slowed down (but, if so, how could anyone in it catch up?)? Plaintiffs' attorney asked Frances Caine, who had been in charge of the EMR classes in San Francisco for several years until 1974, and who had just said that the EMR curriculum *was* regular to a large degree, "But they never catch up?" Caine answered, "If they caught up, they would be out."

The plaintiffs, as we have seen, had a very optimistic view of what schools could do for children. In their remedy memorandum (filed March 9, 1978, p. 12) they asked the court to direct each school district to provide supplemental assistance for every black child removed from EMR and to "continue such assistance until their achievement in reading and arithmetic is equivalent to their grade level." This request may have been just something to give to the judge that he could take away, making other suggested remedies seem more reasonable. But if it was seriously meant, it is really astonishing that any responsible group can imagine a public education program that will bring borderline youngsters to grade level in a system where most *regular* minority students who graduate from high school are more than three years below grade level. This expansive view of education had informed Judge Wright's opinion in *Hobson,* a case well known to all the participants at trial here: "What is needed is not instruction watered down to present levels of ability, but stimulation, enrichment, and challenge" (Wright, 1967, p. 470). There is, of course, a perfectly respectable teaching philosophy that contrasts sharply with this: Start where the child is and work along with step-sizes and at a pace that he or she can handle. Plaintiffs' witnesses were in favor of self-pacing, but they thought the schools could increase its rate so that children who started behind could catch up.

The plaintiffs' witnesses had very little to say at trial about what really went on in an EMR classroom. What was said, by state's witnesses, was uniformly favorable. Caine, as noted, said that the morning EMR classes were entirely academic, though slow-paced. Two of the plaintiff children's teachers, Stepney and Burenstein, described doing numbers, spelling, sentence building, individual reading, phonics, and arts and crafts. To the teachers, the children were simply slow learners; all the state's witnesses involved in EMR programs insisted that children were monitored carefully, and if they seemed to be doing well, were returned to the regular program. (About 10 percent to 20 percent did move on.) Caine tried to have each EMR child in the system read to her at least once a year, and her notes on the plaintiff children (such as "watch him—may be more EH than EMR") indicated an alertness to individual variation over time that supplemented the already high level of individual attention the children got by virtue of class size.

The teachers and supervisors also insisted that they recognized no arbitrary ceiling on the abilities of the children despite their being labeled "EMR." To Meyers, as to most others, the curriculum *was* a very slow form of much of the regular curriculum—it carried a special designation only because it was a special legislative and administrative category with special funding, special teacher certification requirements, and so on. As Meyers said, there had been slow learner classes before the EMR category was ever used. Even Judge Wright, writing in *Hobson* about essentially the same category, defined it in essentially the same way (1967, p. 448), describing it as a "highly simplified, slower-paced version of the standard curriculum," with a heavy emphasis at the high school level on vocational training (p. 449). Goldstein said, when asked how the EMR curriculum differed from compensatory education, that it was better by virtue of better teaching and closer attention.

It may be, and it probably is true, that the state's picture of EMR classes was rosier than a thorough and objective survey of them would justify. But there seems little warrant for considering them as holding tanks or dumping grounds whose curriculum, as plaintiffs would have it, is a series of field trips broken up by sessions with coloring books. Certainly, the evidence would warrant the modest conclusion that children in EMR classes were kept as constructively and happily employed as their almost-as-slow peers in the thirty-pupil regular classes and that the teaching of basic academic skills was serious business for the EMR classes. With the testimomy of Schuetz about the success of his vocational training classes in getting EMR students employed, and by Jones on the better outcome for EMR students in later vocational adjustment than their slow counterparts in the regular high school curriculum, the judge's severe and repeated derogation of such classes is very hard to understand or accept—unless, as seems clear, he regarded the stigmatization involved in assignment to them as a cost exceeding any benefit they might confer, or unless he simply did not understand how slow slow can be.

Stigma, Labeling, and Pygmalion

The plaintiffs' opinion was best summed up, I think, by Jones, who insisted that it was better to be a consistent failure in the regular class than to be labeled as EMR and placed in the special day class. The plaintiffs particularized their view in several ways. First, that the EMR curriculum, even granting what the state sought to show, was insufficiently academic; second, that EMR teachers did not expect much of their labeled pupils and therefore moved slower than they needed to; third, that the label itself lowered the self-concept of the labeled child.

About these three areas much psychological work had been done. Jones, for the plaintiffs, had collaborated with his student Donald MacMillan on a very influential paper of the putative effects of the "mentally retarded" label (MacMillan, Jones, and Aloia, 1974); Meyers, for the state, had collaborated with MacMillan on a large study of mainstreaming former EMR children in California (Meyers, MacMillan, and Yoshida, 1975). In the first of these papers, the authors had concluded that special versus regular class placement had no clear-cut effect on the self-concepts of EMR children. Furthermore, EMR eligible children are sociometrically low in regular classes even when they are not officially labeled.

The Meyers et al. (1975) study was reported quite fully at trial by Meyers himself. It sampled students who were reassessed, decertified (D), and returned to regular classes (RC) following the legislative change to a cutoff of 2 standard deviations below the mean IQ in 1970 and the accompanying mandate to reassess all EMR students. They were compared with students of similar grade placement, sex, and ethnicity who had remained in EMR following their reassessment and with another matched group of RC students in the lower half of the class who had never been referred or placed.

The typical D student, at the time of the study, had entered EMR at age 8.5 and had an average IQ of 70; had remained in EMR for three and a half years; and, at age 15.2, had been back in RC for a little over three years, was assigned to seventh grade, and was reading at a grade equivalent (GE) level of 2.7. The EMR controls had entered EMR at the same age, with an average IQ of 66; had been in EMR a slightly shorter time prior to reassessment; and were reading at GE 2.2. The RC controls were the same age, but on average a half year less over age for their grade placement, and were reading at GE 3.2. The D and EMR students did not differ in grades, citizenship, or years in regular classes prior to placement into EMR. Note that the RCs were themselves far below age and grade level in achievement, and the D's even further behind. The EMRs, however, were the worst in achievement. What confounds this apparent support for the efficacy of mainstreaming is the fact that the D's at the time of reassessment (prior to reentry into RC) had an average IQ of 78, 8 points higher than what it had been when they had been placed into EMR three and a half years earlier; this higher IQ is presumably what helped them to be decertified. The EMRs, on the other hand, had declined from 66 to 64, so that there was almost a standard deviation difference between the two groups in IQ, a fact that could well account by itself for the better D achievement.

This performance of the D's indicates that they were among the slowest of the slow. Still, they preferred RC assignment to EMR, and they were not doing badly by comparison to their less bright EMR controls. It is hard to imagine, however, that by age 18 they would have got much further than grade 4 equivalency. Had they been assigned to classes of higher average achievement, one wonders whether they would have been restigmatized as the class dummies. Even as it was, not only were they slow, but they were also rated by their teachers as lower than their RC controls in social acceptance.

Much was said at the trial about self-fulfilling prophecies: the famous Pygmalion effect. Plaintiffs quoted Rosenthal and Jacobsen (1968) and Beez (1968), which purported to show that young children labeled as smart were then so treated by their teachers that, though their names had been chosen randomly, they did in fact improve their scores significantly on achievement tests. Defendant's witnesses, especially Thorndike and Sattler, inveighed against the Rosenthal–Jacobsen study for its manifest weaknesses (see Thorndike, 1968; at trial he termed the study "bizarre") and stated what was true, that the study was difficult to replicate, even by its authors. Both Humphreys and Meyers had published papers (Yoshida and Meyers, 1975; Humphreys and Stubbs, 1977) in which the power of teachers' expectancies to predict student performance was compared with the power of student performance to predict teachers' expectancies, with the latter effect the sole or predominant one. And Sattler and Gordon also summarized these and other papers that either failed to replicate Rosenthal and Jacobsen or led directly to the result that behavior produced expectation, not expectation behavior. The recent synthesis of findings by Raudenbush (1984) confirms the view that teacher expectancy effects are greater, the less well acquainted the teacher is with the pupil.

Perhaps all the negative comment on the Pygmalion effect got through to the judge: He did not, as Judge Wright had done in *Hobson*, have much to say about it. The Pygmalion effect is one that seems to suit popular myth-making predilections. Most people believe in it, and the blacks in this action certainly did. It may be effective, under some circumstances (for example, Seaver, 1973; Eden and Shani, 1982), but, generally, its applicability to EMR teachers is probably weak or nonexistent.

In another sense, though, plaintiffs may have had a point. In a class homogeneously low, the standard of expected performance is bound to be lower than in a regular class, simply by adaptation level dynamics. The teacher might, therefore, "push" less because she or he does not notice how far behind the children really are. Caine, for the defense, said that, if anything, her teachers pushed too hard; Jones, for plaintiffs, suggested that because special education teachers were unusually nurturant, they probably pushed too little. No data were adduced on the matter, nor does the literature offer much wisdom.

As to the effect of the EMR label (or EMR placement—it is hard to unconfound these) on self-concept, the testimony at trial made easy the judgment that children did not like it. More than that, the Meyers et al. (1975) study made it clear that some D children, at least, would rather fail in the RC than be relabeled. The harder question is whether, *in general*, failure in the RC will hurt the EMR-level child more than the label will. It was agreed that the outcomes of the studies in the literature are mixed. Goldstein, who was (except for the teachers) probably the most positive about special classes for the mildly retarded, focused on studies showing a higher self-concept among EMRs in their own rooms. But there are results of all sorts (see reviews by MacMillan et al., 1974; Gottlieb, 1981; Madden and Slavin, 1983). Two studies (Carroll, 1967; Strang, Smith, and Rogers, 1978) show that the EMR children best off with respect to self-concept may be those who are neither fully mainstreamed nor fully segregated, but who are mainstreamed enough to feel normal and segregated enough to feel equal. The case is plausible, though two studies are not much evidence.

The data on sociometric status of low-IQ children in regular classes are clearer—it was usually quite low, before the movement for supplying special EMR programs took hold, and it is still low for former EMRs now mainstreamed. Gottlieb (1981) reviews some of his own work showing mainstreamed EMR children to be 1 standard deviation below the class mean of the socioeconomic scale, unless there is a special intervention designed to improve the attitudes of others, a step that might reduce the gap by half. He has also shown, however, "that the mean sociometric status of mainstreamed children was significantly lower than that of segregated EMR children when both groups of EMR children were rated only by their nonretarded peers" (p. 119).

Perhaps the most important empirical issue concerns the relative academic achievement of mainstreamed versus segregated EMR children. If mildly retarded children do, indeed, do better in regular classes, the complaint of irreparable harm has validity even if plaintiffs had not been mislabeled initially, and such a finding would warrant mainstreaming all mildly mentally retarded children. The better success of the D students in the Meyers et al. (1975) study is of little moment, since they were intelligent enough to be decertified, as we have seen. As a study of the efficacy of special class placement, it is all too typical of most of the literature. Random allocation studies are rare. Goldstein did one of them (Goldstein, Moss, and Jordan, 1965) and reported that after three years few differences were found between his segregated EMRs and his mainstreamed group. The reviews by Meyers, MacMillan, and Yoshida (1980) and Gottlieb (1981) concluded that few differences exist in the achievement of the two groups. They are alike, each being very low, so that, as Meyers et al. (1980) put it, "at the cost of apparently a weaker self-concept, the mainstreamed students were holding their own on other variables in contrast with the segregated." Madden and Slavin (1983) point out that the effects of class placement may interact with IQ range, such that the students with milder handicaps near the top of the range may reap a net academic benefit by being mainstreamed, while those nearer the bottom might profit more from segregated class placement. Other factors, especially the degree of special help available in regular classrooms, will obviously play a role.

Summary

To sum it up, the differences dividing plaintiffs and defendants came to four. First, how much were intellectual and social incompetence each to weigh in any discussion about categorizing for purposes of education? Second, even granted some agreement on the first issue, at what point along the continuum toward severe, permanent, and comprehensive incompetence is the line to be drawn below which children will be labeled as educable but retarded? The third issue, opinions on which affect the decision on the second, is what sorts of academic improvements can be expected by good teaching of disadvantaged children who are 8 or 9 years old and in the IQ range of 50 to 70? And the fourth question, related to the third, is what *is* the least restrictive alternative for such children? If it involves separate special classes, is there any way to have them without stigma? If it involves regular classes, will or can the state provide sufficient tutorial attention without keeping children out of class most of the time? We will deal with these questions in Chapter 9.

PASE

Definitions

The Illinois definition of MR was just like that in California, except that the words "psychological investigation" replace "as determined by psychological examination." There was never any requirement in Chicago of the sort that so negatively impressed Judge Peckham: No Chicago school psychologist was made to use one of a small set of intelligence or any other tests, though in fact almost all EMR referrals had an IQ test in their file.

The incidence of EMH (EMR) in Chicago was and still is very high, and we must assume that these high rates, obtaining for blacks as for whites, represent characteristics of policy rather than of population. No large city by the end of the decade reported EMR rates as great as those in Chicago. For example, in 1980–1981, rates for blacks, whites, and Hispanics in Chicago were 3.83 percent, 1.74 percent, and 0.83 percent, respectively, for an overall rate of 2.85 percent. Philadelphia, the next highest of the six large cities also reported (see Designs for Change, 1982), had corresponding rates of 2.39 percent, 1.38 percent, and 1.95 percent, for an overall rate of 2.03 percent. Rates in Chicago, in fact, had actually *risen* for black and white populations from 1973–1974 to the year of trial and continued to do so into the 1980–1981 school year—that is, until the consent settlement of the decade-long desegregation suit *(United States v. Chicago Board of Educa-*

tion) resulted in the school board's agreeing in the spring of 1981, to a desegregation plan concerning "educational components."

Table 3 shows data from the pairs of years that bracket *PASE* (filed in 1974 and tried and decided in 1980). Note that whereas the total school population fell by 86,448 (of which about 75,000 were white students), the EMH population scarcely changed, the result being a rise in the overall EMH rate. This was marked among blacks and even more among whites. Among Hispanics, whose presence in the school population rose during this period, the EMH rate fell for reasons we will consider shortly (also in Chapter 8). The proportion of blacks among all EMH students rose a little, from 75 percent in 1973–1974 to 82 percent in 1980–1981, but since the black base rate in the school population also rose slightly, the rise in disproportion was small.

Clearly, neither the CBE nor the state seems to have been concerned to decertify either students in general or black students in particular, a posture quite different from that which had prevailed in California, when as we have seen, both the legislature and the state school board had pushed to reduce and to put into ethnic balance the numbers in EMR classrooms. There are several possible reasons for this difference. First, the passage of strong bilingual education programs by the Illinois legislature in 1976 provided a placement for many low-achieving Hispanic children, and the effect on EMH placements can be seen in Table 3. The Hispanic plaintiffs who were once among the *PASE* plaintiffs left, and the final, second amended complaint sued only for relief for blacks, there no longer having been any Hispanic disproportion.

Second, the sheer size and relative poverty of the black population makes the EMH placement of black children, typically carried out by one or more members of the large black middle class employed as teachers, principals, social workers, psychologists, and CBE officials, less salient as discriminatory and stigmatizing and more salient as meeting a need. Washington, D.C., with a huge majority black population and a large black middle class administering much of it, has a rate of EMH placement similar to Chicago's (Kazimour and Reschly, 1981). Of six large cities surveyed by the office of Civil Rights of the Department of Education (reported in Designs for Change, 1982), and not including Washington, D.C., the rank order correlation between rate of placement of blacks into EMR and black proportion of the school population was .72.

Table 3.   Total and EMH (EMR) Population and Rates for Blacks, Caucasians, and Hispanics in Selected Years in Chicago

	Blacks			Caucasians			Hispanics			City Total		
	Total	No. EMH	EMH Rate	Total	No. EMH	Rate EMH	Total	No. EMH	EMH Rate	Total	No. EMH	Rate EMH
1973–1974	314,089	9,915	3.16	160,848	1,922	1.19	63,730	1,287	2.02	544,971	13,174	2.41
1974–1975	310,800	10,296	3.31	151,290	1,825	1.21	67,508	1,094	1.62	536,657	13,259	2.47
1979–1980	290,021	10,692	3.69	95,528	1,373	1.44	81,945	1,019	1.24	477,339	13,303	2.79
1980–1981	278,645	10,658	3.83	85,683	1,493	1.74	84,228	701	0.83	458,523	13,077	2.85

NOTE: Figures for the city are slightly larger than the sum of the three groups tabled here, because other small ethnic groups are not shown.

Third, and very different from *Larry P.*, the witnesses on both sides had good things to say about the EMH program in Chicago. Chicago is well known for having adopted a mastery curriculum, and since mastery involves self-pacing, it is easy to show that the EMH curriculum in its academic component is a part of the main curriculum, taken slowly. Dale Layman, the plaintiffs' chief witness on retardation and special education, did, of course, support many of the plaintiff views: that the IQ tests were culturally biased; that the IQ score played an inordinate role in determining EMH eligibility; that EMH placement confers stigma; that EMH teachers, influenced by the IQ scores, may expect too little of their charges; and that errors in placement were occasionally made and usually with minority children. She had herself found that of sixty referrals to her, five or six were misdiagnosed as EMH when they should have been called learning disabled (LD), culturally deprived (CD), or educationally handicapped (EH).

But she also praised the EMH curriculum and said that EMH teachers generally follow it and do good work. She liked most EMH teachers she had met and thought that in general the Chicago school system tried to deal with each child at its own level and as an individual. And she, too, used the WISC-R in testing. More importantly, she thought that there was truly an EMH category consisting of biologically normal children who were simply very slow to learn, with a short attention span and limited ability to generalize, who required very patient and concrete teaching, and whose final levels were limited.

This view was obviously very different from the one espoused by all plaintiffs' witnesses in *Larry P.* and by Albee and Powell again in *PASE*. Albee cited Mercer in stating his view that adaptive behavior must be deficient in order to find retardation, that an IQ score of 50 to 70 is not an accurate index of limited intellectual capacity, that "there is lots of research to indicate that under appropriate stimulating environmental circumstances, their [the nonorganically involved low achievers] IQs can be raised dramatically" (RT 156).[4] He opposed the very existence of self-contained rooms for EMH children as places where they "are banished forever to a kind of Siberia of non-academic contact . . ." (RT 175).

For Powell, too, as we have seen, adaptive behavior was a better measure than IQ of innate intelligence, and, just as for Mercer and Albee, the causes of school failure were essentially either clearly organic or they were environmental. If the cause was not organic, then some sort of intervention should be able to remedy the deficit.

At one point (RT 195) Albee quoted with approval what he asserted to be Zigler's view (see Zigler and Seitz, 1982, for a recent statement of it), that, where organic involvement is absent, people with IQs between 50 and 150 are normal. Albee, Powell, and Williams seemed to read the word "normal" in that statement as "potentially equivalent": All that might be needed was some appropriate intervention of the sort they had so much faith in. They did not see such differences as being like differences, say, in height: normal but difficult to change.

The Learning Disability Issue

PASE did feature one diagnostic issue that was not prominent in *Larry P.*, namely, What constitutes a learning disability as opposed to retarded development? Both plaintiffs in *PASE* were tested by Stoner and found to be LD, not EMH, a finding the judge accepted. Plaintiffs here also brought a witness, Brough, who was an LD specialist and who gave each plaintiff a large battery of tests.

The LD category is not well understood, and something of a catch-all (Shepard, Smith, and Vojir, 1983; Campione, Brown, and Ferrara, 1982; see also the more extended discussion in Chapter 8). Furthermore, Brough's credentials and style were unprepossessing; one of his two publications was "Why Riding Is Therapeutic," which appeared, if I read the testimony correctly, in *North American Riding for the Handicapped News*. His testimony concerned a large amount of profile analysis over several tests, the organizing model being the "house of learning," with auditory, visual, and motor integration "rooms." There was much speculation about brain dysfunction, laterality, and dominance.

In reading the transcript, it appeared to me that Judge Grady was fascinated with Brough's testimony; he was full of questions and not at all impatient. Plaintiffs' lead attorney Winter confirmed my view that the judge was indeed very much impressed by Brough, as he was elsewhere during the trial with, for example, discussions of the meaning of differences between Verbal and Performance scores from the WISC, as reported by Stoner.

When the defense in *Larry P.* tried to demonstrate the usefulness of the WISC by referring to the diagnostic utility of subscale "scatter," they got nowhere. Plaintiffs argued in reply that it was the overall score that really mattered, and plaintiffs certainly did not try to remake themselves into LD cases—they insisted, first to last, that they were wrongly classified as retarded when they were normal, by a test that was biased against blacks. In *PASE*, plaintiffs brought in the LD argument, but it served primarily to make the tests seem more useful and so helped defendants. Plaintiffs were, in fact, too successful in their argument. As Judge Grady said (1980, p. 882), "Plaintiffs seem not to realize that their own evidence shows that the two class representatives . . . do not have claims which are typical of the class they purport to represent."[5]

Summary

The two trials differed quite markedly in the way that EMR/EMH was conceived of. In California, EMR was considered a bad program, a dead-end, a dumping ground with little connection to the regular curriculum. In Chicago, EMH was part—the slow-paced part—of the regular, mastery-oriented curriculum and was thought of as an appropriate placement for very slow learning children. In Chicago, unlike California, the issue was less on adaptive behavior and more on school performance, and none of the long definitional arguments about innateness or what *real* retardation was occupied much trial time. Finally, the LD category loomed large in Chicago: Judge Grady was interested in particular strengths and weaknesses as revealed in profiles of test and subtest scores. That same interest in the particular determined his major finding concerning test bias, which is the subject of the next chapter.

Endnotes

1. Humphreys himself, however, was willing to recognize something called "academic" retardation, which was caused by emotional handicap, rearing in another language, or inadequacy of schooling. But it is clear that he regards such cases as but a small fraction of the EMR population.
2. Gordon used the particularly unfortunate example of pygmies being interviewed to see whether there are any good broadjumpers in the neighborhood (RT 7187). There must be more palatable ways to discuss adaptation level in a trial of this sort.
3. As Chapter 9 shows, the current rates are not far from these.

4. He seems here to have changed his mind about the status of the mildly retarded. In 1972 he said "the large majority of retarded children and adults are *not* retarded because of an acquired physiological abnormality, or because of a defect in their metabolism, or because of brain injury, or because their mothers had German measles, or because of the effects of any other infectious disease, or because of any other discovered or undiscovered exogenous or biomedical defects. Rather, the majority of retarded children and adults are produced from the more or less accidental distribution of polygenic factors present in the entire human race."

5. It should be noted that, according to the data of Kaufman (1979), perhaps a seventh of normal children of the plaintiffs' background would have Verbal-Performance score discrepancies as great as theirs. The question is, Does a discrepancy that prevalent qualify as a handicap?

Chapter 6

ARE THE IQ TESTS RACIALLY AND CULTURALLY BIASED?

The central question in these cases concerned actual discrimination—neither judge said that as a matter of law a simple showing of disproportion in racial placement sufficed to prove discrimination, without a showing of intent or at least of unfairness, intentional or not. Judge Peckham found, as a fact scarcely disputed, that the tests were biased. Judge Grady, as he himself noted (Grady, 1980, p. 882), was unpersuaded by the witnesses and arguments that had persuaded Judge Peckham, and their different views of bias, as he saw it, arose because in *PASE*, but not in *Larry P.*, there was a detailed examination of items. That isn't quite true: Hilliard in *Larry P.* dealt at length with items to show their bias, and Judge Peckham believed him. Williams, in *PASE*, alleged bias in many of the same items in similar ways, but Judge Grady was skeptical— hence the "detailed examination," which, as we shall see, did not depend entirely on the testimony of anyone. At no point in the analysis of these opposed outcomes does the issue of judicial temper or style loom larger.

Larry P.

Judge Peckham said that the cultural bias of the IQ test was "hardly disputed in this litigation" (1979, p. 959), echoing his 1972 statement to the same effect: "Defendants do not seem to dispute the evidence amassed by plaintiffs to demonstrate that the IQ tests in fact are culturally biased" (Peckham, 1972, p. 1313). He must have been using "culture" here in the broad sense, just noted, that includes SES and home environment factors intermixed. In any case, the statement is false—there was in fact tremendous dispute about whether the tests were biased. But his definition of bias revealed again his confusion about Intelligence A and Intelligence B: "An unbiased test that measures ability or potential should yield the same pattern of scores when administered to different groups of people" (Peckham, 1979, pp. 954–955).

The issues over which the question of bias was fought were several: the history of IQ testing, the standardization of the tests, the selection of items, the taking into account of the black experience and culture, and, most importantly, the predictive validity of the WISC-R and Stanford–Binet. A final, empirical issue was whether the IQ tests, whatever their nature, really were the cause of the ethnic disproportion in EMR.

These last two issues are related, since if tests are closely related to school success and failure for both ethnic groups, they cannot per se be the cause of disproportionate placement. The folk, or intuitive, definition of bias—How can blacks who haven't been exposed to what the tests test do well?—would call tests biased because all of mainstream America is or has been biased. This view, discussed in Chapter 4, came up often, but, as we have seen, it can be taken seriously only if by intelligence is meant Intelligence A.

History

Kamin's testimony will be familiar to all who have read his book (1974). It sufficiently impressed the judge that he devoted nearly three pages of his opinion (Peckham, 1979, pp. 935–937) to it. In brief, it recounted the use of Binet's test in America by psychologists who thought they were measuring a fixed and primarily innate trait and therefore thought that the racial and ethnic differences they saw among native whites, blacks, and poor immigrants were relatively permanent characteristics. Statements from Goddard, Brigham, Yerkes, and Terman, the racism of which would rarely be uttered today save by Nazis or Ku Klux Klanners, were read into the record as representing the provenance of the American IQ tests. They make one cringe to read them and must have had a similarly repellent effect on the judge hearing them.

There was not much the state could do about this testimony. Two witnesses tried to rehabilitate Terman, whose views did seem to have changed from 1916. Humphreys had been his graduate student and described him as a political liberal and certainly not a racist. Munday, whose company publishes Terman's test, reproved the plaintiffs' attorney for quoting from 1916 and not later, pointing out that similarly damning or more damning statements could be quoted against the Founding Fathers. It was a reasonable point, but it could not have availed much to remove the taint from the origin of the testing movement.

Standardization

The two tests primarily at issue, WISC-R and Stanford–Binet, were standardized on white samples until their revisions in the 1970s. That fact was noted—for example, in *Hobson*—as an indication of cultural bias. In the 1970s, both new standardizations included blacks in approximate proportion to their representation in the population, though Houghton Mifflin had not published a comparison of performance by race, and Munday actually testified, wrongly, that there were no studies of racial performance on an item-by-item basis (RT 4693). In fact, as we have seen, Nichols (1970) had done such a study in a dissertation, quoted for other purposes by Kamin (RT 890–93), in connection with subtest analysis of the WISC. (See later discussion and also Jensen, 1980, p. 565.)

The plaintiffs complained that simply adding low-scoring blacks to the normative sample without changing the test to take account of the black "experience pool" (Hilliard RT 370) served only to raise the average white score, given a grand average of 100—yet another sly move by the oppressor to keep the oppressed down, so it was implied. This argument cleverly puts test defenders into a trap: They cannot win if the tests are standardized entirely on whites, nor can they win if they use blacks in the sample. Doppelt complained of this (RT 5740–5780) when asked to agree that the addition of blacks to the sample simply lowered the mean; he did so, adding that removing children of professionals would have the same effect. His implication was that any normative group can be analyzed into subsets, but it is intended to represent all those subsets in one group. The issue is, again, the difference between the Cleary et al. (1975) conception of a single though heterogeneous society and the Mercer multicultural perspective.

Finally, this colloquy took place (RT 5481):

Mr. Miller: Actually, since we know that blacks do tend to score lower on the average than whites on the IQ tests, by increasing the percentage of blacks in the standardization sample you actually increase the—you give whites a bigger boost?

A: What you are saying, Mr. Miller, is that all the concerns expressed in the past that we should have blacks in the sample were really wrong. We should never have had blacks in the sample which seems a slightly incongruous arrangement.

Q: Well, you didn't answer my question exactly.

A: I don't think we are giving them a boost. We are describing a situation. If it turns out that the whites have a higher score, then this is what has happened.

The fact that test developers had arranged to produce equal scores for the sexes, but not for the races, was a large part of plaintiffs' attack. They claimed, and the judge believed (see Peckham, 1979, pp. 955–957), that the different treatment of sex and race occurred because testers assumed that the sexes were equal but did not assume that the races were. The clear implication is that the developers could also have constructed a test on which there was no black-white difference. Kamin articulated the argument, when asked on direct examination why, in his opinion, the race difference had not been eliminated (RT 875–876):

A. Let me answer the following way. I am struck at the discrepancy in the treatment of the sex difference versus the treatment of the race difference and the treatment of the social class difference for that matter.

I can see no scientific ground why one should eliminate questions which appear to show that one sex is doing better than the other and not eliminate questions which appear to show that one social class is doing better than another or that one race is doing better than the other.

It seems to me this has to reflect the preconceptions of the people who are making up these tests. . . .

Evidently, when they found the items discriminated between blacks and whites or between upper- and lower-class people, judging from the quotations which I have earlier cited, I would imagine that the testmakers felt that these differences simply validated the test as a test of intelligence; after all, Terman had predicted before any data were available that tests would show that blacks are less intelligent than whites.

So I would imagine he would not be particularly upset or alarmed and certainly not surprised if he found these items, indeed, did discriminate between the two races.

Of course, the great distinction between the sex and race cases here is that, on average, there are no or only slight differences in the school performances of the sexes (or, for that matter, in almost any cognitive ability, spatial reasoning perhaps excepted—see Maccoby and Jacklin, 1974), in great contrast to those of the two races in question, or of different social classes. That Kamin, an astute and erudite psychologist, would not have known this is difficult to believe. Even if Terman and Merrill (1937, p. 34) had not made it clear the sex differences were not large or numerous, McNemar's work (1942) would show it. At trial both Humphreys and Munday testified that the sex differences that existed favored one sex or another about equally, as Terman and Merrill had said. There are, in fact, tests of mental ability (e.g., the Ravens Matrices, Thurstone's primary abilities) whose items have not been edited for sex differences that produce equal scores for the sexes (see Jensen's 1980 review). Since there was a large pool of items on which the sexes were close, those evoking large differences could be rejected. For race differences, there were very few items that did *not* produce significant differences, and rejecting those that did, therefore, would leave very little left. The defense went extensively into the failure of the major attempt to construct a test that would be "fair" (produce equal scores for different SES levels)—that is, the Davis–Eels Games (Eels et al., 1951)—to show that what resulted was a test that predicted important criteria less well, while still discriminating between the classes.

Tapping the "Black Experience Pool"

The issue was, How can the "black experience pool" be taken into account in the testing process? The black psychologists suggested that it might be better to have blacks test blacks, but they did not push the point, and Sattler and Gordon marshaled the by then considerable evidence that race of examiner made little or no difference. (See the review in Jensen, 1980.) State experts, by and large, said that they would not do what the black psychologists did to take account of the black experience—that is, alter the items, accept nonstandard answers, give more time, and so on. The general view of state witnesses was that, having given the test in standard fashion, one might then probe, test limits, and take account of background factors in the interpretation.

That sounds reasonable, but if the test is not biased, why should anyone have to make a special interpretation for disadvantaged minority children? That is just what the judge asked Lambert (RT 6646), whose advice to school psychologists was to "be cautious" in interpreting test performance of minority children. In fact, one should be cautious in interpretations of test performance by any child; caution therefore does not translate into a method of taking particular account of black experiences. Conceivably what Lambert and others are suggesting is that one should be cautious in certain cases about inferences having to do with Intelligence A: It is the banker's son and the sharecropper's son all over again, and the difference in interpretation, given the same score, would be that a large and enduring environmental change would be likely to have different effects upon the two. But if that is the case, it was never made clear.

Another way to take account of the black experience is to construct items that tap it or omit items that do not. The well-known BITCH test (Black Intelligence Test of Cultural Homogeneity)[1] (Williams, 1972) has items taken from urban St. Louis argot and is said to be usable "as a measure of one's capacity to learn." In fact, it is a pure information-vocabulary test in multiple-choice format, many of whose terms are relatively common in the general culture (for example, dough, dig, gig, fag, butch, give me some skin, chick, bread, the claps, out of it, old lady) and many of whose items are not (for example, Mothers Day is?, Who wrote the Negro National Anthem?, What is Malcolm X's name?, H.N.I.C. stands for?).[2] The problem with the test is that it does not require any reasoning. In one study its correlations with the WAIS and years of education were not different from zero in white or black samples (Matarazzo and Wiens, 1977). The blacks certainly exceeded the whites on the BITCH, but the relation of their BITCH scores to years of education was $-.33$, while the correlation between WAIS and years of education was .36.

The plaintiffs, though their witness Hilliard mentioned the BITCH, were not offering it as a substitute. They did not, in fact, offer a single item that might tap the black experience, though they were often pressed to do so. They spent their time, instead, criticizing the items on the WISC and WISC-R, chiefly those in the information and comprehension subtests. The strategy was to cite items that seem far from the black experience, like "Who wrote Romeo and Juliet?" or "How far is it from New York to Chicago?" These are items 16 and 24 on the WISC, and 8-year-old low-achieving children of any race would never get close to such items. Hilliard's comments on these are typical: "There are a lot of kids in this country who are intelligent and who could care less about Romeo or Juliet, you know" (RT 158). "I know a lot of intelligent children who . . . could not tell you how far it is from one end of San Francisco to another." Such comments are, of course, applicable to children of all races. There was never any showing how an undefined black culture had some effect, beyond what could be accounted for by psychosocial factors present in every ethnic group, that militated peculiarly against the learning of such matters as the number of days in the week or the four seasons of the year, to take two information items closer to the range of low-achieving 8-year-olds.

Hilliard ambitiously attacked every part of the WISC as biased. Thus, again choosing arithmetic items that are on the difficult side (for example, "Thirty-two is two-thirds of what number?"—item 13 on the WISC Arithmetic Subtest), he said this: "The problem with the arithmetic test has to do with whether or not a child has been taught these things" (RT 161). That is unarguably true, and it also has to do with whether a child has learned these things. The average test age equivalent of that item is over 15 years, and so success is likely a result of what is taught and learned in school. No showing was made that either black culture or racism make arithmetic either worse taught to or harder to learn by blacks.

Of the Similarities Subtest, he was asked about the item, "How are salt and water alike?"—an item passed by the average 13-year-old. The flavor of his style is captured in the following quote:

> *Now, this is where the cultural bias comes in again. None of this judgment about that item or any other item using vocabulary as a base will stand up under the examination of people who are skilled in linguistics.*
>
> *If you understand linguistic principles, that is to say, how language works, what vocabulary means, not from a psychologist's perspective but from a linguist's perspective, then there is no way in the world that you would say this was a standard question that is asked in a standard way or heard and responded to in a standard way by every child.*

> *In other words, vocabulary is not standard, even when people use the same word. So even before you are able to use your mentality to figure out the answer to the problem, you first have to insure that the examiner and examinee understand the word in exactly the same way, or else you will be giving a benefit to the person who understands it in the same way as the examiner and you will be cutting down the person who uses that word in a different way. Now, linguists know this, but apparently testmakers do not.*

Of the item concerning the way liberty and justice are alike, he said this (RT 168):

> *Now, we come to this on liberty and justice. When a child says liberty and justice both are free things, is that a wrong or an unintelligent answer? Now, they get no points on this test for that.*
>
> *There is one level at which that answer might be an unintelligent and, therefore, unabstract answer. There is another level which might be a highly abstract answer, depending on what the child meant by free things.*
>
> *Interestingly enough, this is the way many of our minority youngsters would answer because they use a lot of other things in the symbol system besides the precision in the words.*

Clearly, Hilliard himself had something in his own symbol system besides precision in words. His views on language would appear to preclude not just testing but communication itself.

His discussion of the "burglar" item from Picture Arrangement, in which the examinee is to put four pictures into an order that makes the best story, was similar. The correct order is having the burglar approach a window, raise it, enter and bag the goods, and get caught by a policeman while exiting. Hilliard wished to defend the intelligence of a nonstandard, and wrong, arrangement (RT 194–195):

> *In other words, it assumes that you believe that policemen catch burglars. But what if you assume that policemen watch burglars and help burglars, and sometimes that has happened, you know. I would hope it doesn't happen frequently, but if you happen to be in some places, some children know that things that—for example, drugs are passed, and in some cases policemen, in fact, do watch because everybody in the neighborhood knows where the drugs are. But no one seems to be picked up for dealing in drugs.*
>
> *So if a child happens to accept that value, you know, or happens to believe that, they might actually put this policeman in a different position. They might even make him first before the burglar goes into the room. Again, that might not be the right answer that we want in terms of values, but it doesn't mean, if you take the*

assumption that the child may be working with, that it is an unintelligent answer.

Of the Vocabulary test, he had this to say (RT 289–290):

If you use the vocabulary of children in Iowa and you insist that it is the identical vocabulary that white children in San Francisco or white children in New York speak, or whether the children in Appalachia or white children in Atlanta speak, that means you haven't been traveling because they have different vocabularies. And each child ought to be able to use their own vocabulary to show what they can do.

And, finally, for Block Design, Hilliard said that good performance depends on living in a geometrical world, but he didn't explain how the world of American blacks was less geometrical than the world of American whites.

Hilliard's critique, especially his claim to know how minority children would answer certain items, highlights two characteristics of his testimony, repeated in *PASE* in the testimony of Williams: first, the reliance on anecdote wholly unsupported by evidence; second, the extension of his "expert" status to cover expertness on all matters having to do with blacks, including "the black community" and "black culture." Clearly, Hilliard believed, and we may agree, that experience affects test scores. It is not so clear that there is any way to test his assertion that persons who do not know such things as fractions, or the meaning of "bicycle," "nail," or "brave" at an age when most of their peers do, are intelligent. And it is even less clear how ignorance of such test items is tied uniquely to a black experience independent of the SES and sociocultural effects we have already reviewed.

I asked Condas why she had not objected more to testimony that, from her point of view, certainly was irrelevant to the point of ludicrousness. She said she let it run because she thought Hilliard was making a fool of himself and harming the plaintiffs' case. But she read Judge Peckham wrongly. He found Hilliard persuasive, as his opinion makes clear: "To the extent that a 'black culture'—admittedly a vague term—exists and translates the phenomena of intelligence into skills and knowledge untested by the standardized intelligence test, those tests cannot measure the capabilities of black children" (1979, p. 960). That may be true, but no one showed how, if at all, the American black culture does those things, if by intelligence we assume Intelligence B; and if it does, no black psychologist had any suggestions about how to measure these culturally unique manifestations of intelligence.

There is another way to take the black experience into account, in the book-balancing sense of the term, and that is resort to quota. It had worked in the *Diana* stipulation to control the rate of Chicago EMR enrollment, and the judge clearly had it in mind during the trial. When Munday said that his company was providing different norms for suburban schools and big-city schools, at their request, the judge was quick to break in (RT 5210): "What would that really mean in terms of the use of these tests in scoring? Would it mean that these would be credits or offsets or would it mean there would be different items or a deletion of items?" He was told that it would simply mean a different set of percentile ranks. Later (RT 5266) this brief colloquy took place:

> *The Court:* As I said earlier, I know it is somewhat outrageous and oversimplistic, but you talk about blacks testing about 10 or 15 points lower. Why not just add 10 or 15 points?
>
> *The Witness:* Well, if one were to add the 10 or 15 points, you would be suggesting to people that the child is functioning very much higher than the child is. And, as a matter of fact, the child wouldn't be able to handle school work at that level.

Mercer's ELP system is a quota system, and it does just what the judge suggested: It adds points, like a veteran's preference, the bonus here being given not for time spent in military service but for assignment to low sociocultural status. Gordon testified to data later published by Oakland (1979) that showed that the untransformed WISC-R predicts scholastic achievement with correlations in the .60s, while the ELP produces correlations only in the .40s. As Munday said, adding points produces neither a better student nor a better prediction. This relatively low prediction from the ELP has since been confirmed by Reschly (1978). Though the difference in prediction from the WISC-R was trivial for Anglos and blacks, it was larger for Chicano and Native American Papagos and, overall, the same as that reported by Oakland.

For reasons already indicated, it is unlikely that the judge would have taken Gordon's testimony very seriously. He heard testimony that a testing company provided different norms,[3] and he had seen the *Diana* quota work, at least to resolve disproportion if not to educate Chicano children. That may have been all he needed.

Internal and External Validity

Some data on internal validity came in through the state's witnesses on the issue of what is called the group-by-item interaction. Thus, even though blacks do worse than whites on every item on a test, if the rank order of item difficulties is the same for each group, then no item is unusually easy or difficult for one group as compared with another. Gordon and Sattler reported the results of several such studies (Jensen, 1976; Sandoval, 1979; Miele, 1979) that showed that the item difficulty levels for black children correlate between .95 and .98 with item difficulty levels for whites, that the group-by-item interaction accounts for only 2 percent to 5 percent of the variance in performance, and that even this amount disappears if whites are compared with older blacks (if mental ages are equated). The implication is that, on average, the development of mental ability in black children follows the same course as but at a somewhat slower rate than that in white children.

The phenomenon may be illustrated with reference to the "fight" item: "What is the thing to do if a boy (girl) much smaller than yourself starts to fight with you?" The correct answer is not to fight, but blacks have insisted that in ghetto culture it is correct and adaptive to fight back whenever anyone hits you. Doppelt had comparative data on this item, which showed that blacks passed it at rates less than whites until age 8½, after which time the two rates were about the same, quickly approaching an asymptote of about 95 percent. Doppelt's explanation was that there was essentially no cultural bias; Gordon's would have been, I think, that the blacks took longer to go to asymptote because of lower intelligence; and the plaintiffs claimed that the blacks, once in the Anglo institutions of the public school, then learned the right Anglo answer within two years. (They did not explain, however, why blacks did not also learn the right arithmetic or vocabulary items during the same time.)

Mercer, in responding to the group-by-item argument, said that blacks were shut out uniformly from all parts of the Anglo culture and thus showed equal deficits on all items. Gordon, in response, found it unbelievable to suppose that each and every one of the items of the WISC-R would be equally biased. The question of internal validity had little impact, however. Judge Peckham had far more interest in external criterion validity. As we shall see,

PASE was opposite in its emphasis, with the Mercer–Gordon dispute far more salient.

The chief argument in *Larry P.* about the fairness of the tests concerned their predictive validity. Did they predict as well for blacks as for whites? Here plaintiffs, as we have seen, managed to frame the issues thusly: Do individual IQ tests predict the teachers' grades for black elementary students as well as they do for white elementary students (especially at low IQ levels, and especially in California)? Studies using group tests as predictors, standard achievement tests as criteria, or high school or college students as subjects were deemed irrelevant; studies comparing predominantly black classes with different mostly white classes were disfavored. Studies simply showing very good prediction in an all-black elementary group, without an all-white comparison in the same school or district, were considered invalid, and so on.

To everyone's surprise few studies met these restricted criteria of relevance. The judge did not actually declare other studies to be irrelevant, but he made it clear that they would not weigh much. When Sattler, at his deposition a few months prior to trial, was asked for such studies, he knew of none. State's experts like Thorndike said that they were sure there had been hundreds of such studies—after all, Binet's criterion was teacher-rated school performance—and Humphreys said that the lack of studies in recent decades simply showed that you don't have to keep dropping pebbles from the tower of Pisa to prove the law of gravity. But, in fact, only four studies were put into evidence by testimony or exhibit comparing predictive validity coefficients for blacks and whites when grades were the criterion: Mercer's (by testimony), Goldman and Hartig (1976), Miele (1979), and Oakland (1978). The median correlation of these studies between WISC or WISC-R and GPA was .24 for blacks and .39 for whites. (Only Miele found blacks better predicted, but his study was lost in Sattler's ill-advised and poorly structured attempt to cover ninety-two studies in his testimony.)

Four other studies used group test predictors of GPA and so did not fit the plaintiffs' model (McCandless et al., 1972; Entwhistle and Hayduk, 1978; Trotman, 1977; Thorndike, by testimony); here the average coefficients were 0.45 for blacks and 0.48 for whites. But Thorndike's contribution here, which did stand out since it was not buried in a huge table, was to say that his test predicted blacks at .26 and whites at .41, not much help for the defense.

There were two studies of teacher ratings of academic competence (Goldman and Hartig, 1976; Reschly and Reschly, 1979), and the average prediction of those ratings by the WISC was .40 for each group. One recent study by Reschly, Ross-Reynolds, and Grimes (1981) on random samples of black and white third graders in Iowa shows the WISC-R predicting teacher ratings of competence 0.55 for blacks and 0.60 for whites; this obviously supports the trial evidence on the equal prediction of such a criterion. Another (Svanum and Bringle, 1982) reports correlations between abbreviated WISC scores (Vocabulary and Block Design) and crude teacher ratings of school achievement of 0.33 for blacks and 0.44 for whites, with smaller variances in the sets of black scores.

None of these predictions adduced at trial is strong, but the only ones that show real race differences involve teacher grades, which, in the Riverside, California, data (used both by Mercer and by Goldman and Hartig) included grades for music, PE, art, and health. Such grades, as has been shown, were considered by plaintiffs, but not defendants, to be properly a part of the criterion.

Where standard achievement tests are used as the criterion, the coefficients for the two groups are higher, and nearly equal, so it is clear why plaintiffs fought this criterion so hard. Of seven studies in evidence (six in Sattler's compilation), the average prediction from both individual and group intelligence tests of reading achievement was 0.54 for each racial group (Henderson, Butler and Goffeney, 1969; Henderson, Fay, Lindeman, and Clarkson, 1973; Goolsby and Frary, 1970; Mitchell, 1962, 1967; Oakland, 1978; Reschly and Reschly, 1979). For mathematics achievement, the coefficients were 0.61 for blacks and 0.63 for whites, over five studies (Henderson, Fay, Lindeman, and Clarkson, 1973; Goolsby and Frary, 1970; Mitchell, 1962; Oakland, 1977; Reschly and Reschly, 1979). Similar results supporting the evidence available at trial have been more recently reported in Svanum and Bringle (1982) and Oakland (1983) where WISC or WISC-R and achievement correlations are slightly higher for whites (0.64, 0.71, 0.65) than for blacks (0.62, 0.62, 0.58).

Defendants claimed that the differential prediction of grades was a function of restriction of range in predictor, criterion, or both. Figures 2 and 3, two of Mercer's many exhibits, show the scatter plots of WISC predictions of grades for blacks and whites, respectively. Clearly, blacks have a lower variance on each measure. Still, it is also clear that the Cleary et al. (1975) definition of

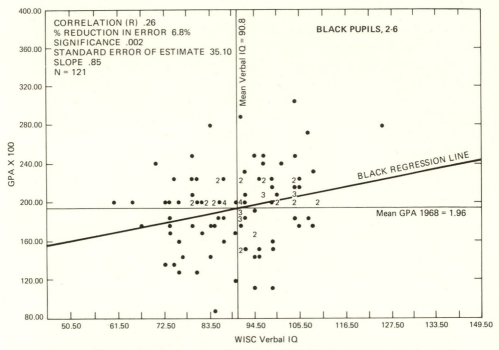

Figure 2. Grade Point Average (GPA) by WISC Verbal IQ, Grades 2-6, Mercer's Riverside Data for Black Pupils.

fairness as coincidence of regression slopes (equal intercepts, equal slopes) for each group is not met, for whatever reason. Mercer regarded these data, shown in Figure 4, as her most important evidence that the IQ test is unfair, since it met defendant's definition head on. (Figures 2 and 3 cover grades 2 through 6, omitting kindergarten and grade 1 data. Figure 4 is based on all the data, K–6.)

There was really scarcely anything to counteract these exhibits. In Sattler's large exhibit of ninety-two studies, two made the point in regression analyses: There were no ethnic differences in regression lines (Hall, Huppertz, and Levy, 1977), or ethnicity did not affect a prediction equation when IQ was entered (Jensen, 1974a). But most of these studies never made an impact,[4] and without scrutiny of the exhibit, the testimony does not call attention to itself.

Reliability is, of course, a feature of fairness, and the judge asked Humphreys, Thorndike, and Lambert about how often the test makes mistakes, especially at the low range. Now it is true that the

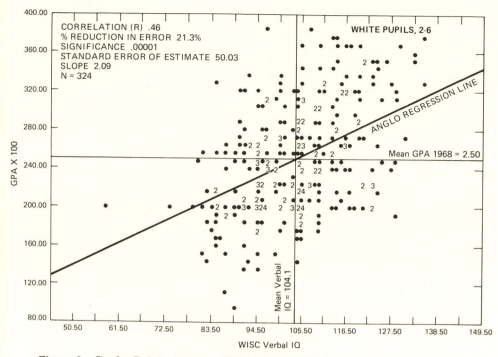

Figure 3. Grade Point Average (GPA) by WISC Verbal IQ, Grades 2-6, Mercer's Riverside Data for White Pupils.

Stanford–Binet, at least, is more reliable at low IQ than at high IQ ranges (Terman and Merrill, 1960), but even with a reliability of .90, persons averaging 69 on a first test will average about 72 on a second. Humphreys, responding to the judge's inquiry, said that of 100 children scoring in the 65–70 range, about five to ten would show large changes over five years. Thorndike had recourse to Table 3.4 of his text (Thorndike and Hagen, 1977), which showed that, for a reliability of .80 and N of 1000 in the bottom quartile, 325 will have moved up on the next testing. If the judge, who was worried about misclassification among low IQ scorers, was seeking reassurance in the algebra of correlational prediction, he wasn't getting any.

To compound the problem for the state, Mercer's chart showed that for blacks at the low end of the IQ range, scores were underpredicted. There weren't many data points down there, and hardly any for whites, but there did appear to be antiblack bias if one focuses on the lines.[5] This impression was reinforced by careful work by plaintiffs' attorney. Lambert had testified about Lune-

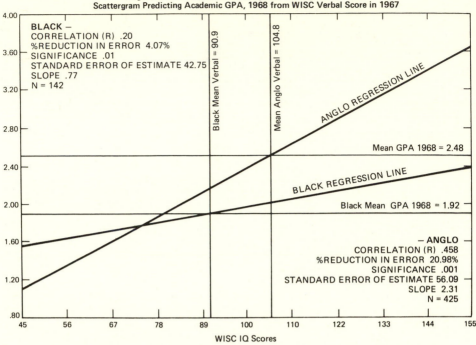

Figure 4. **Regression of GPA on IQ, Separately by Race, Mercer's Data for All Pupils in K-6.**

mann's dissertation (Lunemann, 1974) to the effect that intelligence tests overpredict black achievement scores when a common regression line is used and so are, if anything, fairer to blacks than to whites. But Lunemann himself had said, with respect to very low scores, the following (RT 6622–6623):

> *Black pupils with IQs ranging from 60 to 80 frequently achieved higher scores than their white counterparts and scores which were as high or almost as high as those of black pupils with IQs from 80 to 100.*
>
> *The findings were not consistent and the sample sizes were small. Nevertheless, since low IQ scores, in the 60–80 range, are at least a prerequisite, and occasionally a criterion, for admittance into special education classes such as classes for the educationally handicapped and educable mentally retarded in California, it is important that special precautions be taken in using these IQ scores as any kind of predictive index of future school performance.*
>
> *In fact, the instability and unexpectedly high achievement of these low IQ black pupils tended to support the claim that many*

black pupils have been wrongfully placed in special education classes.

Lambert tried to explain that the low achievement scores being discussed were at chance level, which they were, and that there were very few whites in that range, making any conclusion about bias in the low range quite untenable. She claimed that Lunemann was simply taking an occasion to express a personal conviction, but we may forgive the judge for believing the author himself and for thinking, perhaps, that Lambert's approval of this thesis (for she was on the committee) might impeach to some degree her present criticism of it.

The evidence in the record, and the literature in general at the time, almost all of which was in the record, would lead a prudent reviewer not to reject the null hypothesis of no racial difference in predictive validity of IQ tests for achievement, if not for grades. Studies appearing since the trial reinforce that position. Bossard, Reynolds, and Gutkin (1980) found no difference in regression and very high prediction from Stanford–Binet to WRAT achievement in black and white samples referred to school psychologists and matched on IQ. Reschly and Sabers (1979) found that there were different slopes and intercepts from one ethnic group to another, but that the bias that existed underpredicted whites when a common regression was used. Svanum and Bringle (1982) report that regression of teacher ratings on WISC scores yields the crossing pattern of Figure 4, but that regression of standard achievement test scores onto WISC scores produces overprediction for blacks at every level of WISC scores. These trends in the data on bias in IQ predictive validity are recapitulating that data for employment selection (Hunter, Schmidt, and Hunter, 1979; Hunter, Schmidt, and Rauschenberger, 1984; Linn, 1982) and college selection (Breland, 1979; Manning and Jackson, 1984). In the early 1970s there was much discussion of "differential validity" of SATs or employment tests, but as studies accumulated, the data compelled the conclusion that tests predicted nearly equally for blacks and whites, with whites being underpredicted by a common regression when there was any difference.

But what the judge had before him were Mercer's charts, Lunemann's statement, and a fair bit of vivid evidence that the correlational expression of IQ prediction of *grades* for blacks was smaller than that for whites. Thus his conclusion to that effect

(1979, p. 973) does not seem any more unjustified than would its opposite have been. However, the inference of cultural bias from such a conclusion certainly does seem unjustified, given the strong possibility of restriction-of-range effects and given the evidence of near-equality of prediction when achievement tests or teacher ratings of academic competence were the criteria.

The Role of IQ Tests in Placement

A final question about the bias in the IQ tests was whether the tests were, in fact, the culprits in causing so much black enrollment in EMR. The state's witnesses said correctly that the process of placement begins with teacher referrals and that the disproportion was as bad in initial referral rates as at any point thereafter. According to them, few children referred by teachers for EMR placement are found eligible for it by testing (Lambert said one in five; Bryant, two in seven; Hanson, a quarter or a third; Ashurst and Meyers, 1973, reported 56 percent during the late 1960s when the IQ cutoff for eligibility was 75 to 80 in most of California).

They also distrusted teachers' judgments of intellectual ability. Lambert cited work in which, of 300 children in the second and fifth grades in Berkeley, 15 percent had serious handicaps, but less than 3 percent were referred by teachers. Mercer herself claimed that teachers cannot see the potential of non-Anglo children. Goldstein reported a study in which 40 percent of an IQ-defined gifted group were not identifed as such by teachers or parents; Sattler reported studies showing that 25 percent of children no better than average in IQ were judged gifted, whereas, at the other end, 25 percent of normal children are judged retarded while only 12 percent of children with IQs less than 69 are judged to be retarded.

The state's experts saw as the chief advantage of using the IQ test that it "saved" children who were referred as positively retarded from being labeled and placed in EMR. That is, children whose failure had much to do with emotional disturbance or with poor schooling or with a very specific learning handicap would show up brighter on the IQ test than on school achievement just because of the breadth of coverage on the IQ test. They might then be channeled into educationally handicapped or learning disabilities programs. Similarly, underachieving students might be discovered by IQ tests. For instance, Thorndike posed the example of two students with equally bad reading problems in which it makes a difference if one has an IQ of 110 and the other of 80.

The only real data on teacher referral were in Ashurst and Meyers (1973) and reported by Gordon. The data were again from the Riverside schools, where Anglos were 80 percent of the school population, blacks 8 percent, and Chicanos 11 percent. Of 257 children referred, 48 percent were Anglo, 20 percent black, and 31 percent Chicano; of those placed, 41 percent were Anglo, 20 percent black, and 36 percent Chicano. The large departures from base proportionality clearly came in the teacher referral process and not in the psychological assessment phase.[6]

Thus there seems little doubt of the role of teacher referral. Perhaps the most clinching fact of the nonculpability of the IQ test in creating the disproportion in EMR classes was the fact that several years after the test moratorium in 1974, disproportion was about as great as it ever had been, despite a climate in which, according to those in touch with the field (Hanson, Lambert, Colwell, Brinegar, Meyers, and Bryant), psychologists and others involved in the placement process were highly aware of the *Diana* and *Larry P.* actions, were afraid of legal trouble, but still continued to certify black children for EMR. (They did not certify Chicano children in disproportionate numbers, perhaps because of *Diana*—they simply couldn't, despite what they might think appropriate for the child.)

The judge did not much like hearing this. Consider the following discussion of the absolute drop in minority enrollments in EMR during Hanson's examination by Menocal (RT 3572ff):

The Court: You mean the persons making the assignments decided that they were improperly placing minorities in these classes and that's why it dropped? Is that what you are telling me?

The Witness: Not exactly.

The Court: What are you saying?

The Witness: I'm saying that I think school psychologists, faced with the problems of minority groups, were saying if we have three times, or two times, or whatever factor one might use as far as a ratio, more minorities assigned to our classes than presumably expected, then we'll stop identifying minority groups, period, in many instances. . . .

I think my problem is that the concern is such that a minority pupil, if he is indeed eligible and not able to profit from regular classes, is also deserving of an opportunity for a special class, and many of them were not so afforded that opportunity.

The Court: Why was that?

The Witness: Primarily because I think people were afraid to—

The Court: Afraid of what?

The Witness: We were faced then with litigation—

The Court: Nobody ever ordered that. I don't understand what you are saying.

The judge may technically not have ordered that minority children who were in deep trouble in regular classes be kept there for further failure, but the *Diana* stipulation, and the fairly likely outcome of *Larry P.*, made such a result likely. He seemed to prefer to think, however, that the drop in absolute numbers was entirely the result of a stricter IQ eligibility cutoff and better professional judgment on reevaluation or evaluation of new referrals.

The data show that in the three school years before the test moratorium, 1971–1974, the percentage of black children in EMR classes average 25.5 percent. In the three years following it, 1975–1978, the corresponding figure was 24.5 percent. In the twenty districts enrolling 80 percent of the blacks in California, the percent of blacks in EMR declined from 54 percent in 1976–1977 to 51 percent in 1979–1980 (defense attorney file memo 1980). Given the fact that EMR enrollments were continuing their decade-long drop during this period, meaning that the relatively few children placed would be even further out on the tail of the IQ and achievement distributions, it is small wonder that psychologists found it difficult to refuse placements, despite concerns about litigation. The small drop in black disproportion, despite nonuse of the IQ tests, is pretty thin evidence to find it the culpable instrument, but it was all the judge had, and he took it. (Actually, the drop in proportion of *new* black enrollments in the twenty large districts, from 50 percent to 46 percent, was the fact he used [Peckham, 1979, p. 951].)

PASE

The defense in *PASE* was relatively simple—we have seen how establishing the role of SES and home environmental factors was a

significant part of it. The other main part consisted of establishing
the criterion validity of the tests at issue, and there was plenty of
help from plaintiffs' witnesses. Halligan virtually dared the plaintiffs to challenge the criterion—that is, the school and its curriculum—and, like the *Larry P.* plaintiffs, they never directly took up
that challenge. The case turned on an issue raised in passing by the
defense and pursued relentlessly by the judge, from the beginning
through the closing arguments to the decision: It was the question
of internal validity, here defined as item bias.

Bias in History and Standardization

Kamin, the first witness, repeated his testimony on the history of
testing and the racist attitudes of early test developers, but it went
unchallenged and was finally dismissed by Judge Grady as irrelevant: "One would not be surprised by evidence that their theories
of racial inferiority infected not simply their interpretation of the
test results but the actual structuring of the tests. However, Dr.
Kamin did not make that charge. Neither he nor any other witness
attempted to demonstrate any bias in the test items traceable to
the racist notions of Godard, Yerkes, Terman, and their followers.
If evidence concerning their racial attitudes was offered only to
show why they misinterpreted the test results, the evidence bears
on something which is not at issue in this case" (Grady, 1980, p.
872).

Kamin also brought up the sex issue, adding that tests should be
contrived so that women actually get higher IQs, since they
routinely get better grades in school (assuming that grades are the
primary criterion for intelligence). Here the judge showed his
dominant interest right away, asking whether sex differences were
consistent for all items. Kamin granted that they were not. He
then asked the same question about race differences, and Kamin
granted that they were consistent "across the board" (RT 56–57).

By the time of the *PASE* trial, Gordon had attacked Kamin's
Larry P. testimony (Gordon and Rudert, 1979), entered as Defendant's Exhibit 29 in *PASE*, and Halligan quoted it in cross-
examining Kamin. Part of that quote appears in Judge Grady's
decision (1980, p. 880) where he discussed the relevance of sex
differences to race differences. Nowhere in the record does feed-
back from *Larry P.* play so prominent a role.

Questions of standardization were also at a minimum in *PASE*.

Again, an argument was made by plaintiffs and simply ignored by defendants. Thus, on the one hand, Williams said that one cannot standardize on one group and then apply the resulting items on another. On the other hand, he also dismissed the use of representative samples of blacks in the restandardization of the WISC: "They just threw in 10–12 percent minority people" (RT 450). But that was about as far as that argument went. The defense was standing by its view that a test that predicts a middle-class curriculum is good, not despite, but because of its middle-classness.

The IQ Test as Part of the Curriculum

Regarding the correlation between IQ test and curriculum, the defense received assistance from plaintiffs. Thus Kamin described IQ tests to be versions of school achievement tests—useless, in effect, just because they were redundant. Albee endorsed reading readiness tests and achievement tests as giving good information, without commenting on the black-white difference of a standard deviation that generally obtains with them. Williams, as was his wont, put the case most strongly, the words in the record of trial (RT 607) being approximate quotes from one of his papers:

> *While the controversy continues regarding the unfairness of ability tests, not much is being said about testing's twin companion, the educational curriculum. It is well documented that the tests are biased; similarly, the educational system is biased against black children. Educational tests are used primarily to predict academic success, to evaluate student progress, and to group children in school.*
>
> *The school, then, becomes the main criterion by which the predictive validity of a test is established. What has been left unsaid or underemphasized is the fact that the tests are powerful instruments in shaping educational curricula and teacher expectations. For example, if a teacher's class scores are consistently below the national norm, it is likely she will teach concepts and materials similar to that found in the tests.*
>
> *The reason that educational and ability tests have been able to predict academic tests so well is because of their similarity of content and structure to the educational criterion. The tests are basically mini classrooms. Another way of putting it is that the test items are representative samples of the context and structure of classroom materials. This agreement holds true for all educational tests, IQ, achievement, and aptitude. The relationship between tests and educational materials is isomorphic or point to point. It is therefore imperative that black psychologists, educators, and other*

*professionals break the lockstep in tests and educational systems,
both of which were designed for white children and mainstream
America.*

As we have seen, however, he had little to offer in breaking up
the white middle-class curriculum apart from suggesting ethnic
studies courses and the statement that he was working on a
culturally specific black curriculum. He testified about his BITCH
test but did not propose it as a sample of some universe of
knowledge that ought to be part of school curricula. Judge Grady's
comment (1980, pp. 874–875) was customarily tart: "It would be
possible to devise countless esoteric tests which would be failed by
persons unfamiliar with particular subject matter. Every ethnic
group, every business, trade or profession has its own vocabulary,
its own universe of information which is not generally shared by
others. The fact that it would be possible to prepare an unfair test
does not prove that the Wechsler and Stanford–Binet tests are
unfair."

For Williams, as for all other plaintiffs' witnesses, any test that
yielded group differences, explicitly including competency tests
and bar examinations, was ipso facto biased—the position, let it be
recalled, is that if there are no innate or genotypic differences,
then there should be no phenotypic differences; if there are such
phenotypic differences, then it is a signal of unfairness. Albee put
the argument succinctly: "We know that black children as a group
score approximately 1 standard deviation below the white norms
on these tests, and this simply means that unless you honestly
believe that black children are innately inferior, that these tests are
grossly biased against black children" (RT 177).

Judge Peckham quite clearly bought this confusion between
societal unfairness and a measure of its effects, though it is hard to
say whether he would have agreed with Williams that bar examinations, which famously produce disparate racial impact and which
are inevitably supported by judges against all equal protection
challenges, are biased. But Albee and Kamin surely thought that
bias was equivalent to group difference; the tests are unfair because the test material is not as available to black (or to Appalachian white, as both Albee and Williams argued) as to white
middle-class children. This is the differential exposure hypothesis,
but it has force only if IQ scores are taken as genotypic measures,
which everyone in *PASE* agreed, at least officially, they were not.
As we have seen, however, some plaintiffs' witnesses truly be-

lieved that a proper IQ test should measure genotypic differences, and would do so given equal "exposure." Thus Williams: "You cannot measure a person's intelligence by asking questions based on assumptions; you have to know that a person has been exposed to it, and then you're measuring how well he has learned it. You're not measuring something innate when you ask him what that is" (RT 465).

Judge Grady was plainly skeptical of this difference-equals-bias hypothesis and its underpinning of differential exposure. Thus, to Albee: "If all IQ tests ever measure is exposure as we have defined it, then why isn't it always unfair 100 percent of the time except for the kid who comes out with [IQ] 195? He is not complaining. How about the kid with only 192? As between those two kids, you are blaming one because he did not have sufficient exposure, is that true?" (RT 225). He was also skeptical of the view, as we have seen, that all differences in IQ of apparently equally exposed children are nonetheless due to subtle differential environmental effects. When he asked Albee whether he would be equally comfortable testifying if the case had been brought by white EMH plaintiffs, his answer was "that it would be very easy for me to testify in favor of the test for middle-class white kids because they are the standardization sample from which the tests were derived" (RT 225). But if differential exposure equals bias against low IQ, why does the standardization sample make a difference?

So the defense argument (and the plaintiffs') that the test and the classroom were from the same cultural universe was established. The test was a useful tool in making decisions within the educational part of the universe. This argument was made almost entirely without benefit of data. No laborious attempt was made to demonstrate unequal or equal predictive validity for the two racial groups. The only data entered were those of Richard Berk showing correlations between IQ and achievement scores for his large ($N = 5500$) sample of children referred for psychological evaluation in three school years, 1973–1976. Plaintiffs' Exhibit 81 shows that the correlations of IQ with math and reading achievement were .52 and .50 for blacks and .65 and .63 for whites, with blacks' standard deviations in all variables being about 80 percent of whites'. Referred whites had an average IQ of 89; referred blacks had an average IQ of 77. The black deficit in reading and math achievement was about one-third of the white standard deviation, rather than the two-thirds that obtained for IQ.

But that was it as far as data use went. The plaintiffs themselves introduced data from a standardized achievement battery (the WRAT), and while they might not have settled any argument, there was no argument really to be settled; no pulling and hauling over whether the criterion should be grades alone or about the difference in the size of the correlations. Halligan's witnesses made their points quite without data. The black psychologist Hines made the case succinctly: Tests are clinically useful for assessment in the hands of professionals, especially the WISC with its subtest scatter, and tests and curriculum both represent the dominant culture.

Judge Grady and the Analysis of Item Bias

The concept of scatter leads to the aspect of Judge Grady's decision that has drawn the most fire, his extensive discussion, for 90 percent of his opinion, of each test, item by item, in an apparent armchair analysis of bias and in an obvious breach of the security of the tests. Bersoff (1981, p. 1049) expressed a common reaction of psychologists: "If Judge Peckham's analysis is scanty and faulty, Judge Grady's can best be described as naive; at worst it is unintelligent and completely empty of empirical substance. It represents a single person's subjective and personal opinion cloaked in the authority of judicial robes."

But Judge Grady is far less culpable than he seems. He had pleaded with both sides to supply him with papers concerned with item analysis. As he noted at the end of his opinion, he disagreed with Judge Peckham's opinion because he found in it "relatively little analysis of the threshold question of whether test bias in fact exists." He went on to say what his words throughout the trial had said: "I believe the issue in this case cannot properly be analyzed without a detailed examination of the items on the tests" (Grady, 1980, p. 882).

It is fair to say that neither side came into the trial seeing the analysis of item bias as the main issue. Both sides brought the issue up, however, and Judge Grady, unlike Judge Peckham, forced them to take more interest than they initially had. Halligan, beginning with Kamin, challenged the plaintiffs' theory that blacks suffered an equal deficiency of exposure, owing to cultural difference, to every item of every sort sampled by IQ tests. He read or paraphrased the criticisms of Gordon and Rudert (1979) and asked for comment on the phenomena that include the fact that the same rank order of difficulty of items occurs within each racial group, and the differences between races in rate of correct answers to any item closely mimic age differences within races.

Thus Halligan, cross-examining Kamin (RT 100–101):

> Q. Well, I will submit it to you for comment. That is a very unrealistic a priori. That is very unrealistic to think that every item on a long test is going to represent lack of exposure to information in about the same way and the same degree as any other item. Very unrealistic.
>
> A. I don't think it is unrealistic at all. . . . [F]or example, . . . restricting yourself to one racial group, one or the other, that individual who has a better vocabulary than another is likely to use words of different frequency with the same relative frequencies as the less verbally apt person, and that does not contradict the fact that he knows more words all told and has probably been exposed to more verbal imput than the less verbally exposed.

Note that Kamin answered with respect only to vocabulary words, not about the differences in exposure to vocabulary as distinct from Block Designs, Arithmetic, or Picture Arrangement items.[7]

This approach to internal validity was brought up several times by Halligan, and obviously had an effect on the judge. During closing arguments some seven weeks following the last witness, Lucy Thompson, representing the Office of Civil Rights on the plaintiffs' side, tried to rebut the argument from internal validity studies; this colloquy ensued (Closing Argument 86–88):

> *Ms. Thompson:* In other words, experts have said that it is reasonable to say that cultural bias pervades all questions of the test so that you would expect that white children and black children . . .
>
> *The Court:* This is what Ms. Mercer says in her article, which is in the record.
>
> *Ms. Thompson:* I think that the article that the defendants are using is—the basis for this argument is Jensen's study.
>
> *The Court:* They are using Gorden and Rudert, which in turn quotes Miele and Jensen.
>
> *Ms. Thompson:* There are four articles on that theory. We think that that does not show that the tests are not racially and culturally biased, that it is really consistent with the theory of cultural bias, and we would think that that data is not persuasive.
>
> *The Court:* What does the government say the data show? That

there is across the board lower scores item by item or that there is not such across the board lower scoring?

Ms. Thompson: Apparently white children and black children get more questions wrong of the hard questions and fewer questions on the easy questions, but there is still a third of the black children who receive 15 points lower as a group than white children on the overall scores on the IQ tests. We think that these internal validity studies don't account for that difference. In other words, however you look at what is going on inside the test, you still have this large number of blacks receiving very low scores, and that results in placement in EMH classes.

The Court: That is, I think, a different question than the one you were talking about.

Does the government say it is demonstrated by the studies that have been made that blacks, generally speaking, score lower on each of the IQ test items straight across the board than whites?

Ms. Thompson: I don't think that is what the studies say.

The Court: What do they say?

Ms. Thompson: I think they say that on the questions that white students missed most often, black students also missed those questions most often. This goes to the question of the ranking of the questions. Ranking of the hardest question, and then the next hardest question, and the next hardest question.

The Court: Rank order of difficulty?

Ms. Thompson: Right. I believe that studies show that the rank order is the same for black and white students.

The Court: But that does not have to do with the passing or failing?

Clearly, Judge Grady had done his homework and understood the argument better than Ms. Thompson. But what he wanted, what he pleaded for the two sides to give him, was analyses of the response to particular items, one by one. He had expressed that interest indirectly in his great interest in the meaning of various subtest scores, his fascination with Brough's testimony on LD, and his interest in Williams's testimony. On the penultimate day of the trial, the famous "Fight" item ("What is the thing to do if a boy or girl much smaller than yourself starts to fight with you?") came up. As we have seen, it is often attacked (as in *Larry P.*) as an item that blacks from the ghetto are likely to get wrong because failure to fight back would be a sign of weakness. Halligan read from Gordon and Rudert (1979) to the effect that Miele had found that item

relatively easier for blacks than for whites. Judge Grady interrupted (RT 1732):

> *The Court:* Is there any—has anybody gone to the trouble of
> collecting that kind of data on any items that this one—
>
> *Mr. Halligan:* Hey, here I go. I'm ready. Here we go.
>
> *The Court:* We are getting close to the source of wisdom here, it
> seems.

But Halligan slipped away to studies of internal validity that
reported rank order data on items without providing actual passing
rates for each particular item. A few minutes later the judge said it
all (RT 1736–1738):

> *The Court:* The core issue in the case is whether particular items are
> culturally biased. It seems to me the best conceivable evidence on
> that would be to see whether there is some inconsistency in per-
> formance by race on specific items.
>
> Now, I have had a lot of rhetoric here back and forth on general
> terms on whether "the test is biased or not."
>
> Well, it isn't "the tests." It is a series of specific items, and one
> reason, despite the thing I have said today, my mind is still open on
> this test is that I have got to sit down, item by item, and come to my
> own conclusion in light of all the evidence as to whether there is a
> racial bias, but the proof of the pudding would be in the eating, and
> if somebody gave a test to a thousand black children, and it turns out
> that 962 of them knew that the sun sets in the west, wouldn't I like to
> know that? Or if only 31 of them knew that the sun sets in the west,
> shouldn't I know that?
>
> I mean, surely somebody has given some thought to this matter in
> specific terms over the years. Hasn't anybody ever, in the Chicago
> school system, ever bothered to take the scores and take the tests
> and see how these kids do on these various items? I just can't believe
> that nobody has done that.
>
> *Mr. Halligan:* You know, there are circumstances—
>
> *The Court:* Nor can I believe that several proponents of the plain-
> tiffs' theory of this case haven't done it. I am equally critical of the
> lack of homework on both sides here, if the fact is that this had not
> been done. It seems to me very late in the game to be speculating
> about whether your theory is borne out by hard evidence or not.

Judge Grady made it very easy for all parties to submit "learned
treatises" into evidence. They may be received, under the Federal
Rules of Evidence, Rule 803.18, as exceptions to the hearsay rule.

The problem is that the rule states that they must be "read into evidence, but may not be received as exhibits." Grady simply refused to abide by that limitation, stating (RT 1752–53) that it might be appropriate to a jury, but that he would rather rely on the written word than his fallible recollection of oral testimony.

At the end of the last day on which testimony was heard the judge said, "How long is it going to take you to get the evidence that I referred to last time, namely any studies on this subject, which I happen to regard as pivotal" (RT 1825–1826). This plea never did produce the data he wanted. he got a paper by Mercer (1978) from the plaintiffs, and papers by Miele (1979), Jensen (1976), and Nichols (1970) from the defendants.[8] Of these, only Nichols provided much data, on passing rates by race and age for several items of the Stanford–Binet. Those, with Miele's data and James Doppelt's data (which had been introduced in *Larry P.*) on the "Fight" item, were all that Grady had to work with. Under the circumstances, given his view of the main issue in the case, armchair analysis was better than no analysis at all.

The question is, Since the "Fight" item produces less racial disparity in passing rates than most others, why did Grady include it among the nine items he found biased? The answer, I believe, requires us to examine the only other sources of evidence he had concerning item bias: the testimony of Williams, primarily, and of Hines, a black psychologist and witness for the defense.

Williams's testimony plays a prominent role in the opinion, which was, in the main, inhospitable to it. That testimony, from the point of view of informed social science and psychometrics, is at many points so outrageous as fully to justify almost any degree of suspiciousness. It is shot full of unsupported acecdote, misstatements of fact or at least of consensus, and logical inconsistencies, some of which we have already seen. But the testimony on particular items formed the most salient part of Williams's opinion. Judge Grady included a good deal of it in his decision, sometimes without comment, presumably because he thought Williams's words needed none.

A few examples will serve to illustrate. Item 12 of the WISC-R asks, "Who discovered America?" If a child answers "Indians," the question is rephrased to the form "Yes, the Indians were already there, but who sailed across the ocean and discovered America?" Williams commented (RT 476), "Now, to a Native American child that is absolutely insulting, to say, to really again refuse to accept the fact that Indians were here when Columbus—well, the Indians watched Columbus discover America." Clearly no one is refusing to accept the fact that Indians were here; more to the point, as the judge noted, his objection does not show how the item discriminates against black as opposed to white children.

There is a bit of consecutive testimony (RT 495–498) in which Williams took on several Stanford–Binet items, thus providing a representative sample of his style:

> *On page 96: Finding reasons, 1. Here the child is asked, "Give two reasons why children should not be too noisy in school."*
>
> *First of all, there's not enough information in that particular question. I've had children tell me, "Do you mean at recess?"*
>
> *What am I supposed to say. I tend to say, "No, in school."*
>
> *To me, that question is rather ambiguous.*
>
> *"Give two reasons why most people would rather have an automobile than a bicycle."*
>
> *Well, that's absurd. There are people who do want—I have no data on why people would prefer an automobile to a bicycle, especially in countries where a bicycle is the common modality. You know, there are arguments for bicycles just as there are arguments for cars.*
>
> *And some children are very, very bright and have creative responses on them. But there's only, again, a set of answers that has been predetermined.*
>
> *There's another argument, on page 99, in Similarities.*
>
> *Now, the Similarities test is supposed to measure abstraction, that is, how people form concepts, although there is no validation that the ability to do similarities is necessarily correlated with intelligence.*
>
> *For example, the first one: "In what way are a snake, cow, and a sparrow alike?"*
>
> *Now, it's been a long time since I've heard the word "sparrow." It would seem to me that, first of all, that is a test that is a vocabulary test, that one has to know what those phenomena are before one can really get the similarity.*
>
> *If I don't know what a sparrow is, then I'm penalized from the beginning, and there are many kids who don't know what a sparrow is. They know what a bird is, but not a sparrow.*
>
> *Well, there are a couple of more that I'd like to get to, and then we'll move on to something else. We're moving into the upper levels.*
>
> *I want to give the one about the reasoning. This is on page 107: "My house was burglarized last Saturday. I was at home all of the morning, but out during the afternoon until 5:00 o'clock. My father left the house at 3:00 o'clock, and my brother was there until 4:00. At what time did the burglary occur?"*
>
> *Now, there are a couple of things here. You give the child the card*

and read the question to him. And the correct response is: "If the response is either 'after 4:00' or 'before 5:00,' ask as to explain what he means."

Now, questions of this nature, again, get at reasoning to specific things, here, and is it a question of intelligence if the child does not come up with the correct answer?

Why not—you know, there are other kinds of reasoning problems which, I think, we could come up with which would be much more satisfactory.

In other words, what does this tell? There is no where in the manual that would explain in theoretical forms how this is related to a theory of intelligence if the person can or cannot complete that particular item. And that's at the upper levels.

The judge simply noted the objections in his opinion; his only comment (1980, p. 868) being that, as to the snake-cow-sparrow item, "It would have been helpful to have some documentation of the fact that substantial numbers of 11-year-olds are unfamiliar with the word." He was angry with the plaintiffs, who had found it possible to do an analysis of the school records of more than 5000 referred children, for not doing one of item responses by race.

Had Williams testified in *Larry P.*, he might, like Hilliard, have been more readily believed. But he had the misfortune of drawing a judge who read every manual and every item. Judge Grady knew, therefore, that the items selected for criticism were unrepresentative of the tests (whole subtests were never mentioned) and not representative of difficulty levels. As to representativeness, Judge Grady had this to say (1980, p. 874): "One who had not examined the tests in detail would be left with the impression that Dr. Williams had made a representative random sampling that typifies a cultural unfairness permeating the tests. In fact, the items were carefully selected and were not representative of the tests as a whole. They appear to be the only items Dr. Williams could find among the hundreds contained in the three tests which he thought would illustrate his charge of racial bias."

As to the matter of difficulty level, many criticized items, as we have seen, would never be administered to young children. As the judge said of one such item (1980, p. 840): "Hieroglyphics are not a pressing item for any American child, white or black." In observing that plaintiffs had criticized only one of the dozens of vocabulary words on the three tests, he simply noted that at the lower age levels the words were widely available to all children in schools and elsewhere, just as were simple arithmetic items. He took

Williams to task for criticizing Stanford–Binet Proverbs items intended for superior adults in a trial concerning the testing of slow-learning children.

But the question of the eight Wechsler items and one Stanford–Binet item found by Judge Grady to be biased remains. (Of the Wechsler items, three were from the Information Subtests and five were from the Comprehension Subtests. Four were dropped from the WISC-R.)[9] On what bases did he come to his finding? At least two are obvious: First, the plaintiffs criticized the item; second, so did the defense. That is, the black school psychologist Hines, who worked for the CBE, agreed with Williams that black children are disproportionately likely to say that the stomach growls when asked what it does, to say that the color of rubies is black because "Ruby" is a common name for black women, and to not know what "C.O.D." means. He also agreed that there might be a slight onus on a black child who, finding a wallet, returned it to its owner, since blacks would be more often suspected of having taken it in the first place.

The judge was persuaded on the socioeconomic issues and recognized that in a welfare community children were clearly at a disadvantage in learning about certain matters not taught in school: checks, C.O.D., organized charities, are the instances in the items he found biased. The relatively higher danger of ghetto street life may also have prompted him to agree with Williams that if a child has gone to a store and not found the bread he or she was sent to get, it might be better to return directly home.

What of the famous "Fight" item, the only one on which the judge had data, which data tended to show that the item was neither relatively nor absolutely difficult for black children? I believe that the judge, when he referred (1980, p. 846) to a study that, he said, showed that black children failed the item twice as frequently as white, must have been referring to Doppelt's exhibit (Plaintiffs' Exhibit 55E) on passing rates by race and age. If that is true, he must have used data from 6½-year-olds alone, in which the passing rate for whites was 60 percent and for "nonwhites" 33 percent (90 percent of the nonwhites were black). At age 7½ the two groups are much closer (73 percent to 52 percent), and in the 8½- to 10½-year range nonwhites do better by a small amount (85 percent to 86 percent). Ironically, on the only item for which he was supplied with data, he was too selective of it.

The upshot was that the judge found four items of the Wechsler test currently in use (the WISC-R) and one item of the Stanford–Binet (aesthetic comparison, where he found that the judgment of "prettiness" in faces to be too subjective to be a measure of intelligence) to be "either racially biased *or so subject to the suspicion of bias that they should not be used*" (Grady, 1980, p. 875, emphasis supplied). That phrasing makes clear that he was judging the appearance as well as the fact of bias, and, of course, he is as well equipped to do the former as the average psychometrician. Even his finding of the *fact* of bias, scorned as armchair analysis by psychologists, is justified by the fact that he was forced to do it in the absence of the data he so assiduously sought. We cannot be sure he would have understood the data, and his treatment of the "Fight" item data provides grounds for concern, but the fact is, no one gave him the chance to do the psychometric analyses that everyone bemoans the lack of. He had defined the core issue quite clearly: A test consists of items, so they must be examined.

Conclusion

It was clear in the decisions, quite obviously, that the two judges had differing views about whether the tests were biased. But it isn't merely that one examined the tests closely and the other didn't. It was the decision to do so or not that mattered, and their different decisions in that regard were symptomatic of their different tempers as much as anything else.

Judge Peckham, after all, heard at least as much testimony about items as Judge Grady did. Hilliard's rationales for why wrong responses ought to be credited when they are given by black children were not less imaginative than Williams's. But, while Judge Peckham readily accepted the notion that a different black culture, interpretable only by black experts, could transmute such "wrong" responses into reasonable, even creative ones, Judge Grady was simply unbelieving, even censorious.

For example, to Williams's attempt to justifiy the "wrong" arrangements of a simple picture story in the Picture Arrangement Subtest, Judge Grady said: "Comparing the actual picture cards in these two items to the analysis made by Dr. Williams, I am unable to follow him. The 'Fight' arrangement consists of three cards which, to me, have no possible logical sequence other than the one prescribed by the test author. . . . I am inclined to believe that Dr. Williams simply did not recall what these cards were about" (1980, p. 856). Peckham did not greet Hilliard's very similar testimony about the "burglar" arrangement with any skepticism at all.

One cannot justly assume that in cases in criminal, contract, or tort law, the two judges might not be differently positioned on the tender minded–tough minded dimension. But in this civil rights case it was Judge Grady who asked all the hard questions because he was unwilling in the first place, as we have seen, to accept a separate black culture as being of any greater effect than any other ethnic variant, without clear evidence. As he noted, however, "Dr. Williams did not relate the other characteristics of black culture to performance on the tests" (1980, p. 873). And without evidence of a clear connection between the early racism and any modern test item, he was unwilling to let the historical taint of racism in early test developers stand as evidence of current test bias.

As far as the issue of test bias goes, perhaps the nub of the difference in these decisions is that the times had changed, and so had the judges. The tests and testimony were much the same.

Endnotes

1. In 1970 Williams called it the "Black Intelligence Test Counterbalanced for Honkies," reflecting perhaps the more provocative mood of those days, and in *PASE* that early title was brought out in his cross-examination.
2. Answers: The day the welfare check comes, James Waldon Johnson, Little, Head Nigger in Charge.
3. It isn't clear whether he realized that the different norms applied to different school systems, not different ethnic groups within a school.
4. Among other difficulties with Sattler's presentation, he was interrupted by plaintiffs' attorneys nineteen times in the first thirty-eight pages of his testimony.
5. In fact, the average grade for the four black and one white students with IQ under 70 was just above 2.0 ("C"), well above prediction in four of the five cases.
6. The judge acknowledged in a footnote (1979, p. 950, fn. 51) that teacher referrals might be the source of the disproportions in EMR placements. But he said the IQ test would bias the placement process by "saving" disproportionate numbers of relatively high-scoring whites. The reasoning here is wrong. If the proportions do not change from referral (prior to testing) to placement (following testing), the tests have not contributed to disproportion.
7. When asked by his attorney whether he saw any consistent pattern in the differing magnitudes of race differences on WISC subscales, Kamin said he

could make no sense of it and he didn't know of any psychologist who had really tried to (RT 58). That is a strange statement coming from a scholar who had read, later reviewed, and in the trial actually quoted Jensen's 1980 book, where Jensen certainly did try to make sense of the pattern of differences (they depend, he said, on the "g-loading" of the subtests).

8. Judge Grady also received several papers on the issue of differential validity in the prediction of grades or achievement scores by ability tests. They included, for the defense, the Coleman Report (Coleman et al., 1965), the Cleary et al. (1975) report, and papers by Boney (1968) concerning prediction of high school grades by race using ability tests, and by Guterman (1979) on prediction of achievement in different social classes, and for the plaintiffs, Mercer (1978), which summarizes her arguments that internal validity measures are explicable by the phenomenon of cultural diffusion. Note that none of the defense exhibits meets the criterion imposed in *Larry P.*, that is, that the studies concern primary school children with grades alone as criterion and individual ability tests as predictors.

9. The eight Wechsler items follow:
   1. What is the color of rubies?
   2. What does C.O.D. mean?
   3. Why is it better to pay bills by check than by cash?
   4. What would you do if you were sent to buy a loaf of bread and the grocer said that he did not have any more?
   5. What does a stomach do?
   6. Why is it generally better to give money to an organized charity than to a street beggar?
   7. What are you supposed to do if you find someone's wallet or pocketbook in a store?
   8. What is the thing to do if a boy (girl) much smaller than yourself starts to fight with you?

Chapter 7

THE ROLE OF THE GOVERNMENT

Much of plaintiffs' case in *Larry P.* was devoted to showing that the state knew and (therefore?) intended the disparate racial consequences of using IQ tests for special placement. The strategy was a conservative one: Menocal thought he might have to prove such intent under Title VI of the Civil Rights Act. In *PASE*, with its different history, little of the case concerned governmental intent: The issue was almost purely *test*, not governmental, bias.

Larry P.

Plaintiffs spent much of their case in *Larry P.* trying to establish that the state intended to discriminate against black children by knowingly assigning them in large numbers to an inferior, dead-end education. In reply, the state tried to show that, given disproportionately large numbers of persistent school failures among black children, it acted with care to assign them to the most appropriate education among the existing possibilities (and the *existence* of EMR classes, though they were made by plaintiffs to seem awful, was never the target of legal attack).

Intent in racial discrimination cases, as elsewhere, is a slippery term. The easiest standard of proof is the so-called "effects" test, according to which any disproportion in the allocation of benefits or burdens adversely affecting a protected minority is per se evidence of intent. The next easiest (for plaintiffs) is the tort

150

standard, by which a party is presumed to have intended the natural and foreseeable consequences of its actions. On either showing, a defendant would have actively to prove that there were good (sometimes compelling) nondiscriminatory reasons for doing what he or she did. Finally, plaintiffs might in some cases have to show, to establish intent, that defendants really had a central motive to disadvantage members of minority groups—that is, show real racism. Generally speaking, plaintiffs have an easier road with statutory than with constitutional (equal protection) claims, with school than with employment discrimination claims, and with race than with other (such as sex, alienage) discrimination claims. Plaintiffs in *Larry P.* were on the right side of all of these comparisons.

Defendants relied heavily on *Washington* v. *Davis* (426 U.S. 229, 1976), even appending the test at issue in that case ("Test 21") to their posttrial brief. In that case, black applicants for police training school in Washington, D.C., had been screened out in numbers disproportionately large compared with whites, and they had sued on equal protection grounds. The Supreme Court held that the city had a reasonable nondiscriminatory purpose in demanding minimum levels of performance on a test that was content valid[1] and which predicted grades in police training school. California argued that IQ tests had, likewise, both content and predictive validity.

As we have seen, defendants lost these arguments. Even had they won them, there was no assurance of victory. The failed candidates in *Washington* v. *Davis* were presumably neither officially stigmatized nor trapped in some inferior life. The EMR children were certainly stigmatized, and we have seen how Judge Peckham saw the issue: that the EMR classes really were a burden to the children, not a benefit.

Plaintiffs showed that the state and local school boards had done nothing to alleviate disproportionate EMR enrollment. Reports of ethnic disproportions were simply filed and not investigated. The requirement that the WISC, Stanford–Binet, or Leiter tests be used was pushed through in the face of mounting minority concern about EMR disproportion. A state survey of school district records showed that there were no records of home visits, health history, or required triennial reevaluations in many cases, though the IQ test results were nearly always present.

The witnesses from the OSE insisted, as we have seen, that

there was no "real" disproportion because there were relatively large numbers of black children who needed EMR classes and who were failing badly in the regular classes. They said they simply filed reports because they didn't have the manpower to investigate them or enough political or statutory clout with school boards to bring them into line. That is probably true: They didn't have much effective power over school boards. But it is also true that they didn't think there was anything untoward requiring investigation. They said that the data not present in the files either existed in other sets of files or were taken informally and not written. There is probably some truth in that, too, as far as I could make out from interviews and from an informal memo from Colwell to the San Francisco city attorney, Dan Collins:

> *I approve heartily of this recommendation that there be a central file. The simplest way to do so would be to require that all Pupil Services records relating to the pupil be copied and sent to Doug Boyce.*
>
> *a. As I have indicated to you, Dan, I think our record-keeping stinks and has gotten steadily worse since Alice Henry retired, or roughly since the Suit was filed.*
>
> *b. Given the current disorganization of the District, only a court order is likely to bring this about.*
>
> *c. I don't see how the lack of papers has hurt any of the Plaintiffs, but to satisfy the Legal Profession and protect the District from future lawsuits, we need to live up to Ed Code requirements.*

Judging from the evidence, Colwell's memo, and similar comments made to me by a school psychologist in Palo Alto, districts *were* lax about such substantive matters as reevaluations, assessments of adaptive behavior, home visits, and health histories.

There was never, however, any showing that the records were less scanty for whites than for blacks. One of Menocal's memos to his law student interns, in fact, asked them to look over the city files to see whether the files of black children were more characterized by "IQ only" data than the files of white children. I never saw the result, but I am certain that I would have if the inquiry had been fruitful for the plaintiffs.

As another part of Colwell's memo pointed out, it is not always possible to live up to the Education Code: Home visits are sometimes resisted or very inconvenient, and medical data are ambiguous or unavailable, for example. Even if it were possible, a definition of EMR that relies primarily on school and IQ test performance, as the state's did, will inevitably not stress all the other data required by the code. It seems clear that the state simply did not think there was much they *could* do about the disproportion, and it didn't try. Or, rather, it thought that the provision of the EMR classes *was* what it should be doing.

With sufficient diligence and discovery, one can make virtually any bureaucracy look sloppy: It is standard technique among plaintiffs of all sorts to envisage a perfect world. There are always missing records, inconsistent statements, unkept promises, and feckless attempts. If they occur in the context of a great moral issue, they will look not just sloppy but positively malicious. It is to Menocal's credit that he made this case so convincing, and he thinks that it is this feature that most distinguishes *Larry P.* from *PASE*. Judge Peckham really was angry at the officials of the OSE. He professed astonishment that they seemed to regard themselves merely as custodians of reports. At one time in Brinegar's examination, after Menocal had established that the OSE never investigated or took formal action on district reports of ethnic disproportion in EMR, Peckham interjected with the sarcastic question, "Are you the Assistant Superintendent of Public Instruction and Director of the Office of Special Education?" (RT 4709). At another, he said impatiently to Condas, with reference to the legislature's 1971 resolution deploring disproportion, "Isn't it simple? You are bound by it—you have to make the effort to achieve it" (RT 2153).

The other part of the state's role was, of course, its conduct of the trial itself. Here it did very badly indeed, not from incompetence, but from the nature of civil rights litigation, particularly involving schools. Although six poor black children against the great state of California may seem like David against Goliath, the fact is that the children were represented by lawyers and legal organizations highly skilled in this sort of litigation—repeat players, in Galanter's (1974) terms—and they are (or were at least when this lawsuit was filed) very well funded.

The decision (Peckham, 1979, p. 930) lists ten lawyers for the plaintiffs, representing Public Advocates, the NAACP, the Legal Defense Fund, the U.S. Office of Civil Rights, and Morrison and Foerster, of San Francisco. Of these, five took major roles in the courtroom, each with certain assigned responsibilities for direct and cross-examination, and two others also contributed. For the state, Condas carried nearly the entire load, with the city attorney making only rare and brief appearances. For plaintiffs, there was a

platoon of clerks, interns, paralegals, and United States government functionaries. Just as important, there was Edward Opton at
Morrison and Foerster, a psychologist-lawyer who had been interested in this case for years and who helped guide the strategy of
the plaintiffs on the mental abilities issues. Condas, by contrast,
had one nonlawyer assigned to help her, as well as Sattler, who
read the testimony at a distance and sent back comments sometimes too late for good use in cross-examination. Condas was
as bright and hard-working as any lawyer in the action, but there
was only one of her on her side, and she was a tyro in the world of
complex federal litigation.

Plaintiffs' working files were full of trial team memoranda.
(There having been no trial team for defendants, there were no
such memoranda.) Thus, for example, from Opton, on possible
questions for the examination of Fred Hanson, the last of thirteen
suggestions:

> *13. Does the decline in EMR enrollment in recent years indicate
> that "educable mentally retardation" is not characteristic that a
> child either has or does not have, but rather is a label whose
> meaning will vary according to specific details of the procedure
> schools use to apply the label? (He will waffle. [Press] for a clear
> answer. Is one of those procedural details the criterion score on
> I.Q. tests, i.e., two standard deviations or some other number
> deviations? (It will probably require considerable probing and
> pressing in getting him to admit (or firmly deny) that "educable
> mentally retarded" is a sort of Red Queen's term: it means what the
> Department of Education says it means, no more, no less, and with
> no rationale for the number of children it includes other than the
> Department's decisions to so define it.)*

There were memos on every sort of issue—for example, how to
counter an attempt by defendants to show that HEW had approved the regulations of at least five states that approved the IQ
tests under attack in *Larry P.*[2]; suggestions, and request for
suggestions, for dealing with the defense contention that the lower
IQ-performance correlations in blacks results from restriction in
range; lists of the books that Condas had in her office; and so forth.

Plaintiffs were beautifully coordinated at trial, as well. They had
a set of points to make, and they made them crisply and redun-
dantly. The cross-examiner for each defense witness clearly knew
nearly everything of relevance the witness had written, which, of
course, meant that plaintiffs were in possession of a large number
of prior inconsistent, or seemingly inconsistent, statements or at

least of whatever the experts may have said that might be currently embarrassing. And certain questions and points were made in every cross-examination. Menocal ran a tight ship, and he knew what course he was sailing.

Condas simply could not match this organization. The contrast between the direct testimony of Mercer and Sattler, two vital witnesses, one for each side, was illustrative. Mercer gave, in effect, a practiced talk, illustrated by several well-designed slides. Her counsel never let the testimony run too long without an emphasis-making question, took the role of thick-headed layperson asking for the point to be made still another way, and in general managed the delivery of expert opinion that was punchy and clear. Sattler, on the other hand, rambled through his review of ninety-two studies to the great confusion of everyone. There would be patches as long as six pages where he simply described study after study, without any interruption by Condas and therefore without any clarity about the point he was making. The judge would ask, for example, about predictive validity studies of black students, and eventually Sattler would be talking about some data, fascinating to him, concerning construct validity or what have you. The direct testimony was simply not orchestrated to achieve anything like its potential effect.

The same contrast occurred in cross-examination. Condas was reactive—she would start with apparently prepared questions, but something in the replies would draw her interest, and, in effect, the witness would come to lead the cross-examiner. This effect was especially noticeable with Hilliard and Mercer, who spoke with voluble assurance at all times. Plaintiffs' attorneys followed a pretty clear script, very briskly. Even the style of question differed greatly. Plaintiffs' attorneys rarely deviated from some form of closed question ("You would agree, would you not, that . . ."; "Isn't it true that . . ."). Condas often deviated from the closed question ("How would you go about developing an observational system?"), with the result that her questions provided wonderful opportunities for witnesses to expatiate on their points of view.

The judge was unhappy with the state's meager allocation of personnel to the case. So was Condas, but there was nothing she could do about it. The judge also complained about the chief defendant: "Wilson Riles ought to be here. He has never appeared once in this action. I find that interesting" (RT 244). Riles, of course, had the largest school system in the country to run. He also had a bureaucracy that did not see eye to eye with him; a state board of education (his co-defendants), the political coloration of which changed from year to year; and house counsel that was not allowed to defend him (in California, only the attorney general defends the state). In other words, the state lacked the coherence and the resources of the plaintiffs. This vulnerability of states, especially school systems, to civil rights suits framed by "repeat players" has been amply documented by Griffin and Jensen (1982).

Menocal's interrogation of Riles was implacably aggressive and embarrassing to Riles. It was clearly designed to make Riles seem like some bumbling Uncle Tom coopted by the Anglo power structure, willing to see black children consigned to inferior education, willing to sit on the board of a testing company, and willing as a regent to vote for greater use of standardized testing for admission to California colleges and universities. It was effective stuff, but it may have succeeded too well, assuming that Menocal really did not want the state to appeal. Riles was furious, and at negotiating sessions following the decision he pounded the table in anger and would not submit without appeal to the imposed quota or the finding of discriminatory intent by him and his department.

The appeal was quixotic. The state board, which undergoes continual change in its makeup, voted not to appeal, despite dislike of the quota. Nor did San Francisco appeal. Hence, Judge Peckham's judgment regarding them is final. Riles, at least in theory and certainly by statute (Ed. Code Section 56120) is responsible to the State Board of Education (SBE) to carry out its directives, which with respect to *Larry P.* would be the terms of the unappealed judgment.

Considerable discussion between Condas and SBE functionaries and lawyers about the wisdom of appealing did take place. Condas was not at first in favor of filing (memo to Thomas Griffin of December 11, 1979). She felt that the facts of disproportion, continued with full knowledge by the board and department over a ten-year period, would be read by an appellate court as they had been read by Judge Peckham: as tantamount to intentional discrimination, requiring something like a quota system for amelioration. Unless the data could be attacked (and no one seemed really to think they were in error), she didn't think the case worth appealing. Her last sentence was this: "If [the data are correct], how *do* the districts justify their past practices?" The fact that she was still asking that question indicates, I believe, the little weight she accorded an argument based on broadly conceived psychosocial factors.

In the event, at the oral argument on appeal in November 1981 (just ten years after the case was filed), Condas was asked, even before she began her argument, why Riles was the only defendant and whether he ran the board. That question, as she told me later, did not admit of a satisfactory answer. She said that he, *in effect*, ran the educational system. But the appeals court then inquired about the statutory situation and asked, in light of it, what they could do. I was able to discern no real answer in the ensuing verbiage. And the final preliminary question was, "Isn't the order in *Larry P.* the same as *Diana*?"; that question was repeated at the end of rebuttal in this form: "If you could live with *Diana*, why can't you live with this?" Her answer was that Riles would not have countenanced the original *Diana* stipulations, whose consent decree was entered before he took office in 1971.

Menocal was asked whether the special education of black children would now, because of the quota, be hostage to the decisions of white parents to enroll their children in EMR. He said that the quota really was not a quota, that districts would need only to justify their overrepresentation after a showing of a good faith effort to reduce it.

It is difficult to imagine any district wanting to be involved in any such justification. All they might adduce, again, would be disproportionate teacher referrals, a phenomenon virtually ignored by Peckham, and one that Menocal himself regarded simply as an excuse, according to a negotiating letter he wrote to Thomas Griffin of the legal office of the department of education. Furthermore, if defendant witnesses were correct, and the survey by Kirp, Kuriloff, and Buss (1975) would indicate that they were, the threat of lawsuits or court hearings is a powerful factor for school personnel. It is far easier not to place, or actually to remove, one or two black children in a small district than to justify their enrollment to a court, in a remorselessly adversarial setting.

PASE

In many ways the government defendants in *PASE* had a lighter burden. There had been no legislative resolution against disparate impact and IQ tests; there was no requirement that school psychologists use any of the tests in dispute; the city had not, as had California in *Diana*, agreed to a quota on special education placement, nor had it been subject to a finding of discrimination in pupil allocation. Judge Grady, unlike Judge Peckham, had not issued a preliminary injunction (which implies a decision in advance of trial) against the government.

There was, of course, evidence that the schools were lax in carrying out health histories and assessments of adaptive behaviors, and the Office of Civil Rights of HEW had found the CBE out of compliance with its own plan regarding various aspects of integration, and had denied it ESEA (Elementary and Secondary Education Act) funds as late as April 1979. Furthermore, one plaintiff witness, William Zbinden, had headed an inspection team that had evaluated several districts in 1976–1977 and found several of them wanting in their handling of referrals where the outcome might be EMH—little or no record of a measure of adaptive behavior, for example.

Nonetheless, by September 1979, the State Board of Education had "passed" one of the districts in which a compliance team assessed a random sample of the special education records. And Zbinden himself had said the districts he had inspected were at least minimally up to standards. He also said that in three of the four districts he looked at, the judgment of the psychologist was *not* relied on primarily. Nor did he challenge the IQ tests or claim disproportionate misplacement of black children into EMH.

As we have seen in another plaintiff witness (Layman—see Chapter 5), this trial lacked the intransigent view of governmental venality and malign intent to harm black children that existed in *Larry P*. One reason for the different atmosphere may have been the contextual shift in locus. Chicago was a predominantly black school district. Two important conditions followed from that fact. First, though 80 percent of EMH pupils were black, their base rate in the school population was 60 percent, and the disproportionate excess of 20 percent does not seem large relative to the factor-of-two situation in California.

Second, the CBE was staffed by many blacks in senior and professional positions. Twenty-three percent, or over forty, of the school psychologists were black, as were large proportions of social workers, teachers, and so on. Two of the four defense witnesses (Hines and B. Williams) were black, and it was clear that black professionals (see Chapter 4) used the challenged test. Hines and

Zimmerman testified that it was very unlikely that any black child would be placed into EMH without having been seen by a least one black professional. Even Albert Briggs, the black assistant superintendent testifying for the plaintiffs, testified as to the adequacy of his multidisciplinary staffing approach and to the fact that he had seen to it that the IQ score could not by itself determine the decision about a referred child. No such black professional support for the tests was evident in *Larry P.*, where the defense relied almost entirely on white experts and white bureaucrats and where the black presence generally in the state was far smaller.

In Chicago the city was spending $50,000,000 more for the EMH program than it received from state and federal funds. There was no financial incentive to maintain the program, and there was testimony that more parents wanted their children to get in it and stay in it than there were parents who wanted their children out of it. Judge Grady was impressed by these facts, and other aspects of due process as well. Thus, Barbara Williams, in charge of due process hearings, said that the CBE had never lost an individual rights hearing on appeal.

There was a reversal in the strengths of the opposing team of lawyers in *PASE*, as well. Wallace Winter told me that leading his team proved difficult. There were lawyers from Vermont (to examine Albee), New York (for Kamin), the Child Advocacy Project, and one private firm, along with two of his associates from the Legal Assistance Foundation. With all these players, he had trouble maintaining a coherent main thrust. The defense team consisted of Patrick Halligan and two lawyers from the school board, all of whom spent full time on a defense case whose theory was relatively simple: They had a few points to make and they did so relentlessly. Halligan, in particular, was forceful and vigilant, never permitting his cross-examination to be diverted or distracted from those few points it was designed to make.

Conclusion and Epilogue

Both the context and the times gave plaintiffs in Chicago a far harder row to hoe than plaintiffs in California had had. It is simply more difficult to make the case that black professionals would be using a set of tests that harmed black children, especially given the fact that no test was required to be given. There was no history of legislative concern for disproportion, no requirement for IQ test use, no history of the judge's having dealt in certain ways with the very issues being tried. Add to that fact a weaker plaintiffs' team, a stronger defense team, and a more skeptical judge in Chicago and the change in outcome is easier to understand.

The Ninth Circuit Appellate opinion in *Larry P.* was filed, at last, in January 1984 (the amended version is dated June 1986, after a denial of a rehearing motion, and is referenced as 793 F.2d 969) and upheld Judge Peckham's decision by a 2 to 1 vote. In effect, they found the decision not "clearly erroneous," which is the federal standard. The majority noted that *Diana* had presented (and had settled) the same issues with respect to Hispanic children, and they were impressed with the evidence the state did not care much, if at all, about the minority overenrollment problem, even quoting the legislative declaration of 1971 that the verbal portion of IQ tests underestimates the academic ability of minority pupils. They also cited the 4 percent drop in *new* EMR placements of black children during the test moratorium beginning in 1975 as evidence that the IQ tests had been responsible for the disproportion.

They noted, as they could not have done in the *PASE* record, that the EMR curriculum was very different from the regular curriculum and denied opportunity to develop academic skills. They also noted Kamin's evidence that test developers never tried to equalize the scores of races as they had tried to equalize the scores of sexes; that the race difference in IQ had not been shown to be accounted for by SES differences; and that the remedy, since it did not involve any fixed numerical requirements, was not an impermissible quota.

The dissent claimed that there had been no showing of disproportionately *improper* placement of blacks by virtue of their IQ scores; that is, he said that disproportion alone is not proof and that tests had not been shown to be the efficient cause of placement errors in a complex judgment in which so many variables operated. Further, he noted that the record showed that IQ tests were recognized as protectors against misevaluation and misplacement, and he thought that the finding that really provoked the appeal—that Wilson Riles had purposefully and intentionally discriminated against black children—was clearly contrary to the record. (On this last point the dissent prevailed in the amended opinion, and Wilson Riles was finally exonerated.) Finally, he thought that the remedy did establish an arbitrary constraint, based solely on race, upon the EMR placement process and thus instituted the evil that *Bakke* was meant to avoid. "Though I am mindful," said Judge Enright, "of the 'clearly erroneous' standard of review to be employed—I am left with the definite and firm conviction that a mistake has been made" (dissent from appellate opinion in *Larry P.* v. *Riles*, slip opinion filed January 23, 1984).

The opinion and dissent followed the respective briefs of plaintiffs and defendants and recapitulated both the substantive arguments reviewed in these chapters and several still current legal issues: What is a "quota"? When does disproportion alone supply proof of discriminatory intent? How are burdens of proof to be allocated? More important for comparison with *PASE*, however, is the "clearly erroneous" standard referred to earlier. What it means is that a district court's finding will only very rarely be second-guessed—virtually never if the decision is rationally inferable from the trial record. It also implies, therefore, that the plaintiffs' appeal in *PASE*, filed in 1980 following the decision against them, had little chance of prevailing.

The result, had Judge Grady been upheld in the Seventh Circuit, would have been clear inconsistency of findings in two circuits, and that situation would have made the issue a possibility for resolution by the Supreme Court, though that Court could (and I think most likely would) have avoided it. The conflict was nevertheless foreseeable, and it added uncertainty to the causes of the two winners pro tem, Menocal and the CBE. Menocal did not want Winter to appeal on behalf of *PASE* (because the "clearly erroneous" standard would militate against success), and he argued strenuously with him to that effect. The *PASE* appeal was, in fact, finally dropped in March 1982, when the CBE had agreed to most of what the *PASE* plaintiffs had sued for.

Complex school equity cases have a way of lingering, and *Larry P.* has been no exception. With the appeal finally settled, Menocal moved to have the original judgment modified. The resulting *Order Modifying Judgment* was filed September 25, 1986. It appears to set a possibility of limit on the requirement that the SDE report special education enrollment data by category and ethnicity. That is, if reporting, explanation of disproportions where they exist, and monitoring of and adherence to corrective plans are properly done, then beginning with the 1988–1989 school year the SDE will no longer be obliged to continue reporting to the court.

The real thrust of the order has to do with IQ testing. As of October 25, 1986, IQ tests were no longer to be used for *any* purpose with a black child; nor could an IQ score of a black student transferring into California remain in his or her record; nor could black parents have put into their children's record IQ scores privately obtained; nor could black parents of any sociocultural background whatever ask or insist that the school psychologist administer an IQ test to their children. "There are no special education related purposes for which IQ tests shall be administered to Black pupils" (*Larry P.*, No. C-71-2270 RFP, Order Modifying Judgment, September 25, 1986).

Menocal had been irritated by the continued use of IQ testing for black children. From 1975 until this recent order, the system for assessing possible EMR children had become something of a charade. An IQ test could be used with a child referred for assessment, but if it then appeared that the child might be placed into EMR, everyone had to behave as though no test had been given. However, the fact no score was presented by the psychologist in the placement conference was a tip-off about its nature. From now on, there really won't be any score hidden somewhere in the record.

Endnotes

1. Content validity is the degree to which the items of a test represent relevant aspects of the task to be predicted.
2. The plaintiffs, who wondered in this memo why Condas did not call an HEW official to so testify, won this point because she didn't. She lost the hearsay exception for official records when she had a California official try to introduce these exhibits.

Chapter 8

EFFECTS OF THESE CASES

The real-world net effects of these cases[1] on the cognitive abilities and school retention of what were once known as mildly retarded children in the 65–80 IQ range are, of course, not yet well known since we are too close to the decisions. But something is already known about the shifting of numbers and programs and the changes in modes of assessment.

In California (as of 1984) there were 12,000 to 13,000 EMR children, down from the 1968–1969 high of 58,000. This is a prevalence rate below what is often accepted for the more serious, biologically involved category of trainable mentally retarded (TMR). Indeed, my recent informal survey of state and local special education officials indicated a continuation of the process that began about the time that *Larry P.* was first filed—the qualitative change in the EMR population from the generally normal very slow learner toward the more serious impairment characteristic of the TMR child (see, for example, MacMillan and Borthwick, 1980). Simultaneously, the declassified EMR children have returned to regular classes or to other special education categories, chiefly learning disabled (LD), an umbrella category that now includes about half of all special education placements. In it may be found children with brain injuries, hyperactive children, children with special perceptual or reading deficits, children with emotional disorders, severe underachievers, and, increasingly, slow learners of IQ levels that are in the 65–80 range (see, for example, Campione, Brown, and Ferrara, 1982; Shepard, Smith, and Vojir, 1983).

Table 4 shows the recent prevalence in Los Angeles for various

**Table 4.   Ethnic Composition of Certain Special Education Programs
1983–1984 School Year, Los Angeles Unified School District[a]**

Program		Ethnic Groups				
		Asian	Hispanic	Black	White	Total
EMR:	No.	64	889	842	360	2178
	%[c]	2.93	40.82	38.66	16.53	100
	Rate[d]	0.15	0.32	0.73	0.31	0.39
TMR:	No.	68	826	392	368	1661
	%	4.09	49.72	23.60	22.15	100
	Rate	0.16	0.29	0.34	0.32	0.29
DH:	No.	38	338	165	212	763
	%	4.98	44.30	21.62	27.78	100
	Rate	0.09	0.12	0.14	0.18	0.14
LD.[b]	No.	294	8358	6577	5416	20774
	%	1.42	40.23	31.65	26.07	100
	Rate	0.69	2.98	5.68	4.69	3.74
District Population		42,114	280,106	115,642	115,269	554,848
%		7.59	50.48	20.84	20.77	99.9

EMR = Educable mentally retarded.
TMR = Trainable mentally retarded.
DH   = Developmentally handicapped.
LD   = Learning disabled.
[a]American Indians, Filipinos, and "others" are not shown. Their numbers are included in
the totals, but are very small.
[b]About 800 pupils are receiving Designated Instructional Services: about 7000 pupils in
special day classes and about 13,000 pupils in Resource Specialist Programs.
[c]This refers to the percentage of the category represented by members of each ethnic group.
[d]The percentage of each ethnic group in this category.

ethnic groups in ER (EMR), TMR, DH (developmentally handicapped), and LD categories. Note that the prevalence rates for
EMR are very low, about .3 percent for whites, Hispanics, and
American Indians and about twice that for blacks, who are also
overrepresented in the largest category, LD. Note also that the
segregated classroom is quite common for LD students, and this is
true not only for Los Angeles but for other cities I visited. In San
Francisco in the fall of 1984, blacks were 22 percent of the public
school population, 46 percent of the population of special day
classes, and 54 percent of the clientele of resource specialist
programs, which are typically for LD students. In Alum Rock the
number of special day classes had not decreased since 1969, but
instead of having twenty-one EMR classes of about eleven children
each, there were now some four EMR classes, about seventeen

primarily LD classes, and two diagnostic classes. Obviously, a switch to LD status has by no means guaranteed either mainstreamed or racially integrated status. For the state as a whole, blacks were 9 percent of the school population and 15 percent of the EMR and TMR total in 1984. Since TMR rates are usually *not* disproportionate, the black EMR proportion is still probably close to twice the school population proportion.

Many, perhaps half, of all children removed from EMR classes in California *have* been placed in regular classrooms—which means that they have been returned to the very environments in which they had failed in the first place. The court order requires all returned students to get some transitional help. But since the early 1970s, thousands of children have never been placed in EMR who would have been so placed before that time. Some of these children get assistance as LD students, but many do not because the criterion for eligibility as LD is to be achieving significantly below ability and very slow learners are often achieving close to their limited ability.

The LD category, being a large catchall, is a wonderful locus of ambiguities where monetary constraints, conceptual fuzziness, human need, and politics all meet. California has a cap of 10 pecent of the population to be funded as handicapped. In San Francisco, they simply go over the limit and rely on state tolerance. Alum Rock is in a consortium with other districts so that if one district is under quota, another may go over. Definitionally, the state requires a severe discrepancy between intellectual ability and achievement in one or more of the areas specified in Section 56337(a) of the Education Code, which include listening, reading, writing, and math skills. Severe discrepancy is indexed as any discrepancy in the two relevant (standardized) scores that is 1.5 times the standard deviation of the population of such difference scores. "But if standardized tests are considered to be invalid for a specific pupil, the discrepancy shall be measured by alternative means" (Bulletin No. 36, January 3, 1984, of the Los Angeles Unified School District Student Guidance Services Division). Since the tests may be considered invalid for most minority children, and since the alternative means of assessing ability include adaptive behavior scales, like the ABIC (Mercer, 1979), known to be only slightly correlated with intelligence tests, it is nearly always possible to find the "hook" that will make a child eligible for service. There is some test shopping, too, so that if a discrepancy doesn't appear on the WRAT, for instance, it might on a test like the Woodcock–Johnson, a favorite among professionals trying to legitimate an LD recommendation.

Still, one effect of cutting down the EMR category has been to cast many children adrift in the mainstream, with little or no special help. (At the very least, the much-maligned EMR classroom is small and easy to compete in.) The effect is mitigated to a degree by the presence of compensatory education programs in areas with high rates of school failure, but the special education professionals I've talked to say that dropping out of school after repeated failure is an increasing problem with these once-EMR-eligible, very slow learners. Even the EMR vocational programs in high schools have declined in number, along with the EMR population itself. One goal of the plaintiffs was to get an education that was better than the "survival skills" program that is the focus of EMR curricula. Fewer EMR children are learning survival skills, but there has been no comparable increase in the quality of education for slow learners.

The requirement to answer to a court has made school boards and school psychologists very shy about recommending any minority child for EMR placement, just as Hansen reported at trial in 1977. Psychologists had seen the *Larry P.* quota coming, since it had come already in the *Diana* settlement of 1970 for Hispanic children. Defense Exhibit 1 in the trial was a file of letters written in 1976 from school boards lamenting the loss of a useful instrument (the IQ test) and relating tales about Hispanic parents who fought to have their children placed or replaced into quota-controlled EMR classrooms so they could find a place where they would not fail. As we have seen, disproportionate black placement has persisted, despite the burdens of justification it imposes, and it would seem to be a function neither of tests nor of any current racism. EMR quotas for Hispanics are easier to meet since there are many alternative programs for Hispanic children not available to blacks.

In Chicago, the ban on tests is as thoroughgoing as it is in California. Tests may not be used for any special education category.[2] The consent decree in the large, ten-year-old desegregation negotiation required the CBE not to permit discrimination in any kind of classroom. A plan developed as a result of the decree obliged the Board of Education to desegregate EMR classes and not to use IQ tests for anyone and to provide transition help for children put back into regular classes.

The board's psychologists were assigned to little else except reassessment. They reassessed some 70 percent of the EMH children by 1984, most of them black, and returned about 26 percent to the regular classrooms, so that the total enrollment in EMH declined from about 13,100 in 1980 to 9660 in 1984. Four-fifths of the returnees were black, but since that was their proportion in EMH, there was no change in the size of the disproportion. The data are shown in Table 5, for four different handicapping categories.

The district lost another 43,300 pupils over this quadrennium, most of them white. The proportion of Hispanics rose, and that of blacks stayed the same at just over 60 percent. More than offsetting the loss in the EMH category were increases in all others for a net increase of well over 3000 handicapped children in a smaller school population (several categories are not shown). The picture is all too common in large cities: The schools lose their middle class, and become relatively less white, more poor, and more handicapped.

Note that the only category shown in which blacks were substantially overrepresented in 1984 was EMH. As with the Los Angeles data of Table 4, the TMR and EH/DH proportions are close to base population proportions. The LD rate for blacks in Chicago was not elevated as it had been in Los Angeles, perhaps because the large placement rate for EMH in Chicago was sufficient to include those children who, in Los Angeles, would never get into the restricted EMR category and would have no place to go but LD or a regular classroom.

The last column of Table 5 also invites comparison to its counterpart from Los Angeles shown in Table 4, for the same school year. Chicago, with only 78 percent of the number of students as Los Angeles, nonetheless placed 4.4 times as many of them into EMH, and 1.8 as many into TMR. Only for the LD category was Los Angeles more likely to place a student, with an excess of about 2000 over what proportionality would predict. The increased likelihood of placement in Chicago is not a function of the difference in ethnic composition between the two school populations—the factor of 3 or 4 exists within each of the three major ethnic groups. The difference would appear to inhere in the category standards being applied in the two cities, with Chicago much more willing to use its EMH system.

An advocacy group, Designs for Change, monitors the CBE's compliance. The Designs for Change spokesperson told me that many children have dropped out of school and that the CBE has

Table 5. Change in Composition of Certain Special Education Programs in Chicago, from 1979–1980 to 1983–1984, for Black, White, and Hispanic Children

	Ethnic Groups						District Totale 1983–84
	1979–1980			1983–1984			
Program	Black	White	Hispanic	Black	White	Hispanic	
EMH: No.	10,692	1373	1019	7902	868	862	9661
%a	81.52	10.47	7.77	81.79	8.98	8.92	100
Rateb	3.69	1.44	1.24	3.00	1.28	.94	2.22
TMR: No.	998	329	238	1905	633	504	3097
%	61.60	20.31	14.69	61.51	20.44	16.27	100
Rate	.34	.34	.29	.72	.83	.55	.71
EH:c No.	2226	840	320	3299	1266	513	5108
%	65.28	24.63	9.38	64.58	24.78	10.04	100
Rate	.77	.88	.39	1.25	1.87	.56	1.18
LD:d No.	6535	3317	1587	8281	3312	2430	14,146
%	56.58	28.72	13.74	58.54	23.41	17.18	100
Rate	2.25	3.47	1.94	3.15	4.88	2.65	3.26
District Population	290,021	95,525	85,683	263,282	56,828	91,816	
%	60.76	20.01	17.17	60.62	15.62	21.14	
District Totale	477,339			434,281			

EMH = Educable Mentally Retarded
TMR = Trainable Mentally Retarded
EH = Emotionally Handicapped
LD = Learning Disabled
aThe percentage of the entire category represented by each ethnic group.
bThe percentage of each ethnic group in this category.
cIn the 1983–1984 data, the category is Behavior Disorder.
dIn the 1979–1980 data, the category was called Specific Learning Disability.
eThe Total includes relatively small numbers of Native Americans and Asians.

not increased the size of its LD staff to accommodate this increased demand for services occasioned by reassessment. With straitened finances, and the redeployment of its psychologists to the reassessment job, the CBE has a backlog of demand for special education services, particularly from Hispanics, who are underrepresented (as in California) in almost every category.[3]

In addition to being concerned about the unencouraging results of regular classroom placement, the plaintiffs' advocates in Chicago are unhappy with the new methods of assessment. The CBE is careful to say that, although its psychologists use tests whose outcome *could* be reported in specific numbers, they are in fact used for the psychological observation of individual performance— just, as it were, as a sort of standardized observational technique. It is hard to read through this heavily legalized message, but it sounds as though they are testing without (overtly) scoring. (Given the constraints of the consent decree, it is hard to imagine what else they could do since scores would create norms, which would then manifest a race difference.) Thus, both the Draw-a-Man and the Kohs Blocks tests are used, but no score is reported—the psychologists do not have to write anything down. No labels are applied; rather, a narrative record is provided.

This sounds like what happens in California, where tests are used but not, in certain cases, reported. And, as in California, there is some use of Feuerstein's (1979) test-teach-test method for establishing learning rate and style. In California, the name of Feuerstein is talismanic, and "dynamic assessment" was on the lips of most special education professionals I spoke to. But in San Francisco, where Dr. Harold Dent, a major plaintiff witness in *Larry P.*, is a special education consultant (as he was for the CBE in Chicago), assessment is currently being done, as far as I can tell, with bits and pieces from Feuerstein and with no norms—the professionals appear to be starting from scratch. Meanwhile, storage cabinets are piled high with discarded and forbidden WISC-R kits.

A recent news article (Cordes, 1986) confirms this impression. A dozen of the district's thirty school psychologists have complained to the APA that current procedures violate professional standards, in part, ironically, for the very reasons used by *Larry P.* plaintiffs in bringing suit in the first place: that the individual assessment process, as currently implemented, has not been validated for the purposes for which it is being used. It might pass muster if it did not have disparate impact upon blacks, but, as we have seen, blacks are still disproportionately placed into EMR and segregated LD classes.[4] In particular, Feuerstein's Learning Potential Assessment Device (LPAD—roughly, the test-teach-test method) has not been validated for placing children into special education classes, and its manual states that it should not be so used. This system is, nonetheless, the one preferred by the district.

Dent insists that the test-teach-test assessment offers curricular guidance to teachers, whereas IQ tests did not. His assertion remains to be demonstrated. The Feuerstein items teach discrimination and reasoning, but they are not on their face related to any curricular subject matter. The method involves changing the child's responses, and I do not know of any demonstration of its reliability, to say nothing of its validity. A rate-of-learning measure could in principle be reliable, but as has been shown, it would correlate strongly with IQ.

Since quotas prevent disproportionate placement of minorities into EMR in California, the inevitable increase in subjectivity and discretion of assessors that occurs in the absence of norms will simply add noise to the decision-making process. In Chicago, where there are no quotas, per se, the plaintiffs' advocates are very suspicious of the great fluidity and discretion in the assessment process. Since they feel that the "overplacement" of blacks arose in part from abuse of discretion, they are not happy with the increase in mystery that has replaced reliance on well-known objective tests. The executive director of Designs for Change said she would actually prefer a rule—say, no placement unless the pupil scores less than 2 standard deviations below the norm on a standard test like the Iowa Test of Basic Skills. Note, however, that such reliance, while more objective, is unlikely to remove the racial disproportion—the tests of mental ability on which blacks score 1 standard deviation below whites include school achievement tests. Use of such a rule would therefore not really meet the objections of the black professionals, quoted early in this book, who included achievement tests among their targets.[5]

The use of achievement tests will do most of what the use of IQ tests would do, with the single exception of the unique use for which Binet developed the test in the first place: to help school officials decide why a child is failing, whether for motivational, emotional, or intellectual reasons.

In California, the broad conception of intelligence urged on the court by plaintiffs has won wide official acceptance in the districts I looked at. Thus, among the mimeographed materials I got in San Francisco, in addition to explications of Feuerstein's (1979) dynamic assessment method, were a precis of Gardner's (1983) *Frames of Mind* and literature on Guilford's (1967) structure of intellect model. These views permit a definition of giftedness, for example, that is the counterpart of any definition of retardation stressing adaptive behavior: That is, classes for the gifted can mitigate the ethnic disproportions that sole reliance on IQ would produce, by selecting students gifted in art, music, and dance.

It is possible, of course, that schools should encourage a wider variety of skills than they have traditionally done. Their custodial role in the care and development of the whole child is receiving ever greater attention and support in any economy that takes larger proportions of parents out of the home. The same economy, however, rewards intellectual development. With limited resources, the tensions created by the contending views of intelligence and the appropriate goals for schools will be severe. The politics of race has heightened this tension, and current demands that schools not only do more but do it better will strain them ever more. The next chapter will deal explicitly with the policy implications of these decisions.

Postscript

An article by Susan Landers in the December 1986 issue of the *APA Moniter* (vol. 17, No. 12, p. 18) reports that the dissident school psychologists in San Francisco have prevailed. The Office of Civil Rights, the day following Judge Peckham's extension of his ban of IQ testing for black children (see the Epilogue in Chapter 7), found that the use of the Learning Potential Assessment Device was not acceptable because it was not validated for use in special education placement.

With its favorite device thus also banned, San Francisco, and presumably other districts, will have to rely more heavily upon achievement tests and readiness tests, all of them standardized and all of them having disparate impact upon blacks and other disadvantaged minorities. Since these tests are designed for placement decisions within the regular system (tracking, promotion, and retention), I think it could be argued that they, too, have not been validated for the specific purpose of placing black children into programs for the educable retarded. If no test were statutorily valid for such placement, then only repeated failure could justify EMR eligibility.

This result seems harsh and inefficient. As the omnipresent Dent is quoted in the article, "What are the schools going to do to evaluate the needs of students?"

Endnotes

1. The data here are chiefly the result of several interviews done in late 1984 in California with Fred Hansen and Ken Bill of the Department of Education; Alice Bryant, Psychological Services, Los Angeles Unified School District; Curtis Cooper, Special Education Services, San Francisco Unified School District; John Kingsbury and his staff, Special Education, Alum Rock Unified School District; Gordon Gareth, Special Education, San Jose Unified School District. For information on Chicago, there is an APA monitor article (Cordes, 1983), and I have talked to Sharon Weitzman, a lawyer who directs Designs for Change, a research and advocacy group overseeing the mandated change in special education assessment in Chicago, and with various officials of the Chicago Board of Education.

2. One strategy of the plaintiffs' advocates appears to have been to insist that new tests be developed and validated specifically for diagnosing EMR status. This is an extremely difficult task. A CBE showing that some of their tests discriminated between EMR and "transition" students was objected to on the grounds that the proscribed IQ tests had been used to set up such groups in the first place. If no valid tests could be developed, then adaptive behavior scales could be the main basis of reassessment, and their use is well known (Reschly, 1981) to make a majority of children who are eligible for EMR on an IQ basis ineligible on the adaptive behavior basis. Such an effect had occurred in Champaign, Illinois, with the use of Mercer's (1979) SOMPA system. Ironically, her system could not be employed in Chicago, though she was a consultant there, because it involves one of the forbidden tests, the WISC-R (see Cordes, 1983, for a discussion).

3. It is thought that the availability of English as a second-language program "hides" many Hispanic children who might otherwise be served in LD or EMR programs, both in Chicago and in California. Thus, for example, the establishment of a strong bilingual program in Illinois in the mid-1970s was accompanied by a decrease in the Hispanic EMR placement rate. It went from 2.0 percent in 1973–1974 to 1.2 percent in 1975–1976. One result was the modification of the complaint to exclude Hispanics from the plaintiff class in *PASE*.

4. In the past school year, the report says, blacks constituted 21 percent of special education classes, which is the same two-to-one disproportion that existed in 1971, when *Larry P.* began.

5. I spoke to a black professional in pupil services in Chicago, who would, I am sure, want not to be named. The phone interview was as clear an example of the problems associated with the attempts to settle complex social problems adversarially as I have come across. She wanted me to put in writing exactly what I wanted from them because she had learned long since that "casual conversations with Designs for Change tended to end in court." She says Designs for Change will not be satisfied with any assessment method that does not result in removing over 60 percent of the black children from EMH—that is, achieves the prevalence rate promoted by Mercer in her testimony in *Larry P.* The Iowa Test for Basic Skills won't do this, and, of course, it has not been validated for the purpose of identifying black EMR children (indeed, what has?). In comments responding to criticism from Designs for Change, criticism of the current nonuse of norms, the CBE said, "It appears that DFC's criticism is based explicitly upon its unwarranted preference for an objective test."

The use of adaptive behavior scales would probably result in greater removal of EMH children, but, says my informant, the school personnel hear more complaints from parents who want to keep their children in EMH than from those who want them out.

The two sides in this dispute simply will not communicate except through lawyers—there is no trust whatever that I can discern. It may be all right for hostile parties to impoverish their communication by reliance on lawyers, provided they can cut their ties. But both parties in Chicago are concerned with the educational problems of children, problems that won't go away.

Chapter 9

POLICY IMPLICATIONS
OF THESE CASES

It cannot be said that all of the changes in special education placement were the result of judicial decision. To review other influences, there were strong movements in the early 1970s in the California legislature to achieve mainstreaming and reduce disproportion in EMR; the Congress passed the Education for All Handicapped Act in 1975; the Chicago Board of Education modernized its assessment procedures throughout the 1970s. Courts affected the political process and were affected by it. Mainstreaming was an idea of great political force and probably would have prevailed in any case. Disproportionate representation in low tracks had been the subject of frequent litigation. So the political involvement in these lawsuits was of a piece with these movements: to achieve more equal status for blacks and to mainstream the mildly handicapped in order to reduce the stigma and, perhaps, the educational burden of EMR placement.

But the attack on the most venerable of tests of mental ability, the individual intelligence tests, was new (Bersoff, 1980). That attack was an exercise in black pride, an effort to explain the large difference in performance—since it was clear, after all, that the tests were not the cause of disproportionate placement—that has continued to exist without tests as much as it did before their ban. Both trials also established that there were racially disproportionate achievement rates prior to any IQ testing. If there were any winners in *Larry P.*, it was the black professionals who found the plaintiffs and brought the suit that declared one famous set of measures of black deficit invalid. Indeed, as the recent judicial order of September 1986 has shown, the ban on the use of IQ tests for blacks has spread. But the other targets, the achievement tests, are too close to the curriculum; to attack tests of arithmetic and language skills, however much they correlate with IQ tests, is to attack a vital institution of Western industrialized culture, the school itself.

For special education, the negative results are reduced precision and objectivity of assessment, reduced precision of placement, reduced morale of and faith in the professionals charged with assessment, some downgrading of the once-central importance of developing intellectual skills, and reduced services for slow-learning, non-LD children in the 65–80 range. The positive results are broader and newer kinds of assessment (if there is time for the breadth, and norms for the novel tests) and some fresh thinking about programs for children having difficulty in school.

Courts and legislatures are limited in the effect they can have upon education, especially if by that we mean the development of intellectual skills and not just changes in special education categories or in racial composition of schools and faculties. For example, Wrubel (1979) studied the impact of court directives on schools (including the directives arising out of the *Larry P.* preliminary injunctions) and found very little impact. Kirp et al. (1975) studied compliance with two famous cases concerning education of the retarded—*PARC* and *Mills*—and with the California legislative changes of the early 1970s. They concluded that in no case did much basic change occur in the educational systems, and what little change did occur came only after enormous and sustained effort. Tables 4 and 5 of the previous chapter tell a similar story with respect to the overrepresentation of black children in the EMR/EMH categories in Los Angeles and Chicago.

In particular, courts and legislatures cannot make group and individual differences disappear; neither can they develop the cognitive abilities of children. Students need instruction suited to their current skills, and the slower or further behind they are when they first appear in schools, the more and more intensive the instruction they need. As highly experienced observers have noted (Bereiter, 1985; Resnick, 1979), though the law may call for sundry labels like LD, EMR, and CD (culturally disadvantaged), children differently labeled often have a similar deficit, which requires a similar remedy, such as intensive instruction in reading and other basic skills.

General Requirements

What is needed, then, is more teaching, which means more teachers and smaller student-teacher ratios. As long as budgets are tight, such classes are likely to occur only for special education categories, and the assessment and decision-making apparatus—tests and the like—will continue to be needed. But if we ever came to appreciate the real social return on good early education, in the sense that Berrueta-Clement et al. (1984) have shown for preschool programs (for example, fewer dropouts and less unemployment in late adolescence), then, as Resnick (1979) has pointed out, classes will be small enough to preclude much of the need for classification and testing; the behavior of the pupil and the experience of the teacher will be all that are necessary to guide instruction.

More intensive, low-ratio teaching will also ameliorate a serious problem with mainstreaming. Mainstreaming implies large variability of academic and social behaviors in a classroom. Such variability makes for hard teaching, and there is a point beyond which teachers (and many parents) will not tolerate the effect on the class of laggard intellectual performance or disruption.

Until such changes in staffing are made, we need some improvement in the classification scheme: most importantly, either a program for non-LD children in the 65–80 IQ range in which classes are smaller than average (I assume many self-contained "LD" classes serve this purpose, but, as we have seen, there are tight budgetary caps on funding the LD category) or better assistance to such mainstreamed children even though they do not qualify as LD. That is, resource or "pullout" programs need to be for *any* student in need, not just a certain category of student.

As long as classifying is to continue, professionals ought to be allowed to use whatever instruments they find useful, including WISC-Rs and Stanford–Binets. The irony in California is that blacks are "protected" from EMR placement by quota (or, if the quota is not kept, by the burden of explanation and the threat of lawsuit borne by the school boards), but within the black population so protected, pupils are denied the advantage of being assessed and classified by useful instruments (the IQ tests). One possible effect of leaving assessment to teacher judgment can be seen in the recent report of a controlled study of an early, highly structured educational intervention for very poor "high-risk" black children in North Carolina (Ramey and Haskins, 1981). The first cohorts of their day care intervention group and the corresponding controls are now in public schools. Although the day care group had average IQs at age five, they were almost uniformly grouped into the lowest academic groups by their teachers when they entered public school. Ramey and Haskins say this (p. 109):

We have also come to suspect that the process of schooling is very different for high-risk children and other children attending the public schools. Teachers tend to relegate high-risk children to the lowest academic group, although such placement does not always correspond with the intellectual ability of all these children as measured by standardized tests.

Perhaps one small change would solve several problems, and that would be to stop referring to intelligence tests as such and start calling them tests of developed scholastic ability, or school functioning level, or the like. Such a name change would remove some of the onus of low scores. It is fairly evident that the public attributes something more innate, general, and permanent to "intelligence" than do professionals in the consensus, who regard it as referring to current performance.

Reducing the Black-White Gap

As to the black-white differences, the policy recommendation is difficult because it requires patience. Twenty years ago Moynihan's (1965) policy planning document on the Negro family outlined what he termed "the tangle of pathology" of much of black life: broken homes, illegitimacy, unemployment, welfare, school achievement deficits, and drug use. The report shocked many readers and angered several civil rights advocates for seeming to blame the victim, much as tests are attacked for the bad news they bring. Moynihan's view was that family cohesiveness was the chief, perhaps the only, guarantee against pathology of such scope and dimension and that the main support for families would be better employment opportunities for black males. The relatively superior school performance of the children of poor immigrant Jewish, Chinese, and Japanese families was, to him, evidence of the power of family cohesiveness sustained by the employment and industry of male heads of household.

A generation later, life for blacks has become better for a few and worse for many (Wilson, 1978). It is no longer true, for example, that only a third of black children live in households of which a single mother is the head—today, over half of all black children are in that circumstance, even though the status of the relatively small black middle class has improved substantially. Moreover, the "culture" of the black underclass, now abandoned by the black middle class and by its controlling and ameliorating influences (Lemann, 1986), simply does not teach the social skills, attitudes, motives, and tolerance for delay of gratification that would prepare males to deal effectively with the middle-class enterprises of successful schooling or of responsible work in steady jobs, even were such jobs plentifully available. As long as aptitude and achievement scores are reported for blacks as a group, the large underclass will pull the scores down.

This book does not concern job-training and employment strategies (though we may note that effective ones have not been created on a large scale), to say nothing of altering the culture of the underclass. But given the present economic situation, what, in addition to more intensive regular teaching, might be done to reduce the intellectual deficit that is located mainly in that underclass? The literature supports the use of preschool interventions in which deliberate practice in cognitive skills is given and, in some cases, child-training advice is given to mothers.

Three recent papers have reviewed two decades of research on such preschool interventions (Berrueta–Clement et al., 1984; Lazar and Darlington, 1982; Ramey et al., 1985). In his commentary (pp. 142–151) at the end of the Lazar and Darlington monograph, Ramey sums up in part as follows (Lazar and Darlington, 1982, pp. 147–149):

> *The major finding is that children from preschool programs were less likely to repeat a grade or be placed in special education classes than were their controls. . . .*
> *For the 1976 consortium follow-up data there are not significant differences in IQ between program and control groups and the evidence concerning achievement test data are not very convincing of substantial program effects. . . .*
> *In fact, the mean IQ performance at follow-up for the children from the four projects having more nearly randomized designs is*

> *approximately one standard deviation below the national average,*
> *for both program and control children. . . .*
>
> *It is my opinion that given the complex and little understood*
> *forces operating to sustain lower intellectual performance among*
> *this society's lower socio-economic groups—including limited eco-*
> *nomic opportunities, racial and social discrimination, and genetic*
> *limitations, to mention just a few—we are unlikely to witness full*
> *realization of human potential through limited educational experi-*
> *ments. Therefore, the expectations of success from such efforts must*
> *be constrained by experience.*

Ramey's own project, the Carolina Abecedarian Project, is a strong, well-reported model (Ramey and Haskins, 1981). Low-income black children of low (<85) IQ mothers were enrolled by random assignment as infants at three months of age or were left to their normal circumstances, with the provision of social work, medical, and nutritional supplementary services common to both groups. The day care program was a cognitively and socially oriented program emphasizing language, with a child-staff ratio varying from 3 to 1 to 5 to 1. Children attended six to eight hours per day, five days a week, 50 weeks a year until entry into public kindergarten. The IQ differences (Stanford–Binet) between the day care and control children were about 9, 15, and 12 points at two, three, and four years, respectively; and at five years, day care children had a WPPSI (Wechsler Preschool and Primary Scale of Intelligence) IQ of 98, with the figure for controls being 91. These differences are not the enormous effects reported for the Milwaukee Project (Garber and Heber, 1981), but they are well described and fully reported, and the samples are large.

The Abecedarian Project is not inexpensive, and its effects are modest. The project assesses home environmental and psychosocial factors, which yield equally low scores for both groups in comparison to middle-class homes, so that even the day care children are still spending most of their time in an intellectual and motivational context unlikely either to amplify preschool efforts or to facilitate later school achievement. The alternatives to such projects are weaker interventions such as Headstart or a long wait before the black middle class becomes larger and, where it exists, more firmly established.

I think it will be true for the foreseeable future that school-based improvements in the intellectual repertoires of poor black children will be strongly counteracted by effects of home and neighbor-

hood. A great social shift is needed to change those important
environments. Even with goodwill and determined effort, however, any such shift will take generations. This picture may be
acceptable to those who take the long view or who distrust the
process and consequences of more rapid social shifts. Persons most
hurt by present circumstances, however, are least likely to indulge
in statesmanlike delay of gratification. Present circumstances make
unlikely in the near term any large expenditures either for preschool and school enrichment programs for the poor or for any new
policies designed to strengthen the black middle class. Deficits are
large, budgets are tight, and affirmative action programs are
increasingly subject to critical scrutiny.

In the meantime, some black advocates will continue to deny
that anything is wrong, except with the tests, or with the grading
system and achievement tests that constitute the criteria, or with
the schools. They will continue to believe that if only teachers had
higher expectations of black children, or if only they taught, in
some never specified way, *correctly,* then the black-white gap
would rapidly close.

Two Recent Cases

Let me end this chapter by adverting to two recent conflicts about
race and education. Perhaps they are signs of the times. The first
was in Georgia, a state that has certainly had its share of such
conflict. The legacy of discrimination has left its black students far
behind its white ones on every sort of measure from basic skill
tests, failed by far higher percentages of black than by white
college sophomores, through the National Teacher Exam, where
the same racial comparison holds true. This sort of result obtains
whether the test is classed as an achievement or an aptitude test
and whether or not black professionals have passed on the items in
advance. (See, for example, *New York Times,* October 27, 1983, p.
A27; *Chronicle of Higher Education,* April 18, 1984, pp. 19–20.)

The state and local school districts measure achievement by the
use of several standardized tests, like the California Achievement
Tests and the Iowa Tests of Basic Skills, along with local basic skills
tests and criterion reference tests. Schools also group students by
ability in the various subjects, and they assign mildly retarded
students to EMR classes. It will surprise no reader that blacks

were disproportionately represented both in EMR and in the lower-achieving groups, so that even though schools might be integrated in the body-counting sense, classes were not.

In *Ollie Marshall* v. *Georgia* (CV 482-233, Southern District of Georgia, 1984) the NAACP and forty-five black school children as class representatives sued the state and its nonmetropolitan districts, asking the court to enjoin the grouping and placement practices as being discriminatory, in violation of (among others) the Fourteenth Amendment's Equal Protection Clause and the antidiscrimination provisions of Title VI of the Civil Rights Act of 1964.

Plaintiffs asked for random assignment to classes for regular students (hetergeneous grouping) and, for very slow learners, implementation of the recommendations in the report of the National Academy of Science panel on selection and placement of mildly retarded students (Heller et al., 1982), a document that has attained considerable authority.

On the grouping issue, the judge had much testimony and literature pro and con by well-qualified experts reflecting the mixed state of the literature on teaching. Plaintiffs blamed the white-black achievement gap, which was larger as a function of length of time in school, on the assignment of blacks to lower groups. The state claimed that the home-related factors that produced a gap when the children got to school continued to operate to exacerbate it throughout the school years.

Judge Edenfield believed the state's expert on educational policy and intellectual development, Barbara Lerner. She adduced the conventional wisdom, that "family background" is the single most potent determiner of school achievement, one that increases in importance over the years, and the judge dismissed the plaintiffs' measure of SES (whether the child was eligible for a free and reduced-price lunch) as inadequate. He believed, as had Judge Grady before him, that the disproportionately large presence of black children in compensatory education programs meant that blacks would predominate in *any* track or program meant for slower learners. He also noticed, on his own apparently, that only one of the parents of the plaintiff children had graduated from high school, and, like Judge Grady, he took judicial notice of the large differences between white and black incomes in the defendant districts.

Daniel Reschly also testified for the state with respect to the EMR issue. He opined that adaptive behavior, though it should be measured in a variety of settings, is most importantly assessed in school, since EMR is a school program. Reschly disagreed with the plaintiff proposal that a rigid IQ cutoff standard be employed, a score above which would exclude any child from eligibility. He thought the multiple assessment provisions of PL 94-143 along with their proscription of the use of a "single score" meant that no such score should by itself either include or exclude any child— that is, a child scoring 72 but failing very badly all of his courses might be eligible, in Reschley's opinion. The plaintiffs, like the Chicago monitors, wanted to reduce the discretion of assessers by a strong reliance on the very tests that their clients had such difficulty with. As with any standardized test, of course, a rigid cutoff would not reduce disparate impact.

Perhaps the most interesting parts of the opinion for policy were the judge's remarks on the propriety and scope of judicial power over public education. As a threshhold matter, he had to deal with the issue, whether the disparate impact of the tracking system on blacks, largely as a result of scores on achievement measures, resulted from present discrimination (he said no) or from the present results of past discrimination, a thornier issue. Most observers would agree that present intellectual deficits among black Americans are clearly the legacy of past discrimination, as a general statement. The question then becomes, Who is to decide what, if anything, is to be done to remedy that deficit, a deficit that will linger to some extent for generations? Judge Edenfield relied on *Debra P.* v. *Turlington* (564 F. Supp. 177, 1983), the famous Florida high school competency testing case. In its first phase (474 F. Supp. 244, 1979) Judge Carr had held that the denial of diplomas to the disproportionately large numbers of black students who had failed the basic competency tests was in violation of the Equal Protection Clause because those students had begun their education while the Florida schools were still segregated—that is, the vestige of unlawful discrimination was plain because it was both recent and blatant. But by 1983 Florida students, like Georgia students, had grown up in a legally desegregated school system, and the injunction against the use of the basic competency test was lifted, disparate impact or no.

Every reasonable person knows that changes in a state education code have no effect on the major cause of black disadvantage, which I take to be the denial to their parents and more remote ancestors of access to the middle class whose patterns of thought and motivation prepare their children for its schools. The plaintiffs in *Debra P*. indeed made that argument: that the tests were unfair because the parents of the tested children were less able to help them because they had themselves been victims of inferior segregated education.

Judges Carr and Edenfield agreed that the vestiges of the oppression of blacks would persist for a considerable time. But, as Judge Edenfield put it, "The Court does not conclude that the present effects are attributable to the past, at least to the extent that *the societal problem has a judicially cognizable remedy*" (slip opinion, p. 102, emphasis supplied). He expressed his version of judicial restraint: "The alternative [random assignment to groups] which is proffered by the plaintiff is more appropriately considered by the administrative and legislative units of state and local government. . . . [T]his court, nor any court, is not in a better position than state and local educators to assess the efficacy of the selected educational programs" (slip opinion, p. 120). This sort of view will perhaps gain adherents as the time since *Brown* lengthens and the mischief caused by court-ordered remedies for entrenched and complicated problems becomes ever more apparent (for example, Lukas, 1985).

The second case took place in 1985 in Minneapolis. The school board there, under Superintendent Richard Green, has adopted a policy of "promotional gates," according to which students must pass "benchmark" tests, given at the end of kindergarten, second, fifth, seventh, and ninth grades, in order to move up to the next grade. The test involved at the kindergarten level is like any readiness test: recognizing letters, colors, and numbers, understanding simple concepts, ordering simple numerals, and the like. In the 1984 spring testing, some 300 kindergarten children were not promoted, and they were disproportionately minority children, particularly blacks. (Dr. Kenneth Rustad, of the Department of Guidance and Assessment Services, sent me ethnic data. Passing rates for blacks were about 74 percent in 1984 and 1985, compared with 94 percent for whites, a difference, given normality, just slightly smaller than 1 standard deviation.)

A few black parents wanted to protest such disproportionate failure to be promoted to regular first grade classes but were dissuaded from doing so. The president of the Minneapolis Urban League noted that there had been warnings for two years of such "gates" and considerable contact with parents about pupil progress:

". . . parents began to realize that this was also a quiet indictment of them, of how they had done in preparing the child in the previous five years" (*New York Times*, September 16, 1984, p. 10).

This news item is a poignant illustration of the dilemmas of policy. Black children are on average underprepared before they arrive at school, and school does not repair this relative deficit. Blaming families who are transmitting their own relative lack of experience with middle-class intellectual skills does not seem any more useful than blaming schools or going to court to forbid the use of the test or of the gate-keeping policy that precludes social promotion. All that exist are a few options with modest potential for making matters better: preschool programs, family support systems of the kind discussed by Zigler and Seitz (1982), remedial work after school or during summers (a sixth of the failing kindergarten children passed their test after going to summer school), and more intensive work during regular classes.

The costs of these programs is high, and the results will come but gradually. Impatience will be a constant temptation, both for taxpayers and civil rights advocates. One of the common effects of injunctions and court orders is to stimulate anger and resistance, as we have seen most plainly in the history of court-ordered busing, often to the detriment and with the resegregation of the schools. It is more difficult (at least for this observer) to see how the lawsuits that are the subject of this book did anything good for black children than it is to see harm. Apart from cases of blatant intentional discrimination and well-substantiated harm, courts will, I think, do themselves and the rest of society a service by staying out of the school business.

There is indeed a national crisis in education, especially in the development of useful intellectual and other skills among disadvantaged minority children (Levin, 1985). What is needed is thoughtful leadership, the willingness to spend large sums of money, and a widespread constituency of support that sees that resources devoted today are an enormously cost effective and humane investment. What is not needed are poor policy decisions coming from a forum very ill-equipped to decide them. With that, we turn to our penultimate chapter, on the use of social science in the adversary system of the courts.

Chapter 10

THE ADVERSARY SYSTEM
AS A WAY OF FINDING FACTS

Wolf (1981) and Rossell (1980) have contributed thoughtful analyses of the role of social science in school equity and integration cases, and nothing in the present analysis of this pair of lawsuits would lead one to a brighter conclusion than theirs about the capacity of the court system to make intelligent use of social science.

Social science data are rarely conclusive, so they are uncommonly arguable (particularly in a forum given uncommonly to argument). They confirm enough of common sense to be easily dismissible as *only* common sense. And their data, unlike that of physics or chemistry, are sufficiently accessible to laypeople—that is, so close, incremental, and supplementary to ordinary knowledge—that it is easy for laypeople to distort their meaning or dismiss their value. Everyone is a bit of a psychologist in a way that not everyone is a bit of a chemist. One of the most influential bodies of social science data on jury size, for example, was dismissed by Justice Powell as "numerology" (*Ballew* v. *Georgia*, 435 U.S. 223, 1978). The result is that the value of even the best social science data may be hard to discern even in relatively neutral settings. But in settings when adversaries are seeking not truth but victory, then what modest value social science data have can easily be wholly nullified.

Adversarial Versus Scientific Truth Finding

The fact that a consensus on some matter exists in social science (see Snyderman and Rothman, 1986, for evidence of the consensus

185

among 661 experts concerning intelligence, race differences, and test use) does not mean that it will be noncontroversial. Kamin, in his *PASE* testimony (RT 107–108), compared the controversy over test bias with the disagreement among psychiatrists concerning the insanity of some defendant and said that the disagreement in each case implied shaky evidence. His argument exemplified two faults. First, Kamin compared applications of general principles to particular cases in a field (psychiatry) marked by ambiguities of definition and diagnosis with evidence about a set of general principles themselves in a field where definitions of predictor, criterion, and bias are readily operationalized and amenable to sophisticated analysis. In a less partisan climate he would have been less likely (I hope) to have done so. Second, he takes the sheer fact of controversy, regardless of the merits of the two sides, as precluding the possibility of consensus. Evolution is a still controversial theory, and well-credentialed experts can be found to argue against it; nonetheless, a consensus exists among well-qualified experts.

The problem in court is that if there are two marginally qualified experts against the scientific consensus and 200 well-qualified experts for it, the court is often likely to hear just two on each side. And if one side represents popular myth (for example, "of course tests are biased against blacks—they've had little chance to learn what is tested"), then the odds against the scientific consensus get longer. Unfortunately, the most valuable consensus, in the sense of providing useful information, is precisely the one that contradicts the popular myth.

Even where the subject of expert testimony is hard science, the court is a less than ideal forum for finding the truth of some matter. The adversarial procedure means that one position is presented at a time, without answer, comment, or discussion, sometimes (as in *Larry P.*) for weeks. Cross-examination of the experts on one side is done not by peer experts but by a lawyer whose skill in the subject is a hastily acquired patchwork and whose skill in cross-examination will vary enormously with the luck of the draw and the money available. Even direct testimony may be poorly evoked or weakened by procedures that control admissibility of evidence and trial conduct. Sattler was interrupted some twenty times in the first half-hour of his testimony, in a clear effort to disrupt the continuity of presentation of evidence of criterion validity of IQ tests, evidence that was potentially very damaging to plaintiffs' case in *Larry P.* In a scientific forum that would not happen.

Thus Judge Peckham heard over two months of plaintiffs' witnesses relentlessly building their case before the other side called a witness. It is possible that really brilliant cross-examination might have blunted the effect, but fact-finding should not have to depend on so thin a reed. Fundamental terms such as *culture, intelligence, bias,* or *retardation* never got defined very clearly; concepts like correlation or the effect of restriction of range on correlation never were adequately understood by the judges. Judge Grady, during closing arguments, asked, "What's the correlation between an IQ of 60 and GPA?" (Closing Arguments, 134). The defense attorney, with unusual courage, said, "With all due respect, Judge, that is a nonsensical question." It is not customary, however, for attorneys to tell judges that they are either stupid or missing the point. In contrast, in the scientific forum the bracing effect of pointing out error is uninhibited by the presence of robed authority.

One very significant difference in these two trials was in the willingness of the judges to accept a broad range of social science data. Judge Peckham was faced with the choice of finding either test bias or racial genetic difference as the cause of IQ score differences, neither side having made much of a case for SES or home environmental causation. Had he accepted the general evidence of test validity and nonbias at all levels of education, especially in predicting standard achievement scores, he could scarcely have found much if any bias at the levels at issue in the trial. So, as we have seen, he adopted the strategy of other governmental agencies (like the EEOC) confronting test differences that threaten opportunities for minorities: He particularized the validation requirements so much (insisting on evidence of prediction of teacher grades rather than achievement test scores for young, low-achieving, black children of California) that the large quantity of data available generally on the prediction of black school achievement became almost irrelevant, even though the great weight of the evidence before and since the trial denies the plaintiffs' view.

Judge Grady, on the other hand, pleaded with both sides to give him any and everything they had on race differences in item passing rates. Furthermore, he accepted scholarly articles, supplied to him at the end of the trial, on general issues of race bias in prediction as well as on internal analyses. The defense had printed a booklet of excerpts from testing experts on criterion validity and other matters, and to this was added the papers by Jensen (1976), Miele (1979), and the thesis of Nichols (1970). We have seen that these papers, along with that by Gordon and Rudert (1979), were influential on the decision.

For a judge to call for papers that had never been testified to and subject to cross-examination is unusual. (They came in by affidavit, as having been relied upon by the defense expert who offered them.) Judge Grady's style was to be very open to information and to ask many pressing questions to both sides, though more to plaintiffs than to defendants. It is possible for a judge to make his own record with questions, or to call his own expert, or to go beyond the record on his own, as Judge Grady did in perusing the tests. But while such methods may eventuate in better approximations to the truth, they depart from the purer forms of the adversary system. Marvell (1980), discussing one of these cases among others, put it thus:

> *Whether courts can (or should) obtain supporting case facts outside the record is uncertain. The law seems to say a judge can go outside the record if he wants to, but again it may be unfair to the opposing party. In* United Shoe, *a famous antitrust case, Judge Wyzanski hired an economist as his law clerk to analyze the competitive situation in the shoe industry. This provoked a lot of criticism, because it was done outside the adversary system and the lawyers had no input. Also, at one time there was talk about having technical experts as clerks in the U.S. circuit courts (Commission on Revision of the Federal Court Appellate System 1975) but the suggestion was squelched because it was felt that lawyers should have a chance to answer any information presented. The issue, I think, still remains unclear. Does a judge misuse social science research if, when hearing a criminal case without a jury, he goes home and reads about the research on eyewitness testimony? I don't know the answer.*
>
> *Most of the debate about how social science information should come to the courts is in the area of social facts. Some say a court misuses social science material not included in the record. That's absurd, I think. The record is an awful place to get social science information when making law; the testimony is unorganized, presented in question-and-answer format, and often out of date by the time it gets to the final appellate court. It's hard to get the best experts to testify. And there are often large imbalances in the amount of material brought in by the opposing sides. Others claim that the court can go outside the record but not outside the briefs;*

but you get some of the same problems here, especially lack of competent expert information from both sides.

In my opinion, a judge misuses social science information as social facts if he fails to do a lot of work on his own to investigate it; the chances of being misled are great, and because new law is made, the consequences of using misleading information can be substantial. This is one of the key problems in Larry P. v. Riles. *Only the plaintiff presented social science information, and the judge apparently did not check out the plaintiffs' material. He should have, even though the result was only a temporary injunction (which, by the way, remained in effect for seven years).[1]*

Science is, among other things, skepticism of attitude. Some judges appear to be more tough-minded (like Judge Grady) than others (like Judge Peckham), but whether trials like these draw such judges is a matter of chance. It is not foreseeable that judges will be systematically trained to think routinely in terms of base rates and control groups, to check representativeness, to insist on data rather than anecdotes, to say nothing of doing their own research. There is little enough of that even among social scientists, and we cannot expect that judges, not to mention juries, will save social science either from the inadequacies of the adversary system or from those of its "experts" for whom politics may mean more than science.

Problems with the Use of Experts

Indeed, one egregious flaw in the adversary system is its use of experts. There are two major problems. First, "expert" has a much broader meaning in the court than in the judgment of peers. Thus, the two chief critics of intelligence tests from the point of view of black culture, Hilliard (in *Larry P.*) and Williams (in *PASE*), had expert status in the area of test bias in court by virtue of being both psychologists and black, but they have little or none among psychologists who specialize in testing—they lack the training and the scholarship to qualify as scientific experts in that field.

Some of what they had to say was the stuff of everyday discourse—beliefs and anecdotes, unchecked by reported fact, many of which have been mentioned: about the Afrocentricity of American black culture; the ease of repairing the school achievement deficit in children (Hilliard said there were data, never presented, to show three years gain in only thirty-two hours of remedial training); the power of teacher expectancy (Williams's story of the Florida teacher who, mistaking high locker numbers for IQ scores, expected so much from her class that they did very well); the invalidity of the WISC. Sometimes the two witnesses simply had facts wrong as in Williams's claims, for example, that scholastic ability tests usually underpredicted black scholastic performance, or that there is test bias against Asians, or that Galton invented the normal curve.

Various plaintiffs' experts ignored or did not know that there was little or no effect of race or dialect of examiner on IQ scores of blacks, that the Rosenthal–Jacobsen (1968) study did not report a change in teacher behavior and was in several respects inadequate, that the Coleman Report did not show improved black performance from placing formerly segregated blacks into mainly white classrooms, and so on. Without an unusually knowledgeable lawyer or a format in which other experts can challenge mistakes, qualify generalities, or expose half-truths, these misstatements simply pass into the record for later reflection by the judge. Judge Peckham, a believer, swallowed Hilliard and Powell pretty much whole. Judge Grady, a skeptic, dismissed most of what Williams and, later, Powell had to say.[2]

The second difficulty with using experts adversarially is captured by Cronbach's (1975, p. 12) epigrammatic statement: "There is a fundamental difference between the style of the advocate . . . and the style of the scholar. An advocate tries to score every point, including those he knows he deserves to lose." Attorneys do not hire experts whose testimony will not help them, and they tempt even those qualified experts who agree with them to say both more by way of certainty and conclusion, and less by way of limitation and qualification, than they would do in the company of knowledgeable and critical peers. The theory appears to be that the several partial truths encouraged by zealous adversarial combat will add up to the whole truth. That might be the case if there were a critical discourse among the experts to bring out the weaknesses of each position, but there is no provision for such a colloquy in court.

The best example of the expert-as-partisan in these lawsuits is probably Kamin, a man whose knowledge of the intelligence test literature is vast (see, for example, 1974) but whose selection of data to make the environmentalist argument, even outside the courtroom, has been frequently remarked (Fulker, 1975; Loehlin et al., 1975; Scarr, 1976). His attempt to persuade the courts in each case that the treatment of sex differences should be a model for the interpretation of race differences has been discussed (see Chapter 6).

Judge Peckham had been impressed with Kamin's testimony, citing it favorably, and ignoring the contrary testimony of Humphreys or Munday. Judge Grady, however, dismissed Kamin's testimony with a quotation from Gordon and Rudert (1979). It is possible that the judges' preestablished opinions and intellectual styles, or their early established theories of the cases and the selective assessment of evidence that would have followed, led them to their different conclusions. For anyone interested in good social science having its day in court, that is cold comfort.

Are Improvements Possible?

What can be done? Courts are a part of the political process and, like legislatures, are affected by political movements. If dominant political forces concur in the belief that ability tests are unfair to blacks, then so much the worse for the tests. But in cases like these, judges are making complex social policy decisions by themselves. Most other political decision makers can get some help obtaining and evaluating evidence on complex issues: The Congress has staffs and research organizations, and the President can have advisers as nonpartisan as he would like. In lawsuits such as these, however, even if panels of qualified experts could be convened to observe and critique the evidence given in them, it is doubtful whether the adversary system could accommodate so nonadversarial a mechanism. After all, if Judge Wyzanski can be criticized for hiring an economist, imagine the hue and cry if he had hired a panel of them.

It is bad enough that the courts are not just occasionally inhospitable to facts; it is worse that they sometimes reject them outright. Judge Roth, presiding over the remedy hearings in *Bradley* v. *Milliken* (338 F. Supp. 582, 1971), the Detroit school integration case, refused to take testimony on the possibility and size of the "white flight" that might ensue from his huge school integration order (Wolf, 1981). And if the Constitution said what he said it said, he was right; if departure from proportionality of race in schools is fundamentally wrong, then it is irrelevant that there might be costs associated with achieving it: *fiat justitia ruat coelum*. As one of *PASE* plaintiffs' attorneys said in her closing argument, "The only other explanation [of black disproportion in EMR] other than a problem with the evaluation and placement would be that black children are intellectually inferior to white children. We think that that explanation is contrary to the Constitution and all the federal statutes" (Closing Arguments, p. 70). And, as noted, Judge Peckham's softer rejection of evidence for IQ-achievement validities was a similar political proscription of data.

The point here is not that courts are necessarily worse than legislatures. If the citizens of a democracy want to protect their myths or their special interests, then we must not be surprised to see legislatures and courts act to do that. In some respects we may even prefer courts for these functions. We generally attribute greater wisdom to them than to legislatures, even though the latter have greater resources, owing perhaps to our need to feel that a decision we can do little about, because its source cannot be called to account, is a better one.

Psychologists, knowing some myths not to be true, will need to find a way to educate judges and legislators. To improve expert testimony, they should see, first, that cases are ably defended. That means lots of money and, in complex cases such as these, several good attorneys coherently led and ably advised by good consultants. A team like that will go some ways toward showing up the inadequacies of nonexpert "experts," and it can spend the time needed to effect clarity of the presentation of its case.

Second, no expert should mislead by commission or omission. The best way to inhibit resort to half-truth or outright error is probably to report it as quickly as possible both to professional peers and to the public. Many inexpert "experts" will not care much—the major constituency for Hilliard and Williams was not psychometricians but blacks and civil rights activists. Nevertheless, other, better qualified psychologists might be concerned to be widely known as partisan in the use of data. Even here, of course, the more partisan the psychologist, the less likely it is that he or she will be affected by the opinion of other usually more prudent peers.

Beyond all that, citizens, including judges, are educated by the cumulative force of data. It is vastly easier to argue in 1985 that ability tests used for employment or scholastic selection and placement are equally valid for blacks and whites than it was in 1975, when many of these cases were begun or in progress. (See, for example, Sattler, 1982; Hunter, Schmidt, and Rauschenberger, 1984; Manning and Jackson, 1984; Wigdor and Garner, 1982; Heller et al., 1982.) The message, again, is that patience is what is required, along with fidelity to the scientific canon that forbids misrepresentation. Patience is a scarce resource in a world that cannot take its issues back to the lab or seminar but must decide them when they are brought. Scientists, however, need not live by the rules of that world, any more than that world needs to live by the rules of scientific procedure.

Endnotes

1. Marvell is referring to the preliminary injunction phase of *Larry P.* (1972), in which it was indeed true that the city put up little defense.
2. As his opinion (506 F. Supp. 836 and footnote 3) shows, he was quite unimpressed by some of the experts: "In some instances, I am satisfied that the opinions expressed are more the result of doctrinaire commitment to a preconceived idea than they are the result of scientific inquiry. . . . I have not disregarded the expert testimony in this case, but neither do I feel bound by it. The factual determinations to be made are well within the capability of any competent trier of fact." At one point in the trial (RT 1558) plaintiffs' attorney objected to a defense witness answering a question about the cultural bias of intelligence tests, on the ground that the witness, a school official, was not a qualified psychologist. Judge Grady overruled, saying, "The fact that someone wears a hat that says 'psychologist' should not overly impress anyone who has sat through two weeks of this trial."

Chapter 11

SUMMING UP

The impetus for this examination of the litigation over the role of IQ testing in categorizing black children for purposes of special education was the outcome in *Larry P.*, which violated the scientific consensus, and the contrary outcome in *PASE*, which added inconsistency to perversity in the adjudication of a scientific issue in psychology.

I have tried, by detailed reference to the conduct and testimony of the two lawsuits, to show why each came to its own set of findings, astonishing and contradictory as some of them seemed. It may be useful here, by way of summary, to review the factors that were most determinative of the outcomes and systematically to compare the two trials with respect to such factors.

There were two groups of influences. The first were contextual, having less to do with social science evidence and its effects than they did with law and politics. They had rather to do, that is, with the winds of political pressure, the personalities of such major participants as judges, the relative strengths of the opposing teams, and the differences in demography. Here are some of them that may differentially have affected the outcomes in these cases, and may therefore make hazardous any attribution to the role of social science as the basis for outcome.

Differences in Context

First, Larry P. was filed and initially argued during the heat of the desegregation controversy in San Francisco in 1971 and 1972, and sympathy for black causes was arguably greater at that time and that place than in Chicago in 1980.

The decade of the 1970s had begun with great successes in the cause of black civil rights. It had become clear, at least since the Moynihan (1965) and Coleman et al. (1966) reports, that simple desegregation would not go far to improve the distressed conditions of most American blacks. The Supreme Court, in *Griggs*, had in effect approved the stringent views about appropriate uses of ability tests prevailing in the Equal Employment Opportunity Commission (EEOC), and it endorsed the view that disparate impact alone built at least a strong presumption of discrimination.

The Court also endorsed the widespread use of integration in a show of faith in the power of integrated schools to (among other things) improve the achievement levels of black children. Finally, the impetus for mainstreaming retarded and other handicapped children, seen in such famous cases as *Hobson* v. *Hansen, Mills*, and *PARC* and represented in psychology by Dunn (1969) and Hobbs (1975), was running at full tide.

As the decade wore on, the limits of mainstreaming the retarded, of busing, and of integration itself became clearer. The Supreme Court gave less and less deference to the EEOC in cases concerning disparate impact and test validity, and it slowed the momentum of affirmative action in school integration in cases arising in Detroit and Pasadena. Reviewers like St. John (1975) and Stephan (1978) questioned the value of integration in helping black children. And scholars—for example, Gottlieb (1981) and MacMillan and his colleagues (MacMillan, Jones, and Meyers, 1976; Meyers, MacMillan, and Yoshida, 1980)—reviewing the effect of mainstreaming on EMR children, found little, if any, effects on their achievement and mixed effects on self-concept.

By 1980, at any rate, the mood was different. The city of Chicago was nearing the end of a decade of negotiation with the government concerning integration, but by 1980 there were far fewer white students to integrate than there had been in 1970. By 1980, also, the Chicago Board of Education had revised its procedures to reflect the requirements (at least on the books) of careful and legally mandated assessment of the handicapped, including the mentally handicapped.

Second, in *Larry P.* the state began by entertaining the notion of genetic difference as a cause of racial IQ difference. They eventually disavowed this defense in favor of an "agnostic" position, but its odor permeated the trial. In *PASE* there was never any question of using such a defense, and the name of Arthur Jensen was scarcely heard in the land.

Third, Chicago was, as just noted, a predominately black school district. Two important conditions ensued. First, because the district was 60 percent black in school population, the degree of disproportionate enrollment of black children into EMR classes was limited—it was 80 percent, but that is not much compared with the factor-of-two rates of disproportion in California. Second, black school officials testified for the defense in *PASE*, and some forty black psychologists used the challenged tests; it was clear that they found the tests useful in assessing black children. In California the defense was carried primarily by white bureaucrats and experts.

Fourth, the sides were more evenly matched in *PASE* than in *Larry P.* The defense in *Larry P.*, a huge case, was carried essentially by one lawyer, with little help, against a platoon of very competent public interest and private pro bono lawyers and their assistants. In *PASE*, the Board of Education assigned three lawyers, with their assistants, to the case, and the case was smaller in scope and complexity. Conversely, the plaintiffs' team was less cohesive and less coherent in attack.

Finally, the judges were different, both in temper and in case-relevant history. Peckham is well known to be a liberal judge. It is not conceivable that given the choice he was given, between finding test bias or genetic inferiority of blacks, he would not have chosen the former.

Judge Grady was skeptical in general and of plaintiffs' claims in particular. He simply dismissed the notion of cultural difference-not-deficit offered to him. He was quite familiar with the deprivations of much of black life in Chicago and of their effects, and he castigated both sides for pussyfooting around these conditions and effects.

Judge Peckham had also presided over two cases directly relevant to the issue of *Larry P.* One was *Diana*, which was resolved by various consent decrees, including an explicit quota controlling the number of Chicano children placed in EMR classes. The other was the preliminary injunction phase of *Larry P.* itself, in which Judge Peckham had found as an undisputed fact that IQ tests were culturally biased and which had resulted in a ban of IQ tests for use in placing black children into EMR classes. The judge, in short, had ample precedent for his final decision in his own earlier ones and would, like most of us, have been predisposed to cognitive consistency. Judge Grady had no such history of prior commitment on the issues.

These differences in judicial temper, style, and history may not have been critical to the differences in trial outcome, but I cannot say that there is any factor that outweighs their importance.

Differences in Argument and Evidence

The second group of factors had to do with the ways the two cases were presented. What were the differences in content and style, and what difference did they make?

First, the cases in *PASE* were briefer, and the two sides less intransigently unaccommodating, than in *Larry P.* There were not the same extended discussions of stigma and self-concept, or of mainstreaming and its effects, or of the inadequacies of EMR education. In *PASE*, EMR classrooms were granted, even by plaintiff witnesses, to be appropriate for many EMR pupils; in *Larry P.* plaintiffs scorned the use of EMR classes for *any* pupil. In *Larry P.* black witnesses had no use for tests and no stake in the state school bureaucracy. In *PASE* one of plaintiffs' chief black witnesses had a senior position on the CBE (and two of his subordinates testified for the defense). In contrast to the nonstandard and unprofessional testing done by black psychologists in *Larry P.*, the retesting of plaintiff children in *PASE* was done by an experienced black school psychologist using standard procedures, an expert who found the WISC-R useful despite its putative bias. The flow of examination in *PASE* was less often disrupted by objections.

Second, both sides in *PASE* had the materials of *Larry P.* The *PASE* defense had more to learn from the mistakes of its counterpart in *Larry P.* than the plaintiffs did. Most especially, the defense learned to stress four arguments either not made or not prevailing in *Larry P.*: the socioeconomic (SES) basis of black deficit; the relevance of tests for schools, even though both tests and schools might be in some sense biased; internal evidence against test bias; and the appropriateness of a narrow definition of intelligence. These constitute the substantive issues to which we next turn.

Third, plaintiffs in *PASE,* following the successful line in *Larry P.,* attacked the notion that poverty and its nutrition and health correlates could account for much, if any, of the black IQ deficit. That is about as far as defendants in *Larry P.* took the SES argument; indeed, they criticized the evidence for environmental effects in cross-race adoption or intervention studies. But in *PASE,* defendants were able to show associations between "poverty pockets" in the city of Chicago and the presence of federal compensatory education programs (Headstart, Title I), as well as the rate of EMR placement. Furthermore, in Chicago a black middle class existed in numbers sufficient to show a low rate of EMR placement where it was concentrated.

Moreover, in *PASE* it was defendants, not plaintiffs, who introduced the Scarr and Weinberg (1976) adoption studies, and the effects of interventions to show how improved home and school conditions were associated with higher black IQs. (The same studies in *Larry P.* were used by plaintiffs to show the effects of acculturation into the "Anglocentric" world.)

The most dramatic evidence used by defendants in *PASE* was the thesis of Nichols (1970), which showed virtually no difference in IQ between black or white samples matched in SES. In *Larry P.,* conversely, several defense experts testified to the common findings that the black deficit is large even in samples matched in SES, and plaintiffs' attorneys quite deliberately evoked and emphasized such testimony since it took away the SES explanation of race difference and left the judge with the choice of finding either test bias or genetic inferiority.

Fourth, the defense in *PASE* hammered home the point that IQ tests did help to predict school performance. They welcomed the plaintiffs' view that ability tests, school grades, and achievement tests were all part of the same culture and virtually invited the plaintiffs to attack the criterion—that is, the schools. In *Larry P.* Jane Mercer had done that, and her views received, if not open acceptance, at least some consideration from Judge Peckham. In *PASE* Robert Williams suggested adding various minority studies units to curricula but had little else to offer. The defense simply granted that school children in Chicago were not being trained for life in (at various times) Greece, China, Tasmania, or (in Judge Grady's final comparison) "another planet." Judge Grady did not appear to feel it his place to establish curricula, or to pronounce the standard curricula biased against blacks, or even to suggest that it might be changed.

And where in *Larry P.* there was some persuasive evidence that IQ tests predicted black grades less well than white grades (as well as evidence that tests predicted equally well), evidence in *PASE*, provided by plaintiffs themselves, indicated that the prediction of achievement scores for low-achieving blacks in Chicago was quite strong (correlations about .50 with relatively restricted range), even though smaller than that for low-achieving whites (correlations about .60). The *PASE* plaintiffs' use of standardized achievement scores as a criterion was in marked contrast to the rejection of any criterion save grades alone by the *Larry P.* plaintiffs. Finally, the Gordon and Rudert (1979) review, demonstrating strong and roughly equal criterion validity in both racial groups, was by 1980 available to Judge Grady.

Fifth, internal validity was established by reference to work that demonstrated no race-by-item interaction in IQ test items, even while showing large race differences on virtually all items. It is clear from his opinion, in which he actually quotes from their paper (506 F. Supp. 880), that Judge Grady was impressed with the arguments of Gordon and Rudert (1979) against the "cultural diffusion" hypothesis, which states, roughly, that the reason blacks do less well than whites on virtually every item is that there is a black-white cultural barrier across which all items of information from the Anglocentric culture pass with nearly uniform delay. This view requires that such tests as Block Design or Ravens Matrices be as culturally "loaded" as tests of vocabulary and information. Such a view is regarded as implausible by most psychometricians, and Judge Grady, following his survey of several hundred items, obviously did not believe it either.

Judge Grady was interested in the tests at a far more microanalytic level than Judge Peckham, and he was, therefore, fascinated by testimony at the item or subtest level, starting with the very first witness, Leon Kamin. By the end of the trial he was not satisfied that he had been given good evidence on the race-by-item issue, and so he called for papers on the subject, which he quite evidently read, along with the tests. This is a case of preestablished intellectual style forcing, and not merely hearing, the evidence.

Sixth, the cases differed on two last points, each having to do with defining intelligence. First, Judge Peckham, repeating Judge

Wright's error in *Hobson* v. *Hansen*, accepted the plaintiffs' view that an unbiased intelligence test must measure innate potential. This view comports, of course, with the notion that the tests are biased against blacks because they do not truly capture some aspects of black intelligence. The reading in *PASE* was that intelligence was *developed* intellectual abilities, primarily related to schooling and validated, as we have seen, by scholastic achievement.

The second aspect of conceiving intelligence in which the two cases differed radically was the scope of its definition. Plaintiffs in *Larry P.* adopted a broad view of intelligence as being successful adaptation to several environments, of which school was merely one. Even with respect to school, it was not simply academic performance that measured adaptation, it was success in the role of student, including deportment, music, art, and so on. Thus grades were better measures of adaptation than achievement tests, and adaptive behavior in the home and community was as good as scholastic intellectual performance in indexing intelligence. In *PASE*, however, Judge Grady questioned the significance of nonintellectual adaptive behavior for intelligence. As far as he was concerned, IQ tests didn't by any means measure all of life's important qualities. But they measured something relevant to success in school, and that, to him, was the issue, as success in the home or athletic field was not.

Matters Related to Policy

The different outcome of these two lawsuits did not eventuate in different educational policies for special education in the school districts involved, because Chicago adopted most of the changes, including the proscription of IQ tests for use in EMR placement, ordered in California.

IQ tests have been replaced in both jurisdictions by a potpourri of bits and pieces of assessment procedures and instruments. The injunction to remove black children from self-contained EMR classes has been followed, on a larger scale in California than in Chicago, with the following effects:

1. EMR pupils are more than ever at the low end of the 50–70 IQ range, are more than ever suffering some degree of organic impairment, and are less than ever mainstreamable.

2. Racial disparities are as large as ever.
3. LD classes have included more and more of the students who fifteen years ago would have been in EMR classes, and a larger percentage of them are self-contained.
4. Many mildly retarded children who would have been EMR-eligible fifteen years ago are now not eligible for any special help and are coping as well as they can in regular classrooms. Relative to what might have happened under earlier regimes, some of these children will do better and some worse. The proportions of each sort of outcome will depend in part on the average level of abilities in the classrooms in which they are placed.
5. Though intellectual assessment in special education is still being done, it is often being done with methods less reliable than the IQ tests they have supplanted.
6. Some new methods of assessment are likely to prove valuable, and nonredundant with IQ tests, for educational placement.

With respect to the issue of race and class differences on tests of mental ability, these differences are likely to be pervasive and to endure for several generations to come. Since schools are the main arenas for intellectual performance, and school credentials the main touchstones of capability for employment at various levels, the inevitability of disparate impact on blacks of *any* scholastic ability or achievement measure will produce, with equal inevitability, complaints of bias in, and attack upon, the predictors and the criteria.

The group disparities will cease to exist when blacks and other disadvantaged groups are brought thoroughly into the very middle class of which schools are so characteristically a part. The means for doing this are fundamentally matters of economic behavior and policy, over which courts have little control. Courts can try to make over or take over school policies, but, barring egregious wrongs, they are relatively unsuccessful when they do.

The courts provide an unusually inappropriate forum for the resolution of complex social science issues. The main reason is that the adversary system, at least in the kind of complex equity cases this book is concerned with, is a primitive way of getting to an approximation of the truth. Responsive sharing of information and argument among persons competent in the areas that touch on some controversy—for example, the model used by the National Academy of Science in its recent reports on ability testing (Wigdor and Garner, 1982) and on special education placement (Heller et al., 1982)—is the ideal, and, where the need for legal change seems urgent, legislatures are likely to approximate it better than courts.

REFERENCES

ARLIN, M. 1984a. Time variability in mastery learning. *American Educational Research Journal 21*, 103–120.

ARLIN, M. 1984b. Time, equality, and mastery learning. *Review of Educational Research 54*, 63–86.

ARLIN, M., and WEBSTER, J. 1983. Time costs of mastery learning. *Journal of Educational Psychology 75*, 187–195.

ASHURST, D. I., and MEYERS, C. E. 1973. Social system and clinical model in school identification of the educable retarded. In R. K. Eyman, C. E. Meyers, and G. Tarjan (eds.), *Sociobehavioral studies in mental retardation. Monographs of the American Association on Mental Deficiency 1*, 150–163.

BARATZ, S. S., and BARATZ, J. C. 1970. Early childhood intervention: The social science base of institutional racism. *Harvard Educational Review 40* (1), 29–50.

BEE, H. L., VAN EGEREN, L. F., STREUSSGUTH, A. P., NYMAN, B. A., and LECKIE, M. S. 1969. Social class differences in maternal teaching strategies and speech patterns. *Developmental Psychology 1*, 726–734.

BEEZ, W. V. 1968. Influences of biased psychological reports on teacher behavior and pupil performance. *Proceedings of the 76th Annual Convention of the American Psychological Association 3*, 605–606 (Summary).

BEREITER, C. 1985. The changing face of educational disadvantagement. *Phi Delta Kappa 66*, 538–541.

BEREITER, C., and ENGELMANN, S. 1966. *Teaching disadvantaged children in the preschool*. Englewood Cliffs, N.J.: Prentice-Hall.

BERNSTEIN, B. B. 1971. *Class, codes, and control*. London: Routledge and Kegan Paul.

BERRUETA-CLEMENT, J. R., SCHWEINHART, L. J., BARNETT, W. S., EPSTEIN, A. S., and WEIKART, D. P. 1984. Changed lives: The effects of the Perry Preschool Program on youths through age 19. *Monographs of the High/Scope Educational Research Foundation* (No. 8).

BERSOFF, D. N. 1981. Testing and the law. *American Psychologist 36*, 1047–1056.

BERSOFF, D. N. 1980. Regarding psychologists testily: Legal regulation of psychological assessment in the public schools. *Maryland Law Review 39*, 27–120.

BLAU, Z. S. 1981. *Black children/white children*. New York: Free Press.

BLOOM, B. 1968. Learning for mastery. *Evaluation Comment 1*.

BONEY, J. D. 1968. Predicting the academic achievement of secondary school Negro students. *Personnel and Guidance Journal 44*, 700–703.

BOSSARD, M. D., REYNOLDS, C. R., and GUTKIN, T. B. A. 1980. A regression analysis of test bias on the Stanford–Binet Intelligence Scale. *Journal of Clinical Child Psychology 9*, 52–54.

BRADLEY, R. H., CALDWELL, B. M., and ELARDO, R. 1977. Home environment, social status, and mental test performance. *Journal of Educational Psychology 69*, 696–701.

BRELAND, H. M. 1979. *Population validity and college entrance measures*. New York: The College Board.

BROMAN, S. H., and NICHOLS, P. L. 1975. *Early mental development, social class, and school-age IQ*. Paper presented at the meeting of the American Psychological Association, Chicago (September).

BROMAN, S. H., NICHOLS, P. L., and KENNEDY, W. A. 1975. *Preschool IQ: Prenatal and early developmental correlates*. Hillsdale, N.J.: Lawrence Erlbaum.

CAMPIONE, A. C., BROWN, A. L., and FERRARA, R. A. 1982. Mental retardation and intelligence. In R. J. Sternberg (ed.), *Handbook of human intelligence*. New York: Cambridge.

CARROLL, A. W. 1967. The effects of segregated and partially integrated school programs on self-concepts and academic achievement of educable mental retardates. *Exceptional Children 34*, 93–96.

CLEARY, T. A., HUMPHREYS, L. G., KENDRICK, S. A., and WESMAN, A. 1975. Educational uses of tests with disadvantaged students. *American Psychologist 30*, 15–41.

COLEMAN, J. S., CAMPBELL, E. Q., HOBSON, C. J., McPARTLAND, J., MOOD, A. M., WINFIELD, F. D., and WORK, R. L. 1966. *Equality of educational opportunity*. Washington, D.C.: U.S. Office of Education, OE 38001.

CORDES, C. 1986. Assessment in San Francisco. *APA Monitor 17*, No. 4, 16–17.

CORDES, C. 1983. Chicago school reassessment renews debate on role of tests. *APA Monitor 14*, No. 3, 14–15.

CRONBACH, L. J. 1984. *Essentials of psychological testing*. New York: Harper & Row.

CRONBACH, L. J. 1975. Five decades of public controversy over mental testing. *American Psychologist 30*, 1–13.

CRONBACH, L. J. 1969. Heredity, environment, and educational policy. Harvard Educational Review 39, 338–347.

Designs for Change. 1982. *Caught in the web*. Designs for Change, 220 State Street, Suite 1616, Chicago.

DUNCAN, O. D. 1986. A socioeconomic index for all occupations. In A. J.

Reiss (ed.), *Occupations and social status*. New York: Free Press, pp. 109–138.

DUNN, L. M. 1968. Special education for the mildly retarded—is much of it justifiable? *Exceptional Children 35*, 5–22.

EDEN, D., and SHANI, A. B. 1982. Pygmalion goes to boot camp: Expectancy, leadership, and trainee performance. *Journal of Applied Psychology 67*, 194–199.

EELLS, K., DAVIS, A., HAVIGHURST, R. J., HERRICK V. E., and TYLER, R. W. 1951. *Intelligence and cultural differences*. Chicago: University of Chicago Press.

ENTWHISTLE, D. R., and HAYDUK, L. A. 1978. *Too great expectations: The academic outlook of young children*. Baltimore: Johns Hopkins University Press.

FEUERSTEIN, R. 1979. *The dynamic assessment of retarded persons*. Baltimore: University Park Press.

FILLER, J. W., ROBINSON, C. C., SMITH, R. A., VINCENT-SMITH, L. J., BRICKER, D. D., and BRICKER, W. A. 1975. Mental retardation. In Hobbs, N. (ed.), *Issues in the classification of children, v. I*. San Francisco: Jossey-Bass.

FISHER, A. 1978. *Four approaches to classification of mental retardation*. Paper presented at the annual meeting of the American Psychological Association, Toronto (August).

FRAZIER, E. F. 1950. Problems and needs of Negro children and youth resulting from family disorganization. *Journal of Negro Education 19*, 276–277.

FULKER, D. W. 1975. Review of *The science and politics of IQ* by L. J. Kamin. *American Journal of Psychology 88*, 505–519.

GALANTER, M. 1974. Why the "Haves" come out ahead: Speculations on the limits of legal change. *Law and Society Review 9*, 95–151.

GARBER, H. L., and HEBER, R. 1981. The efficacy of early intervention with family rehabilitation. In Begab, M. J., Harwood, H. C., and Garber, H. L. (eds.), *Psychosocial influence in retaded performance, v. II*. Baltimore: University Park Press.

GARBER, H., AND HEBER, R. 1977. The Milwaukee Project. In P. Mittler (ed.), *Research to practice in mental retardation*. Baltimore: University Park Press, pp. 119–127.

GARDNER, H. 1983. *Frames of mind*. New York: Basic Books.

GAUDIA, G. 1972. Race, social class, and age of achievement of conservation on Piaget's tasks. *Developmental Psychology 6*, 158–165.

GETTINGER, M. 1984. Individual differences in time needed for learning: A review of the literature. *Educational Psychologist 19*, 15–29.

GETTINGER, M., and WHITE, M. A. 1980. Evaluating curriculum fit with class ability. *Journal of Educational Psychology 72*, 338–344.

GETTINGER, M., and WHITE, M. A. 1979. Which is the stronger

correlate of school learning? Time to learn or measured intelligence? *Journal of Educational Psychology 71*, 405–412.

GLASS, G. V. 1978. Standards and criteria. *Journal of Educational Measurement 15*, 237–261.

GOLDMAN, R. D., and HARTIG, L. K. 1976. The WISC may not be a valid predictor of school performance for primary-grade minority children. *American Journal of Mental Deficiency 80*, 583–587.

GOLDSTEIN, H., MOSS, J. W., and JORDAN, L. J. 1965. *The efficacy of special class training on the development of mentally retarded children*. (U.S. Office of Education Cooperative Project No. 619). Urbana: University of Illinois.

GOOLSBY, T. M., JR., and FRARY, R. B. 1970. Validity of the Metropolitan Readiness Test for white and Negro students in a southern city. *Educational and Psychological Measurement 30*, 443–450.

GORDON, R. A. 1980. Labelling theory, mental retardation, and public policy: *Larry P.* and other developments since 1974. In W. R. Gove (ed.), *The labelling of deviance: Evaluating a perspective*. Beverly Hills, Calif.: Sage.

GORDON, R. A. 1975. Examining labeling theory: The case of mental retardation. In W. R. Grove (ed.), *The labeling of deviance: Evaluating a perspective*. New York: Halsted Press, pp. 83–146.

GORDON, R. A., and RUDERT, E. E. 1979. Bad news concerning IQ tests. *Sociology of Education 52*, 174–190.

GOTTLIEB, J. 1981. Mainstreaming: Fulfilling the promise? *American Journal of Mental Deficiency 86*, 115–126.

GRADY, J. 1980. Opinion. PASE v. Hannon. *Federal Supplement 506*, 831–883.

GRAY, S. W., and KLAUS, R. A. 1970. The early training project: A seventh-year report. *Child Development 41*, 909–924.

GRIFFIN, T. M., and JENSEN, D. N. 1982. *The legalization of state educational policymaking in California*. Project Report No. 82–A2, Institute for Research on Educational Finance and Governance, School of Education, Stanford University, Stanford, California.

GROSSMAN, H., ed. 1973, 1977. *Manual on terminology and classification in mental retardation*. Washington, D.C.: American Association on Mental Deficiency.

GUILFORD, J. P. 1967. *The nature of human intelligence*. New York: McGraw-Hill.

GUTERMAN, S. S. 1979. IQ tests in research on social stratification: The cross-class validity of the tests as measures of scholastic aptitude. *Sociology of Education 52*, 163–173.

HALL, V. C., and KAYE, D. B. 1980. Early patterns of cognitive development. *Monographs of the Society for Research in Child Development 45*, Serial No. 184.

HALL, V. C., HUPPERTZ, J. W., and LEVI, A. 1977. Attention and achievement exhibited by middle-and-lower class black and white elementary school boys. *Journal of Educational Psychology 69*, 115–120.

HEBB, D. O. 1949. *The organization of behavior*. New York: Wiley.

HEBER, R. 1961. A manual on terminology and classification in mental retardation (rev. ed.), *American Journal of Mental Deficiency*, Monograph (Supp. 64).

HECHINGER, F. M. 1982. About education. *New York Times*, December 28, p. C4.

HELLER, K. A., HOLTZMAN, W. H., and MESSICK, S., eds. 1982. *Placing children in special education: A strategy for equity*. Washington, D.C.: National Academy Press.

HENDERSON, N. B., BUTLER, B. B., and GOFFENEY, B. 1969. Effectiveness of the WISC and Bender-Gestalt Test in predicting arithmetic and reading achievement for white and nonwhite children. *Journal of Clinical Psychology 25*, 268–271.

HENDERSON, N. B., FAY, W. H., LINDEMANN, S. J., and CLARKSON, Q. D. 1973. Will the IQ test ban decrease the effectiveness of reading prediction? *Journal of Educational Psychology 65*, 345–355.

HERRNSTEIN, R. J., 1982. IQ testing and the media. *Atlantic Monthly* (August), p. 68–74.

HESS, R. D., and SHIPMAN, V. C. 1965. Early experience and the socialization of cognitive modes in children. *Child Development 36*, 869–886.

HILLIARD, A. G. 1979. Standardization and cultural bias as impediments to the scientific study and validation of "intelligence." *Journal of Research and Development in Education 12*, 47–58.

HOBBS, N., ed. 1975. *Issues in the classification of children*. San Francisco: Jossey-Bass.

HUMPHREYS, L. G. 1984. General intelligence. In C. R. Reynolds and R. T. Brown eds., *Perspectives on bias in mental testing*. New York: Plenum.

HUMPHREYS, L. G. 1979. The construct of general intelligence. *Intelligence 3*, 105–120.

HUMPHREYS, L. G. 1971. Theory of intelligence. In R. Cancro, ed., *Intelligence: Genetic and environmental influences*. New York: Grune & Stratton pp. 31–42.

HUMPHREYS, L. G., and STUBBS, J. 1972. A longitudinal analysis of teacher expectation, student expectation, and student achievement. *Journal of Educational Measurement 14*, 261–270.

HUNT, J. McV. 1961. *Intelligence and experience*. New York: Ronald Press.

HUNTER, J. E., SCHMIDT, F. L., and RAUSCHENBERGER, J. 1984.

Methodological, statistical, and ethical issues in the study of bias in psychological tests. In C. R. Reynolds and R. T. Brown, eds. *Perspectives on bias in mental testing*. New York: Plenum.

HUNTER, J. E., SCHMIDT, F. L. and HUNTER, R. 1979. Differential validity of employment tests by race: A comprehensive review and analysis. *Psychological Bulletin 86*, 721–735.

JACKSON, G. D. 1975. Another psychological view from the Association of Black Psychologists. *American Psychologist 30*, 88–93.

JENSEN, A. R. 1980. *Bias in mental testing*. New York: The Free Press.

JENSEN, A. R. 1976. Test bias and construct validity. *Phi Delta Kappa 58*, 340–346.

JENSEN, A. R. 1974a. Ethnicity and scholastic achievement. *Psychological Reports 34*, 659–668.

JENSEN, A. R. 1974b. How biased are culture-loaded tests? *Genetic Psychology Monographs 90*, 185–244.

JENSEN, A. R. 1970. A theory of primary and secondary familial mental retardation. In N. R. Ellis (ed.), *International Review of Mental Retardation*, Vol. 4. New York: Academic Press, pp. 33–105.

JENSEN, A. R. 1969. How much can we boost IQ and scholastic achievement? *Harvard Educational Review 39*, 1–123.

JENSEN, A. R., and FIGUEROA, R. A. 1975. Forward and backward digit span interaction with race and IQ: Predictions from Jensen's theory. *Journal of Educational Psychology 67*, 882–893.

KAMIN, L. J. 1974. *The science and politics of IQ*. Potomac, Md.: Lawrence Erlbaum.

KARNES, M. B., HODGINS, A., and TESKA, J. A. 1968. An evaluation of two preschool programs for disadvantaged children: A traditional and a highly structured experimental preschool. *Exceptional Children 34*, 667–676.

KAUFMAN, A. S., and DOPPELT, J. E. 1976. Analysis of WISC-R standardization data in terms of the stratification variables. *Child Development 47*, 165–171.

KAZIMOUR, K. K., and RESCHLY, D. J. 1981. Investigation of the norms and concurrent validity for the adaptive behavior inventory for children (ABIC). *American Journal of Mental Deficiency 85*, 512–520.

KIRP, D. L. 1982. *Just schools*. Berkeley: University of California Press.

KIRP. D. L., KURILOFF, P. J., BUSS, W. G. 1975. *Legal mandates and organizational change*. In N. Hobbs, ed., *Issues in the classification of children, v. II*. San Francisco: Jossey-Bass.

KLAUS, R. A., and GRAY, S. W. 1968. The early training project for disadvantaged children: A report after five years. *Monographs of the Society for Research in Child Development 33* (4, Serial No. 120).

KLINEBERG, O. 1935. *Negro intelligence and selective migration*. New York: Columbia University Press.

KLITGAARD, R. 1985. *Choosing elites*. New York: Basic Books.

LAMBERT, N. M. 1981. Psychological evidence in *Larry P*. v. *Wilson Riles:* An evaluation by a witness for the defense. *American Psychologist 36*, 937–952.

LAMBERT, N. M. 1978a. The Adaptive Behavior Scale—Public School Version: An overview. In W. A. Coulter and H. W. Morrow, eds., *Adaptive behavior: Concepts and measurements*. New York: Grune & Stratton.

LAMBERT, N. M. 1978b. Application of adaptive behavior measurement in the public school setting. In W. A. Coulter (Chair), *What's new with adaptive behavior: Current/future status in assessment*. Symposium presented at the meeting of the American Psychological Association, Toronto, Canada.

LAMBERT, N. M. WINDMILLER, M., COLE L., and FIGUEROA, R. A. 1975. Standardization of a public school version of the AAMD Adaptive Behavior Scale. *Mental Retardation 13*(2), 3–7.

LAZAR, I. and DARLINGTON, R. 1982. Lasting effects of early education. A report from the consortium for longitudinal studies. *Monographs of the Society for Research in Child Development 47*, Serial No. 192.

LAZAR, I., SNIPPER, A. S., ROYCE, J., and DARLINGTON, R. B. 1981. Policy implications of preschool intervention research. In M. J. Begab, H. C. Haywood, H. L. Garber, eds., *Psychosocial influences in retarded performance*. Baltimore: University Park Press.

LEMANN, N. 1986. The origins of the underclass. *Atlantic Monthly*, Part I (June), pp. 31–55; Part II (July), pp. 54–68.

LERNER, B. 1978. The Supreme Court and the APA, ERA, NCME test standards: Past references and future possibilities. *American Psychologist 33*, 915–919.

LEVENSTEIN, P. 1970. Cognitive growth in preschoolers through verbal interaction with mothers. *American Journal of Orthopsychiatry 40*, 426–432.

LEVIN, H. M. 1985. The educationally disadvantaged: A national crisis. *The State Youth Initiatives Project Working Paper #6*, Public/Private Ventures, 399 Market St., Philadelphia.

LINDBLOM, C. E., and COHEN, D. K. 1979. *Usable knowledge*. New Haven: Yale.

LINN, R. 1982. Ability testing: Individual differences, prediction, and differential prediction. In A. K. Wigdor, and W. R. Garner, eds, *Ability testing: Uses, consequences, and controversies*. Washington, D. C.: National Academy Press.

LINN, R. L. 1975. Test bias and the prediction of grades in law school. *Journal of Legal Education 27*, 293–323.

LOEHLIN, J. C., LINDZEY, G., and SPUHLER, J. N. 1975. *Race differences in intelligence*. San Francisco: Freeman.

LONGSTRETH, L. E., DAVIS, B. CARTER, L., FLINT, D., OWEN, J., RICKERT, M., and TAYLOR, E. 1981. Separation of home intellectual environment and maternal IQ as determinants of child IQ. *Developmental Psychology 17*, 532–541.

LUKAS, J. A. 1985. *Common ground*. New York: Knopf.

LUNEMANN, A. 1974. The correlational validity of IQ as a function of ethnicity and desegregation. *Journal of School Psychology 12*, 263–268.

MACCOBY, E. A., and JACKLIN, C. N. 1974. *The psychology of sex differences*. Stanford, Calif.: Stanford University Press.

MACMILLAN, D. L., and BORTHWICK, S. 1980. The new educable mentally retarded: Can they be mainstreamed? *Mental Retardation 18*, 155–158.

MACMILLAN, D. L., JONES, R. L., and MEYERS, C. E. 1976. Mainstreaming the mildly retarded: Some questions, cautions, and guidelines. *Mental Retardation 14*, 3–10.

MACMILLAN, D. L., JONES, R. L., and ALOIA. G. F. 1974. The mentally retarded label: A theoretical analysis and review of research. *American Journal of Mental Deficiency 79*, 241–261.

MACMILLAN, D. L., and MEYERS, C. E. 1980. Larry P.: An educational interpretation. *School Psychology Review 9*, 136–148.

MADDEN, N. A., and SLAVIN, R. E. 1983. Mainstreaming students with mild handicaps: Academic and social outcomes. *Review of Educational Research 53*, 519–569.

MANNING, W. H., and JACKSON, R. T. 1984. College entrance examinations: objective selection or gatekeeping. In C. R. Reynolds and R. T. Brown (eds.), *Perspectives on bias in mental testing*. New York: Plenum, pp. 189–220.

MARVELL, T. 1980. Misuses of applied social research. In M. J. Saks and C. H. Baron, eds., *The use-nonuse-misuse of applied social research in the courts*. Cambridge, Mass.: Abt Books.

MATARAZZO, J. D., and WIENS, A. N. 1977. Black Intelligence Test of Cultural Homogeneity and Wechsler Adult Intelligence Scale scores of black and white police applicants. *Journal of Applied Psychology 62*, 57–63.

MCCANDLESS, B. R., ROBERTS, A., and STARNES, R. 1972. Teacher's marks, achievement test scores, and aptitude relations with respect to social class, and sex. *Journal of Educational Psychology 63*, 153–159.

MCNEMAR, Q. 1942. *The revision of the Stanford–Binet Scale*. Boston: Houghton Mifflin.

MERCER, J. 1973. *Labelling the mentally retarded*. Berkeley: University of California Press.

MERCER, J. R. 1979. *System of Multicultural Pluralistic Assessment technical manual*. New York: Psychological Corporation.

MERCER, J. R. 1978. Test "validity," "bias," and "fairness": An analysis from the perspective of the sociology of knowledge. *Interchange* 9, 1–16.

MERCER, J. R. 1975. Psychological assessment and the rights of children. In N. Hobbs, ed., *Issues in the classification of children, v. I.* San Francisco: Jossey-Bass.

MERCER, J. R., and LEWIS, J. F. 1978. *System of Multicultural Pluralistic Assessment.* New York: Psychological Corporation.

MEYERS, C. E., MACMILLAN, D. L., and YOSHIDA, R. K. 1980. Regular class education of EMR students, from efficacy to mainstreaming. In J. Gottlieb, ed., *Perspectives on handicapping conditions.* Baltimore: University Park Press.

MEYERS, C. E., MACMILLAN, D. L., and YOSHIDA, R. K. 1975. *Correlates of success in transition of MR to regular class. Final report.* Pomona: University of California, Los Angeles, Neuropsychiatry Institute, Pacific State Hospital (ERIC Document Reproduction Service Nos. EC 081 038 and EC 081 039).

MIELE, F. 1979. Cultural bias in the WISC. *Intelligence 3,* 149–164.

MITCHELL, B. C. 1967. Predictive validity of the Metropolitan Readiness Tests and the Murphy-Durrell Readiness Analysis for white and Negro pupils. *Educational and Psychological Measurement 27,* 1047–1054.

MITCHELL, B. C. 1962. The Metropolitan Readiness Tests as predictors of first-grade achievement. *Educational and Psychological Measurement 22,* 765–772.

MOYNIHAN, D. P. 1986. *Family and nation.* San Diego: Harcourt Brace.

MOYNIHAN, D. P. 1965. *The Negro family: The case for national action.* Washington, D.C.: U.S. Government Printing Office.

MYRDAL, G. 1944. *An American dilemma.* New York: Harpers.

NICHOLS, P. L. 1970. The effects of heredity and environment on intelligence test performance in 4 and 7 year white and Negro sibling pairs (Doctoral dissertation, University of Minnesota). *Dissertation Abstracts International,* 1971, *32,* 101B–102B (University Microfilms No. 71-18, 874).

NICHOLS, P. L., and ANDERSON, V. E. 1973. Intellectual performance, race, and socioeconomic status. *Social Biology 20,* 367–374.

OAKLAND, T. 1983. Joint use of adaptive behavior and IQ to predict achievement. *Journal of Consulting and Clinical Psychology 51,* 298–301.

OAKLAND, T. 1979. Research on the Adaptive Behavior Inventory for Children and the Estimated Learning Potential. *School Psychology Digest 8,* 63–70.

OAKLAND, T. 1978. Predictive validity of readiness tests for middle and lower socioeconomic status Anglo, black and Mexican American children. *Journal of Educational Psychology 70,* 574–582.

PAGE, E. B., and GRANDON, G. M. 1981. Massive intervention and child intelligence: The Milwaukee Project in critical perspective. *Journal of Special Education 15*, 239–256.

PATRICK, J. L., and RESCHLY, D. J. 1982. Relationship of state education criteria and demographic variables to school system prevalence of mental retardation. *American Journal of Mental Deficiency 86*.

PECKHAM, R. F. 1979. Opinion, *Larry P.* v. *Riles*. *Federal Supplement 495*, 926–992.

PECKHAM, R. F. 1972. Opinion, *Larry P.* v. *Riles*. *Federal Supplement 343*, 1306–1315.

RAMEY, C. T. 1982. Commentary. In I. Lazar and R. Darlington. Lasting effects of early education: A report from the consortium for longitudinal studies. *Monographs of the Society for Research in Child Development 47*, Serial No. 192.

RAMEY, C. T., BRYANT, D. M., and SUAREZ, T. M. 1985. Preschool compensatory education and the modifiability of intelligence: A critical review. In D. Detterman, ed., *Current topics in intelligence*. Norwood, N. J.: Ablex, pp. 247–296.

RAMEY, C. T., and HASKINS, R. 1981. The causes and treatment of school failure: Insights from the Carolina Abecedarian Project. In M. J. Begab, H. C. Haywood, and H. L. Garber, eds., *Psychosocial influences in retarded performance*, v. II. Baltimore: University Park Press.

RAUDENBUSH, S. W. 1984. Magnitude of teacher expectancy effects on pupil IQ as a function of the credibility of expectancy induction: A synthesis of findings from 18 experiments. *Journal of Educational Psychology 76*, 85–97.

RESCHLY, D. J. 1982. Assessing mild mental retardation: The influence of adaptive behavior, sociocultural status, and prospects for nonbiased assessment. In C. Reynolds and T. Gutkin, eds., *A Handbook for School Psychology*. New York: Wiley.

RESCHLY, D. J. 1981. Evaluation of the effects of SOMPA measures on classification of students as mildly mentally retarded. *American Journal of Mental Deficiency 86*, 16–20.

RESCHLY, D. J. 1980. Psychological evidence in the *Larry P.* opinion: A case of right problem—wrong solution? *School Psychology Review 9*, 123–135.

RESCHLY, D. J. 1978. *Comparisons of bias in assessment with conventional and pluralistic measures*. Paper presented at the annual meeting of the Council for Exceptional Children, Kansas City, Missouri.

RESCHLY, D. J., and RESCHLY, J. E. 1979. Validity of WISC-R factor scores in predicting achievement and attention for four sociocultural groups. *Journal of School Psychology 17*, 355–361.

RESCHLY, D. J., ROSS-REYNOLDS, J., and GRIMES, J. 1981. *State norms for IQ, adaptive behavior, and sociocultural status: Implications for nonbiased assessment*. Des Moines, Iowa: State Dept. of Public Instruction.

RESCHLY, D. J., and SABERS, D. L. 1979. Analysis of test bias in four groups with the regression definition. *Journal of Educational Measurement 16*, 1–9.

RESNICK, L. B. 1979. The future of IQ testing in education. *Intelligence 3*, 241–253.

RESNICK, L. B., WANG, M. C., and KAPLAN, J. 1973. Task analysis in curriculum design: A hierarchically sequenced introductory mathematics curriculum. *Journal of Applied Behavior Analysis 6*, 679–709.

REYNOLDS, C. R. 1983. Regression analysis of race and sex bias in seven preschool tests. *Journal of Psychoeducational Assessment 1*, 169–178.

ROSENTHAL, R., and JACOBSON, L. 1968. *Pygmalion in the classroom*. New York: Appleton-Century-Crofts.

ROSSELL, C. H. 1980. Social science research in educational equity cases: A critical review. In *Review of Research in Education 8*, 237–295.

ROSS-REYNOLDS, J., and RESCHLY, D. J. 1983. An investigation of item bias on the WISC-R with four sociocultural groups. *Journal of Consulting and Clinical Psychology 51*, 144–146.

RYAN, W. 1965. Savage discovery: The Moynihan Report. *The Nation 201*, 380–386.

ST. JOHN, N. 1975. *Desegregation outcomes for children*. New York: Wiley.

SANDOVAL, J. 1979. The WISC-R and internal evidence of test bias with minority groups. *Journal of Consulting and Clinical Psychology 47*, 919–927.

SAPP, G. L., HORTON, W., MCELROY, K., and RAY, P. 1979. An analysis of ABIC score patterns of selected Alabama school children. In *Proceedings of the National Association of School Psychologists/California Association of School Psychologists and Psychometrists*, San Diego (April).

SATTLER, J. 1982. *Assessment of children's intelligence and special abilities* (2nd ed.). Boston: Allyn & Bacon.

SCARR, S. 1981. *Social class, race and individual differences in intelligence*. New York: Plenum.

SCARR, S. 1978. From evolution to *Larry P.*, or what shall we do about IQ tests? *Intelligence 2*, 325–342.

SCARR, S. 1976. Review: *The science and politics of IQ*. *Contemporary Psychology 21*, 98–99.

SCARR, S., and WEINBERG, R. A. 1976. IQ test performance of black children adopted by white families. *American Psychologist 31*, 726–739.

SCOTT, L. 1979. *Identification of declassified students*. Paper presented at annual meeting of the American Psychological Association, New York (August).

SEAVER, W. B. 1973. Effects of naturally induced teacher expectancies. *Journal of Personality and Social Psychology 28*, 333–342.

SHEPARD, L. A., SMITH, M. L., and VOJIR, C. P. 1983. Characteristics of pupils identified as learning disabled. *American Educational Research Journal 20*, 309–331.

SHIFF, M., DUYME, M., DUMARET, A., STEWART, J., TOMKIEWICZ, S., and FEINGOLD, J. 1978. Intellectual status of working-class children adopted early into upper-middle-class families. *Science 200*, 1503–1504.

SHONKOFF, J. P. 1982. Biological and social factors contributing to mild mental retardation. In K. A. Heller, W. H. Holtzman, and S. Messick, (eds.), *Placing children in special education: A strategy for equity*. Washington, D.C.: National Academy Press.

SHUEY, A. M. 1966. *The testing of Negro intelligence*. New York: Social Science Press.

SKEELS, H. M. 1966. Adult status of children with contrasting early life experiences: A follow-up study. *Monographs of the Society for Research in Child Development 31*, No. 105.

SKODAK, M., and SKEELS, H. M. 1949. A final follow-up study of one hundred adopted children. *Journal of Genetic Psychology 75*, 85–125.

SKODAK, M., and SKEELS, H. M. 1945. A follow-up study of children in adoptive homes. *Journal of Genetic Psychology 66*, 21–58.

SNYDERMAN, M., and ROTHMAN, S. 1986. Science, politics, and the IQ controversy. *The Public Interest*, No. 83, 79–97.

SOMMER, R., and SOMMER, B. A. 1983. Mystery in Milwaukee: Early intervention, IQ, and psychology textbooks. *American Psychologist 38*, 982–985.

STEPHAN, W. 1978. School desegregation: An evaluation of predictions made in *Brown* v. *Board of Education*. *Psychological Bulletin 85*, 217–238.

STRANG, L., SMITH, M. D., and ROGERS, C. M. 1978. Social comparison, multiple reference groups, and the self-concepts of academically handicapped children before and after mainstreaming. *Journal of Educational Psychology 70*, 487–497.

SVANUM, S., and BRINGLE, R. G. 1982. Race, social class, and predictive bias: An evaluation using the WISC, WRAT, and teacher ratings. *Intelligence 6*, 275–286.

TALLEY, R. 1979. *Evaluating the effects of implementing SOMPA*. Bloomington: School of Education, University of Indiana, Center for Innovation in Teaching the Handicapped (November).

TERMAN, L. M., and MERRILL, M. A. 1960. *Stanford–Binet Intelligence Scale*. Boston: Houghton Mifflin.

TERMAN, L. M., and MERRILL, M. A. 1937. *Measuring intelligence*. Cambridge, Mass.: Houghton Mifflin.

THORNDIKE, R. L. 1968. Review of *Pygmalion in the classroom*. *American Education Research Journal 5*, 708–711.

THORNDIKE, R. L., and HAGEN, E. P. 1977. *Measurement and evaluation in psychology and education* (4th ed.). New York: Wiley.

TROTMAN, F. K. 1977. Race, IQ, and the middle class. *Journal of Educational Psychology 69*, 266–273.

TUDDENHAM, R. D. 1970. A "Piagetian" test of cognitive development. In W. B. Dockrell, ed., *On intelligence*. Toronto: Ontario Institute for Studies in Education, pp. 49–70.

TUDDENHAM, R. D. 1948. Soldier intelligence in World Wars I and II. *American Psychologist 3*, 54–56.

TULKIN, S. R., and KAGAN, J. 1972. Mother-child interaction in the first year of life. *Child Development 43*, 31–41.

VERNON, P. E. 1979. *Intelligence: Heredity and environment*. San Francisco: W. H. Freeman.

WARNER, W. L., MEEKER, M., and EELS, K. E. 1949. *Social class in America*. Chicago: Science Research Associates.

WECHSLER, D. 1975. Intelligence defined and undefined: A relativistic appraisal. *American Psychologist 30*, 135–139.

WEICKART, D. P., EPSTEIN, A., SCHWEINHART, L., and BOND, J. T. 1978. *The Ypsilantic preschool demonstration project: Preschool years and longitudinal results*. Ypsilanti, Mich.: High/Scope Educational Research Foundation.

WERNER, E. F., HONZIK, M. P., and SMITH, R. S. 1968. Prediction of intelligence and achievement at ten years from twenty months pediatric and psychologic examinations. *Child Development 39*, 1063–1075.

WHEELER, L. R. 1942. A comparative study of the intelligence of East Tennessee mountain children. *Journal of Educational Psychology 33*, 321–334.

WHITE, K. R. 1982. The relation between socioeconomic status and academic achievement. *Psychological Bulletin 91*, 461–481.

WIGDOR, A. K., and GARNER, W. R. 1982. *Ability testing: Uses, consequences, and controversies*. Washington, D.C.: National Academy Press.

WILLIAMS, R. L. 1972. *The BITCH-100: A culture-specific test*. Paper presented at the meeting of the American Psychological Association, Honolulu, Hawaii (September).

WILLIAMS, R. L. 1970. Black pride, academic relevance and individual achievement. *Counseling Psychologist 2*, 18–22.

WILSON, W. J. 1978. *The declining significance of race: Blacks and changing American institutions*. Chicago: University of Chicago Press.

WOLF, E. P. 1981. *Trial and error*. Detroit: Wayne State University Press.

WOLF, R. 1966. The measurement of environments. In A. Anastasi, ed., *Testing problems in perspective*. Washington, D.C.: American Council on Education.

WRIGHT, J.S. 1967. Opinion, *Hobson* v. *Hansen*. *Federal Supplement 269*, 401–510.

WRUBEL, P. 1979. *An assessment of the impact of the courts on local school boards*. Stanford, Calif.: Institute for Research on Educational Finance and Governance.

YEATES, K. O., MacPHEE, D., CAMPBELL, F. A., and RAMEY, C. T. 1983. Maternal IQ and home environment as determinants of early childhood intellectual competence: A developmental analysis. *Developmental Psychology 19*, 731–739

YOSHIDA, R. K., and MEYERS, C. E. 1975. Effects of labelling as educable mentally retarded on teachers' expectancies for change in a student's performance. *Journal of Educational Psychology 67*, 521–527.

ZIGLER, E., and SEITZ, V. 1982. Social policy and intelligence. In R. J. Sternberg, ed., *Handbook of human intelligence*. New York: Cambridge, pp. 586–641.

INDEX